How To Preach The Miracles

Why People Don't Believe Them
And What You Can Do About It

Cycle A

John E. Sumwalt

CSS Publishing Company, Inc., Lima, Ohio

Scripture quotations are from the *New Revised Standard Version of the Bible*, copyright 1989 by the Division of Christian Education of the National Council of the Churches of Christ in the USA. Used by permission.

Library of Congress Cataloging-in-Publication Data

Sumwalt, John E.
    How to preach the miracles : why people don't believe them and what you can do about it, Cycle A / John E. Sumwalt.
        p. cm.
    ISBN 0-7880-2457-4 (perfect bound : alk. paper)
    1. Miracles—Sermons. 2. Common lectionary (1992). Year A. 3. Lectionary preaching. I. Title.

    BS2545.M5S86 2007
    226.7'06—dc22

                                                                    2007011191

For more information about CSS Publishing Company resources, visit our website at www.csspub.com or email us at custserv@csspub.com or call (800) 241-4056.

Cover design by Barbara Spencer
ISBN-13: 978-0-7880-2457-3
ISBN-10: 0-7880-2457-4   PRINTED IN U.S.A.

In loving memory of
Carolyn Perry Sutherland

Table Of Contents

Acknowledgments

I am indebted to CSS Publisher Wesley Runk for persuading me to write this book, a project I had never thought of doing and didn't think I wanted to do. It has proved to be an enriching experience beyond measure. Equally important has been the encouragement and painstaking editing work of the love of my life, Jo Perry-Sumwalt. It is to her dear sister, Carolyn Perry Sutherland, this book is dedicated. When I write of the miracle of resurrection, I think of her and others I love who wait just over the horizon.

The support and love of our daughter, Kathryn; her husband, Mark Hornickel; our son, Orrin; and our West Highland Terrier, Chloe, are a large part of the joy that energizes my work. The congregation of Wauwatosa Avenue United Methodist Church, our staff, and my partner in pastoral ministry, Jan Beutin, are also a part of that joy. They have contributed in numerous ways by conversations after sermons, by sending articles, and by suggesting books to read.

My friend, Mike Rother, came along at just the right time to share key insights that have been integral to the development of some of the ideas presented here. He had an uncanny way of dropping by just when I needed him, and before I even knew I needed something he had to offer.

I am especially thankful to Jack Kaufman, John McLaughlin, Tyler Pease, Jo Perry-Sumwalt, Daniel Sumwalt, Francis McDonough, Rosmarie Trapp, Laura Wassink, Susan Ivany, J. Robert Stimmel, Verna Windrem, Vanessa Bruce Ingold, Donna Mrozinski, Alice Rippen, Mike Rother, Pamela Christensen, Clayton Daughenbaugh, Larry Winebrenner, Karen de Jong-Dermann, Thom M. Shuman, Pamela J. Tinnin, Stan Granot Blythe Duncan, Nancy Bauer-King, Rebecca Coan-Henderleiter, Earl Kammerud, Nancy Nichols, Marilyn MacDonald, Cindy Thompson, the family of the late Eric Monteith, and the family of the late Randall Nulton, for entrusting me with their stories — and to Timothy Haut for sharing his wonderful poems, *Miracle* and *The All Of Love*.

Foreword

If you are an active participant in the life of a congregation you may have noticed that there is a great silence in the church today. And the silence does not grow out of an effort to make space in worship or in the lives of the gathered congregation for divine presence.

Rather, the silence is around the passages of the Bible that tell the stories of miraculous events that seem to punctuate the life and ministry of Jesus. Our contemporary culture has convinced many that anything that cannot be fully understood, analyzed, weighed, and explained is not real. Of course, if this were true, we would have to dismiss the experience of love and even our very thought that denies the existence of that which is beyond our understanding, because our thoughts and the love we experience cannot be measured, weighed, or fully understood.

The silence is due in part to cultural pressure to conform and in part to our discomfort with anything we cannot fully explain or understand, and perhaps most of all due to our denial that at our core, at the very center of life, we are spiritual beings. When this spiritual center is nourished and related to the divine Spirit, we gain the capacity to see, understand, and now and then experience the miraculous.

John Sumwalt has prepared a resource that will assist those who preach and teach the scriptures to open the eyes and ears of the reader and listener to see and hear the truth carried in the miracle stories of the Bible. With contemporary stories and insights into ancient texts, the author invites the reader into the mystery of God's active, palpable presence in the world. When we decide to live daily in God's presence, we are in position to once again see, hear, believe, and experience the miraculous in our daily lives.

Who could ask for more?

Rueben P. Job

Miracle
(Luke 5:12-13)

Watch!
His hand stretches out,
touches the foulness of flesh,
the fetid sores,
the autograph of evil
scrawled on a tear-streaked face.
There is silence all around.
The crowd gasps, wonders,
holds its breath
at such holy courage.
In a millisecond of grace,
this hand
reaches across an infinite chasm
which only love can cross.
This is the miracle:
the waiting
in breathless, sacred silence
to see what love will do.

Timothy Haut

Timothy Haut is pastor of the First Congregational Church (UCC) of Deep River, Connecticut. He is a graduate of Yale Divinity School and was ordained in 1972. Timothy has several books of poetry in the works and waiting for publication.

Take The Miracle Survey

(answer yes or no)

_____ Do you believe in miracles?

_____ Have you experienced a miracle?

_____ Do you know someone who has experienced a miracle?

_____ Have you ever prayed for a miracle?

_____ Have you received a miracle in your life or in the life of someone you know as a result of prayer?

_____ Do you believe the miracles of Jesus really happened?

_____ All of them

_____ Some of them

_____ None of them

_____ Does it make you angry when people talk about the miracles they have experienced in their lives?

13

Do you think that belief in miracles is: (Check those that apply)

_____ Magical thinking

_____ Superstition

_____ Communal hysteria

_____ Mental illness

_____ Ignorance

_____ Faith

_____ Common sense

How would you define a miracle?

_____ The direct intervention of God or an angel.

_____ An unlikely occurrence of good that is a result of natural forces.

Give your own definition of a miracle:

_____

_____

_____

_____

Do you believe:

_____ People must have faith before they can receive a miracle?

_____ Miracles can happen to anyone including nonbelievers?

What would it take for you to believe in miracles?

_____ Scientific proof

_____ Seeing with your own eyes

_____ The witness of someone you trust

_____ The witness of hundreds of people

_____ The witness of scripture or church authorities

_____ Nothing could ever convince me

What are some miracles you have experienced in your life?

_____

_____

_____

_____

_____

_____

In his book, *Troublesome Bible Passages*, Volume 2, Randy Cross defines a miracle as "... nothing more nor less than the in-breaking of God's love and power in this world. Sometimes it happens through what we normally call miraculous occurrences, but it is not limited in any way to those supernatural events. It occurs anytime our lives are blessed with the assurance of God's love."[1]

---

1. Randy Cross, *Troublesome Bible Passages*, Volume 2 (Nashville: Abingdon Press, 1997), p. 58.

Permission is given to copy the Miracle Survey for use in worship services, classes, and research projects.

Introduction

Pass out the Miracle Survey the next time you preach about one of the miracles of Jesus. Give people about five minutes, and, while they are giving their answers, write down your best guess about how you think they will respond. What percentage of the congregation will say they believe in miracles? What percentage will admit they have experienced a miracle? How do you think most of those present in worship that day will define a miracle? Ask the organist to select some appropriate miracle music to play during the survey time.

Have the ushers collect the survey forms and make a show of putting them in a sealed "Miracle Box" with a promise that the results will be tabulated by a team of three or four trusted members that you have made arrangements with before the service. A white box with the words "MIRACLE BALLOT BOX" stenciled in big red letters adds to the fun.

Then go ahead and preach your miracle sermon. Begin by giving your predictions of the survey results. Promise you will give the actual results the following Sunday. You may be sure you will have the congregation's undivided attention throughout the sermon and attendance numbers will increase the following week. That will be considered a miracle by some and you will get an extra "Atta boy" or "Atta girl" for cleverly creating a little attendance spike.

Preaching is miracle work for both the preacher and the congregation. For one thing, it's a miracle that anyone chooses to preach, and it's a miracle that anyone chooses to listen, much less to hear. And, for another thing, miracles happen when miracles are preached. Marilyn MacDonald tells of a small miracle that occurred while she was preaching one Sunday.

> *In one church where I served as a supply pastor for a few months, there was an elderly lady (she was 92 at the time) who could hear some of the time, but not always. She therefore requested a "copy" of my sermons*

so she could follow them on the Sundays when she was
unable to hear. I told her that I did not have completed
manuscripts that I preached from, but would give her
some of the resource material that I used so she could
read that for her message on days she could not hear.
One Sunday, I provided her with the "resource mate-
rial" (including a rough draft of the sermon) prior to
worship. After the service she greeted me with, "I think
I got a better sermon out of that material than you did!
I could hear today!" We had a good chuckle together.[1]

When I preach about miracles, I assume about half of the 300 listeners present in our services on an average Sunday morning, believe in miracles and about two-thirds do not. I was never very good at math, but in this case there is some logic to my nonsense. Let's call it "the miracle gap." Many of those who say they believe in miracles on a Sunday morning in church would give a different answer if asked by a coworker at the water cooler on Monday morning or at the bar after a round of golf on Saturday. Most of us who live in North America keep our religious beliefs and our every day basic assumptions about what is real in separate compartments.

I also know that of the one-half to two-thirds of those present who don't believe in miracles, some of them will bristle at the very mention of the idea. Those who speak of miracles in our scientific age are viewed by some as purveyors of superstition and magical thinking. "Just the facts, ma'am." Get someone to crunch the numbers, then get back to us. What's the bottom line? That's all we need to know. There is little room for mystery in the laboratory or the boardroom, and people who live in those worlds during the week don't like to have it spooned out to them on Sunday mornings.

Mona Lisa Schulze writes about the worship of information in her book, *Awakening Intuition*.

We want to figure everything out. The human tendency
is to seek information, to grasp for the concrete, to fill
in the details. Knowledge is power, after all, and if we
have it, we can help ourselves. Yet not all knowledge is

accessible all the time ... In the end ... there are some
things we simply can never know.[2]

All of us who live in this age of reason and progress are tempted to believe it is only a matter of time before we will indeed know how to "figure everything out." It takes a lot to knock us off our high-tech high horses. A 9/11 or a Katrina gives us pause for a little while; churches fill up for a few Sundays and every one sings "God Bless America" with more fervor, but in a few days or weeks we are back on our high-speed browsers, Googling our way through cyberspace, searching endlessly for the perfect site that will provide whatever is missing in our lives that will make us whole. And, ironically, this is the entry point for those of us who preach miracles.

People who are so hungry for information that they keep inventing faster and faster ways to find it are ripe for a word from the one who said, "The harvest is plentiful, but the laborers are few" (Matthew 9:37). What is ultimately being sought by the masses that crowd the internet highways is the same thing people were seeking that day Jesus looked out on a crowd and "... had compassion for them, because they were harassed and helpless, like sheep without a shepherd" (Matthew 9:36).

Thomas Merton tells about standing on a street corner in Louisville one day in the early 1960s. As he watched shoppers go by, he says he was "... suddenly overwhelmed with the realization [perhaps like Jesus had when he saw his crowd] that I loved those people, that they were mine and I theirs, that we could not be alien to one another even though we were total strangers." Merton observed "... If only everybody could realize this! But it cannot be explained. There is no way of telling people that they are walking around shining like the sun."[3]

The task of the miracle preacher is to invite people into this mystery that we are, into the Spirit world in which we all live, but which few of us are able or willing to see. People come to worship with deep yearnings for the holy — a longing for something they cannot name — and a feeble hope that maybe, just maybe, there really is a God who is rooting for them, and then go home to football and NASCAR, and a culture that is both oblivious and hostile

19

to the idea of miracles. We become discouraged and cynical, our senses dulled by the mind-numbing rationalism that pervades modern living; we don't see the divine shining through all things. To paraphrase Yogi Berra, "If people don't want to open their eyes and see the light, there is nothing we can do to stop them."

What is the preacher of miracles to do? We can begin, like Jesus did, by telling stories of the mysterious, saving presence of God. This is the realm in which Jesus did his miracle work, a dimension of reality that cannot be Googled or downloaded, but is readily accessible to those who are hungry for it. "Blessed are the poor in spirit, for theirs is the kingdom of heaven," he said (Matthew 5:3).

In her book, *Why People Don't Heal and How They Can*, Caroline Myss suggests there is something to be learned from what we don't know and can't find out: "The purpose of the mysteries of our lives may well be to lead us out of our dependence on human reasoning and its limited ability to account for why things are the way they are and to acceptance that Divine intelligence is actually in control of our lives."[4] We moderns live with the illusion that we control our own lives, and it is difficult to accept that while we do indeed have free will, God is active in our lives, and in more than a passive way.

Alice Walker, the award-winning author of *The Color Purple*, tells of a time in the 1990s when she gave up writing for good. "I began to feel that writing was wonderful, but I was once removed from everything I experienced," she says. "I wanted just to show up at places and with people as nothing but myself, not as a writer." For three years she didn't write a word. "Then one day, I was walking through this house and started feeling very strange. I sat on a bench in the sunroom and I felt as though I was being physically informed that I didn't get to decide when I stop (writing). Who informed me, I couldn't say. But I felt it. I nodded, went to Mexico, and every morning I wrote poems. I haven't stopped writing since."[5]

Jesus spoke of this mysterious activity of God in his parables, though they were often misunderstood even by those closest to him. The disciples asked Jesus, "Why do you speak to them in parables?" And Jesus answered, "The reason I speak to them in parables is that 'seeing they do not perceive, and hearing they do not listen, nor do they understand' " (Matthew 13:10, 13).[6]

More likely, Jesus responded to this kind of question with another parable, much like the composer who played a piano sonata for his students, and when asked the meaning of the piece, sat down at the piano and played it again. "That's what it means," he said. The story is the message. It says something that cannot be said or explained in any other way. Jesus tells a number of parables that are quite troubling and probably meant to disturb the hearer. The parables of "The Unmerciful Servant" (Matthew 18:23-34), "The Laborers In The Vineyard" (Matthew 20:1-16), and "The Unjust Steward" (Luke 16:1-8), are three that come to mind. I would love to ask Jesus to explain their meaning. "Jesus, what in the world were you trying to say?" I am sure I would be disappointed with his response, as the disciples often were, because they just didn't get it, at least not at first: not until much later, when they looked back after the resurrection with a new perspective.

Miracle stories, those found in scripture and those drawn from contemporary events, have a similar effect. They take us into a different realm by challenging our understanding of reality, and thus for many, they are indeed confusing and often disturbing.

Why tell stories that people find confusing and don't understand? Why tell stories that are upsetting? Upsetting people is the point. Eugene Lowry, author of the narrative preaching classic, *Doing Time In The Pulpit*, teaches that the preacher must first create some disequilibrium when preaching a sermon, and then bring resolution to the tension in the conclusion. He says, "You don't have to do that when preaching a funeral sermon because they just rolled the disequilibrium down the aisle."[7]

When Jesus told a parable it was his intention to create disequilibrium. How else could he get people who were content with the world as it was to see the new thing God was doing? When people entered into Jesus' stories they were caught up in the "new thing" God was doing, grasped by something powerful that turned their familiar world upside down and inside out. They could never again look at life in quite the same way. The parable is a window into the new order that Jesus is both announcing and bringing about.

21

In miracle preaching the story of the miracle creates the disequilibrium, and this can be the catalyst for a miracle in the lives of the hearers. Martin Buber told how stories can convey real healing power.

> A story must be told in such a way that it constitutes help in itself. My grandfather was lame. Once they asked him to tell a story about his teacher. And he related how his teacher used to hop and dance while he prayed. My grandfather rose as he spoke, and he was so swept away by his story that he began to hop and dance to show how the master had done. From that hour he was cured of his lameness. That's how to tell a story.[8]

That's how to preach a miracle! Miracles happen when miracles are preached. People are healed physically and spiritually. The telling of miracle stories is therapeutic for all involved. Hearers can be healed as much as tellers. After the trauma of the crucifixion and the shock of the resurrection, the disciples told the story as much to convince and heal themselves as to proclaim the miracle of Jesus alive.

Tim O'Brien, author of *The Things We Carried*, a Vietnam War-era novel, said writing novels about Vietnam is a way of dealing with the mysteries of that war that are still unresolved for him.

> The moment of trauma, whether combat-related, a product of childhood abuse, or a wrenching divorce that severs a relationship, can only be understood in successive viewings ... the human mind tends to circle and re-circle tragedy. Each pass provides a new perspective for explaining the inexplicable or resolving elements of a mystery, like changing the lenses on a camera.[9]

This is what the disciples were doing, circling and re-circling, trying to make sense of Jesus' tragic death and startling reappearance in that locked room. They were terrified when they saw Jesus in his resurrected body. He came to them suddenly, seemingly out of nowhere (John 20:19-23). They thought he was a ghost (Luke 24:36-43). Others, when told, refused to believe it. They wanted to see and touch. And when they did see, discovered he looked very much like he did before he died, was solid to the touch, yet able to pass through walls.

This resurrection miracle transformed and energized the disciples and made it possible for them to give witness to it against great odds. We face even stiffer resistance today in the modern world.

Milwaukee Journal Sentinel columnist and author, Philip Chard, spoke at our Lenten lecture series last year about his crusty, farmer father, saying he was a Presbyterian atheist who did not believe in life after death. His father used to say, "When you're dead, you're dead!" Modern disciples of Jesus have the almost-impossible task of giving witness to the resurrection to people who don't believe in life after death. "When you're dead, you're dead." 'Nuff said!

Raymond Moody told a colleague about plans to do research on life after death and was told pointedly: "There goes your career."[10] Belief in life after death is outside the officially sanctioned concept of reality, was then, is now, even among many Christians.

We moderns and post-moderns are like those who doubted just after the resurrection. We want to see and touch for ourselves. We would like to have proof. Give us something tangible, statistics, data, the results of carefully controlled experiments, at the very least; we want rock-hard facts. 2,000-year-old anecdotal evidence is not enough. Even the eyewitness accounts of contemporaries, neighbors and friends, spouses and children, will not persuade most of us that life after death is part of the God-created nature of reality.

John Wesley taught his Methodist followers to inquire regularly about each other's spiritual health. They were to ask one another, at least weekly in their class meetings, "How is it with your soul?" The question makes an assumption that not everyone who frequents Christian worship is willing to make — that there is such an entity as a soul, that I am a soul and you are a soul, a spiritual being as well as a physical being. The French theologian, Teilhard de Chardin, said, "We are not human beings on a spiritual path, we are spiritual beings on a human path." In his book, *Denial of Soul*, M. Scott Peck defines soul as "... a God-created, God nurtured, unique, developable, immortal human spirit." Peck declares a soul is a person's "essential spirit" and because it is spirit it cannot be codified or measured.[11] The soul is a mystery as the creator of souls is a mystery. Jesus said, "Do not fear those who kill the body but cannot kill the soul ..." (Matthew 10:28).

Most of us don't live as if we believe we are eternal souls. We live as if we are a body with a life span of seventy to a hundred years. We prepare carefully for retirement. We have pension plans, carefully selected investments, IRAs, mutual funds, stocks and bonds, and maybe even social security.

We have long, sober conversations about the best way to make ourselves secure in old age, to insure our present standard of living right up to the moment that the hearse comes to haul away our remains. We laugh when we see the bumper sticker, "The One With The Most Toys Wins," but it is not too far from the way we live. Many of us who live in the Western world have so many possessions that we cannot, or will not, allow ourselves to see beyond this world and what we have in it. There is so much more to see and know.

In his book, *Carpe Diem*, Tony Campolo tells about a Franciscan monk he met at conference where he was to be the featured speaker. The monk was there to lead meditation and worship, some of which was to occur outside on the grassy hills and in the woods surrounding the conference center. Tony was trying get into the meditating but nothing was happening for him. So one day he took the monk aside and told him about his frustration. He received quite a surprising response. His Franciscan friend told him he "... did not know how to experience nature as a sacrament." He said when you are trying to meditate in a natural setting, "... listen to God. Ask Him to speak to you through his creation.... Look closely at something long enough, and you will find that it begins to look back at you."[12] That night, Tony went outside, found a place to meditate and followed the monk's instructions. He fell fast asleep and awoke to a glorious sight.

24

... everything around me was ablaze with God ... I felt
myself bombarded by the Holy Spirit. Holiness was
coming from under and over and around everything ...
the glory of the Lord was burning in the bushes around
me ... I was already raptured and I was already tasting
the world that is to come.[13]

I remember visiting my father, Leonard, in a nursing home during the last several weeks before he died in September of 1998. Each day he sank lower as he fought a losing battle with Parkinson's and heart disease.

I recall how saddened I was by his suffering, the loneliness of the nursing home, the physical and emotional pain as he experienced loss after loss of functions he had taken for granted all his life. I recoiled at his bursts of anger. I knew all about the stages of dying, but knowing what's coming, and why, did not make it easier to bear. This four-year veteran of World War II who had dodged bullets in the sand dunes of North Africa and on the mountains of Italy was not going "gentle into that good night," and I was struggling with the meaning of it all.

The last time I visited Dad in his room at Pine Valley Manor, near Richland Center, I found him in a sweeter mood, more malleable, the anger and defiant resistance against the relentless progression of the diseases forgotten for a moment. His birds were singing in their cages and he was playing on his mouth organ an old hymn that I remember well. I sang with the birds as he played.

Count your blessings, name them one by one,
Count your blessings, see what God has done,
Count your blessings, name them one by one,
Count your many blessings, see what God has done![14]

It was a moment of grace, a fleeting epiphany for me, and I think also for Dad. Just for a moment the sweet familiar tune of that old gospel hymn took us to that place of trust and peace that the disciples must have known when Jesus gave them glimpses of the kingdom. We were given "a taste of the world to come," though I didn't recognize what it was at the time.

25

Renita Weems tells about "mystery breaking into our domain" in her book, *Listening To God*.

> ... *we rarely recognize what we ought to recognize at the moment we ought to recognize it ... It usually takes us hours, days, weeks, months, perhaps years for most of us to realize, that we were visited by an angel. We are usually too preoccupied with our own thoughts, own prejudices, own self interest to notice.*[15]

Transcendent experiences open our eyes to all that is around us. We begin to see with what is called our "third eye" or "sixth sense." It allows us a view of the unseen world, unseen by most of us most of the time, and just as real as the one we can see, touch, taste, and hear. It becomes visible in fleeting moments of grace, often for no apparent reason.

I woke at 3 a.m. a few years ago to answer nature's call, got out of bed, and was just about to walk toward the bathroom when I noticed a figure, a spirit that had the form of my wife, Jo. The spirit was moving toward the bed where I could see Jo's head on her pillow and her body clearly under the covers. Jo's spirit was outside of her body. It blew my mind and I still don't fully understand it, nor did Jo have an explanation or memory of it when I told her what I had seen later that morning. I do know I have always had a good grasp of reality and I know I wasn't dreaming. I have read that we have a silver cord that connects the spiritual body to the physical body — and that sometimes we leave our physical bodies while sleeping and wander about in our spiritual bodies. I never would have believed it if I hadn't seen it for myself.

Ken Gelhaus, tells about an unusual epiphanal moment that came as a most unexpected answer to prayer.

> *My mother's oldest sister lived in Spring Green, west of Madison. After her husband died, my parents, who lived in Madison, used to visit her often — and help with house and lawn tasks. My father died in '74 and my mother was limited to a nursing home, so Joan and I picked up the caregiver roles as best we could. One*

26

summer day, I was driving by myself from Stoughton,
where we lived at the time, to Spring Green. It was re-
ally, really hot (we had no AC in the car); and I was
really, really tired. Driving Highway 14, I came to a
place where bridgework was being done. To do the work,
the traffic was routed off 14 up into the hills. Hot! Tired!
Pressed for time — and now a detour! Perhaps you can
imagine my mumbling, grumbling, complaining. Finally,
I prayed something like, "Lord, if you really want me
to help my aunt this afternoon, you're going to have to
help me make it through." In moments there came a
refreshing cool shower — not outside the car, just in-
side, just on me. The car seat did not get wet, my clothes
did not get wet, my hair did not get wet; but I was cooled
and mightily refreshed by a "shower of blessing." Such
a thing had never happened to me before, nor has it
since, but I am most thankful that it did then![16]

Once you have an experience like this you are never the same. You have looked over the edge of the world as we know it and there is no going back, not completely anyway; the other world and its incomparable wonders are etched forever in memory.

According to family lore, my great-great-grandmother, Catherine Isbell, was once unconscious and near death with pneumonia at a time when doctors were few and far between. When the doctor finally arrived at her homestead out on the prairie in Oklahoma, he took one look at her and gave her an injection in the arm. When she regained consciousness she was angry; "Ohhh, I was almost in heaven. I could see over there and it was beautiful, and then the devil came along and poked his spear in my arm, and here I am back in the world!"

Tony Campolo wrote, "Once one has experienced the transcendent ... one can never again be content with the world the way it is."[17] The apostle Paul was very likely describing such a near-death experience when he wrote:

And I know that such a person — whether in the body
or out of the body I do not know; God knows — was

caught up into Paradise and heard things that are not
to be told, that no mortal is permitted to repeat.
— 2 Corinthians 12:3-4

Spiritual writer, Phyllis Tickle, was transformed by a near-death experience when she was expecting her first child in 1955. She said it was "... inexpressibly beautiful, suffused with a joy far beyond the paltry reaches of that word." Phyllis tells that she has never been the same since. She does not fear death, and she said it has removed from her own spiritual life, "... much of what institutional religion and formal dogma use as glue for holding the faith and faithful together." But her experience became a point of contention between her and her physician husband who simply could not understand what she was "babbling about." Over the years, Phyllis says, she has learned to forgive him and to understand how her experience was a threat to his soul, how it "... threatened everything he believed in...."[18]

Those who have life-changing experiences of God's presence are often so filled with joy and so excited that they can't wait to tell someone, only to discover their dear ones don't want to hear it and are threatened by the very idea.

Jean Callihan describes how shocked she was at ordained clergy friends who discounted a profound healing in her life that occurred on a Christmas day after a long, difficult illness that left her incapacitated for nearly three years.

Christmas Healing
Jean Callihan

In the fall of 1986, at the age of 41, I contracted the Epstein-Barr virus. I was very sick — unable to sit up or walk, unable to understand language because I could not remember more than about three words in succession, and unable to do the simplest math. My recovery was very slow, not measured day to day or week to week, but month to month. By June 1989, I was finally able to work full-time again, but I tired easily and experienced similar, though less severe, intellectual problems. I continued to recover slowly and

28

was able to begin seminary at Louisville Presbyterian Theological Seminary in 1993, at the age of 47.

My education was often a struggle because of recurring debilitating fatigue and resulting intellectual difficulties. My prayer during those days was "God, you have gifted me and called me to this task. I don't see how I will have the strength to do it, but I know you will only give me work I am able to do." During my first semester of classes I had two experiences that shook me. When I took biblical Hebrew, I had the eeriest feeling that I knew the language and had spoken it before. And I began to lose my faith as I studied deeply the Old Testament. Both of these experiences frightened me. For many months I prayed for "some small, definitive reminder that you are really there" and not just a figment of the frightened imaginations of primitive people.

At the same time in 1994, I was serving a part-time field education chaplaincy at a nursing home. As the holidays approached I was unable to afford (both monetarily and health-wise) a trip to be with family and friends. I was determined to have a good Christmas season even though I would be one of the few students left on campus. I spent Christmas day at the nursing home leading Christmas services and chatting with the residents. After work, I drove to the home of one of the other student chaplains and spent time with her and her family.

When I finally got back to campus I was exhausted in every way. But I fixed my Christmas feast and, almost too tired to eat, sat down with it in front of my television. While I was channel surfing, I came across a show in which an actress was playing an angel and was suspended over a stage by cables. The cables broke, but she didn't fall. What in the world is this show? I wondered. I stayed on that channel to find out. Eventually the credits began to roll and the words "Touched By An Angel" rolled across the screen. The very moment those words appeared I felt a strange sensation in my mid-section. I focused on the sensation to see if I was going to be sick. As I focused and attempted to define what was happening, I became aware that it felt like a cross between a large ball of light and electricity. This all happened the moment the words came across the television screen — much more quickly than I can describe it — and in that moment, I knew I had been healed. And I was.

I have never had another symptom in the nearly twelve years since. I am working full-time at an often stressful and tiring job as a therapist. I love it and I am good at it.

A footnote to my healing story involves who believed it and who did not. I did not talk about what happened until I saw that all of my symptoms were indeed gone. Then, as I began to talk about it, I noticed that any ordained minister I told was skeptical or rejected my claim, but non-ordained people of faith were moved and believed. What's up with that?[19]

I wrote of my own conflicted experience of the holy in *Vision Stories*. It was just after I had gone to bed, late on Maundy Thursday evening, in the year 2000; a thought came into my head that I would be able to see a spirit if I simply looked. I opened my eyes and saw something indescribably beautiful about two feet above my head. It was a bright, luxurious purple, then deep azure blue, radiant, dynamic, pulsating: a being of light and energy moving slowly closer and closer. As it drew near, I tried to communicate through thoughts, asking who or what I was seeing, and the meaning of the visitation. There was no discernable response. Then the spirit touched me, more like flowed into my being. I felt warmly loved. The warmth moved over and through my body like liquid love. It was exhilarating, like nothing I have ever experienced before. The vision lasted three or four minutes.

The memory of this encounter with the holy still warms my heart. I continue to experience it as a healing presence. I am healthier physically, emotionally, and spiritually than I was before I opened my eyes that night. Most of the painful symptoms of a debilitating illness I had suffered periodically for seven years have abated. The vision is a "blessed assurance" of the presence of God, an answer to prayers for healing, and a beacon to light my way in the years to come. I am grateful beyond words.

What I can express about my vision I have learned to say carefully to people I have reason to believe might be receptive. Some people don't know what to say when they hear of an experience like this. Others dismiss it as foolishness. We live in a culture that is not vision-friendly.

Still, like it or not, believe it or not, the eternal breaks into our lives on a regular basis. Jesus got it right, "... the kingdom of God has come near ..." (Mark 1:15b). His resurrection and continuing presence with us is proof of that, if only we could learn to trust it.

Karen Steineke tells of being baptized at our church in suburban Milwaukee when she was 21 years old.

> *As the pastor was performing the rite, I began to feel a warmth around me suffused and without form. I looked up to see the form of Jesus with an overpowering light surrounding him. For what seemed like minutes I was suspended in time and space. I felt such love and awe. I remember my tears, and, as we left the chapel I tried to hide them from my husband because I was so overcome with a feeling one cannot describe.*[20]

There is a committal prayer in *The Book of Common Prayer* which affirms that God, in Jesus, has "brought life and immortality to light."[21] Reflecting on the prayer, Brian Donst, a Canadian colleague, wonders if Jesus has "revealed" in his resurrection something that has always been a reality in our world.

> *The prayer seems to suggest that resurrection is a fact of life, the problem being that we do not have the eyes to see it or the heart to trust it, and our salvation consisting in part of our having our eyes and hearts opened to see and trust it.... Perhaps the resurrection was one more instance of something God does all the time. Perhaps resurrection is built into the very structure (Logos) of the universe and of life, and the major difference between Jesus and us is that Jesus (because of his intimacy with God) knew and trusted it, whereas we (because of our alienation from God) do not.*[22]

Resurrection is the miracle that shapes the lives of all of us who choose to walk with Jesus. Trusting it is a leap of faith into the "kingdom come" that Jesus has revealed. This new way of being doesn't come easy, and when it does it is like being hit upside the head with a baseball bat, shocking and world shattering.

Keith R. Eytcheson Sr. tells about an unexpected visitation while driving one day. His nephew, who had committed suicide days before, "... appeared in front of the car, seemingly suspended in mid-air. I stared in shock as he said to me, 'Tell them I'm okay.' Then he disappeared." Keith writes, "I drove ahead, pulled the car over, and began to weep...."[23]

An experience like that is the beginning of a paradigm shift. Suddenly there is another dimension of reality to consider. But it is very difficult to change a personal worldview when most everyone else in the culture clings to the old.

I learned a new word in a book about reincarnation of all things. The word is "consilience." Jim B. Tucker, a professor from the University of Virginia, gives a definition in *Life Before Life: A Scientific Investigation of Children's Memories of Previous Lives*: "The need for consilience — the ability of new knowledge to be woven into the fabric of current understanding — helps to filter out erroneous belief — but it can also keep new insight from being accepted." He gives the examples of Galileo who suffered humiliation at the hands of the inquisition in 1633 for his shocking idea about the earth revolving around the sun, of the "... failure of scientists to recognize the existence of meteorites despite reports by farmers of rocks falling from the sky," and of Ignaz Semmelweis, a Hungarian obstetrician in the 1800s, who was vilified for "... producing data that showed that death rates during childbirth dropped significantly if doctors washed their hands...."[24]

Up until the middle of the 1850s, physicians didn't wash their hands vigorously before examining patients because they didn't know germs could be transmitted from person to person. Semmelweis noticed that the death rate among newborns was significantly higher on wards where physicians examined expectant mothers after doing autopsies. When he required the young doctors to disinfect their hands before obstetric examinations the death rates decreased dramatically. One would think the world would welcome such good news, but in fact, Semmelweis was dismissed from one position and when he proved his theory again in another hospital, was ridiculed publicly by a leading pathologist and suffered a breakdown. He was admitted to a mental institution where he died soon after in 1865 at the age of 47.[25]

The need for consilience often keeps us out of the mainstream of life where the Spirit is doing its saving work. It usually takes a society several generations to fully integrate radical new ideas. In *A History of Scientific Ideas*, Charles Singer tells how dramatic new discoveries impact the scientific world very slowly.

> *It seems as though a new method of approach can gain admittance to science or to philosophy only by transforming itself into something like the shape of one already existing. It must be attuned to the times. Its success depends on its maintaining itself, sometimes in disguise, until its achievements are so great and so incongruous with the form in which they have been expressed that recognition of its true shape, becomes at last inescapable.*[26]

Just after I signed a contract to write this book in April of 2006, I went with three young leaders of our congregation to a workshop intended to attune us to the changes that are coming in the church. We were among about 100 other United Methodists from all over Wisconsin, gathered in a church basement on a Saturday morning to listen to a Harvard professor talk about immunity to change. Dr. Robert Kegan told us that most individuals and organizations are immune to deep and lasting change in spite of the best intentions. He said, "Even though we might have a sincere commitment to change, even though we might know in our hearts that we stop whatever it is that is killing us or we die, many people unwittingly apply productive energy toward a hidden competing commitment. The resulting internal conflict stalls the effort in what looks like resistance but is in fact a kind of personal immunity to change."

Dr. Kegan gives the example of the employee who is dragging his feet on a project, because he fears if he does it too well he might be given an even tougher assignment, which he fears he won't be able to handle. This fear is a competing commitment, which prevents him from ever becoming a more productive employee though he may say to himself that he wants to change. Says Kegan, who works with businesses to implement change in individuals and organizations, "Without an understanding of competing commitments, attempts to change employee behavior are virtually futile."

What Professor Kegan offers is a process for helping people uncover their competing commitments, to identify the underlying assumptions driving these commitments and begin to change their behavior so that, ultimately, they can accomplish their goals.[27]

Christians today have a competing commitment with a prevailing cultural view that is skeptical of miracles, a view that has come from a mistaken conclusion that the scientific discoveries of the past 300 years have debunked the miracles of the scriptures. In his 1976 book, *The Other Side of Silence*, Morton Kelsey asserts, "Science needs to go back to its sources and learn how to think, and what to think about all over again." He quotes Paul Feyerbend who suggested "... scientists need to develop their imaginations and open up their limited view of what makes up reality." Kelsey points to meditative prayer as one way of becoming open to the reality that is overlooked by scientists.

> *At present we tend only to see data which fits and is useful to the system of thinking about reality in which we were raised. One of the most important reasons for developing meditative techniques is to open us so that we can see realities from which we have been cut off by today's single-minded, intellectual objectivity.*[28]

Kelsey does not deny the importance of science in helping us to measure and analyze the nature of physical reality. He just wouldn't stop there. There is another reality beyond the physical world if only we will open our senses to it. Kelsey "... rejects equally the one-sidedness of the West, and the one-sidedness of the East which finds illusion in both the inner and outer world." He recommends that we open ourselves to "... an objective psychic or spiritual world which appears to be independent of the individual psyche and apparently extends beyond it."[29]

The apostle Paul dealt with immunity to change in his first letter to the Corinthian church when he was having it out with those who were denying the resurrection. He began with the witness of the church naming Peter and all the others, 500 on one occasion, who had seen the risen Christ. Then Paul "brings it home," as they call out to preachers in African-American churches, "bring it on home now."

> *Last of all, as to one untimely born, he has appeared also to me. For I am the least of the apostles, unfit to be called an apostle, because I persecuted the church of God. But by the grace of God I am what I am, and his grace toward me has not been in vain.*
> — 1 Corinthians 15:8-10a

We may be sure that he told of his Damascus road encounter with Jesus in vivid detail, again and again, wherever he preached. God's grace toward Paul was not in vain, because it was not for Paul alone; it was also for the thousands who would hear his story from his own lips and the billions of us who have been born since who have read his words in scripture. It is this "bring it on home" part that is missing in most mainline worship services today.

Too many preachers have been warned not to share their personal experiences lest they draw attention to themselves and distract from the gospel. Ralph Waldo Emerson said just the opposite in an address to a graduating class at Harvard Divinity School in the late nineteenth century. He told them about a preacher who caused him to consider forgoing public worship.

> *He had no word intimating that he had laughed or wept, was married or in love, had been commended or cheated or chagrined. If he had ever lived or acted we were none the wiser for it. The capital secret of his profession, namely to turn life into truth, he had not learned ... The true preacher can be known by this, that he deals out to people his life — life passed through the fire of thought. But of the bad preacher, it could not be told from his sermon what age of the world he fell in; whether*

35

he had a father or a child; whether he was a freeholder
or a pauper; whether he was a citizen or a country-
man; or any other fact of his biography.[30]

Do we dare speak of our visions and miracles from the pulpit?

Since 2000, I have collected over 200 vision and miracle sto-ries for the three books I edited in the "Vision" series for CSS Publishing Company. I have told many of these accounts in story concerts and Vision seminars, and, almost always someone ap-proaches me afterward and says very quietly, "Something like that happened to me once." They will then tell me of their experience, and when they have finished I often hear these same six words, "I have never told anyone before."

Sometimes these experiences of the holy have occurred sixty or seventy years ago. They are clearly the most sacred moments of their lives, a memory treasured and pondered in the heart, called up in moments of crisis as a source of strength, and they have never told anyone. Our culture discourages speaking about transcendent encounters, and consequently many of us cannot say with Paul, "... his grace toward me has not been in vain" (1 Corinthians 15:10).

Reynolds Price wrote about an encounter he had with the liv-ing Christ in his most recent book, *Letter to a Godchild.* Price is now in his seventies and this event occurred almost twenty years ago, when he was 51. He had been diagnosed with cancer of the spine, which at that time, in the early 1980s, could not be com-pletely removed by surgery. He was preparing to receive five weeks of radiation treatment with the hope that it would prevent inevi-table paralysis. The treatment itself could lead to paralysis and the alternative was to wait while the tumor paralyzed his legs, arms, hands, and eventually lungs, which would result in his death. The vision came while he was propped up in bed a few days before the radiation was to begin. He suddenly found himself on the beach of a large lake that he somehow knew was the Sea of Galilee. He is certain that he was not dreaming and he doesn't know how he came to be on that beach, but he has no doubt about the reality of what happened there.

... in a moment, a man I knew to be Jesus had silently beckoned me into the water with him. In another moment — still silent — he was washing the foot-long wound from the failed surgery ... At last Jesus spoke only a four-word sentence — "our sins are forgiven." ... *I pushed him on for the answer I most wanted — "Am I also healed?" As if I'd forced it from him, he said only, "That, too." And though he gave no obvious sign of anger at my question, he said nothing more and waded back to land....*[31]

Reynolds believes he was healed in that moment, though he proceeded with the radiation treatments. Two years later, a surgical technique became available that made it possible to remove all of the cancer. He thinks now that having the radiation might have been a mistake, that perhaps he should have trusted that his healing was complete, and thus avoided the subsequent paralysis of his lower body. He also leaves room for the possibility that the miracle came, in part, through the radiation and surgery. In any event, he has lived almost twenty years after being told that he probably could not live long.

Reynolds has published his stories in previous books and has received many letters from well-adjusted persons who have had similar "transcendent experience," who almost always tell him, "... that they'd never previously revealed their experience to anyone else for fear of ridicule."[32]

There is power in personal witness, and it is not so much that it convinces people who don't believe in miracles, as it gives confidence to people who have experienced miracles that it is at last safe to tell their own stories, and not least, to trust the validity and power of their miracles.

In December of 2005, a young mother wrote to me in response to a vision survey I sent out. She wrote about some powerful life-changing experiences that she had shared with only three trusted people in her life. She said she wanted to tell her pastor but was afraid he wouldn't understand.

37

I have had three experiences that have been unexplain-
able by scientific standards ... I (have) such a hard time
describing them ... It's like trying to describe color that
doesn't exist. It's like going 90 mph on roller skates
when you have never skated before, or like slipping off
the world and into another dimension where none of
our rules (gravity, time, and the like) apply. It's confus-
ing, and it's terrifying ... I feel a sense of isolation, be-
cause I cannot share them with others. I fear they will
think I'm making them up, or that I'm crazy. I assure
you, neither is true.[33]

After reading an account of her visions, which were indeed among the most remarkable I have known, I wrote to her that her visions were similar to others I had heard and to some visions found in the Bible. She replied, "It is a giddy sort of relief to find that this sort of thing does in fact happen to 'everyday people.' "[34]

There are many people like this young woman, as Marcus Borg tells in his book, *The God We Never Knew.*

In a number of workshops, I have asked people whether
they have had one or more experiences that they would
identify as an experience of God and, if so, to share in
small groups. On average, 80% of the participants re-
port that they have never before been asked that ques-
tion in a church setting or given an opportunity to talk
about it.[35]

When I preach I know there are many in the pews who have had experiences of the divine and could tell of miracles and visions if they thought their testimonies would be welcomed, or at least not mocked. I always try to tell stories that will affirm their experiences.

I also know that on any given Sunday, especially on Christmas Eve and Easter, there are a significant number of souls who will grimace at the slightest mention of miracles. I have seen it happen many a time, including at funerals when I talk about resurrection. I know that on Easter Sunday more than half of those singing "Christ

The Lord Is Risen Today," often with great gusto, don't believe a word of it, and there is little I can do or say that will change their minds, God bless 'em. But I might be able to plant a seed that will some day find a way to grow through the crusty layers of doubt that encase the hearts of so many modern "when you're dead, you're dead," skeptics.

We have a small pine tree growing out of the side of the bluff across the creek from our farmhouse. In time, as its roots go deeper into the cracks, and it grows into a towering beauty like the mother pine that preceded it on the bluff, the rock will crack, making way for the growing tree. In the same way, the gospel has a way of breaking through crusty souls, slowly over time, like a steady stream that eventually hollows out a great canyon. And sometimes, much more often than we might think, our rock-hard hearts are melted suddenly by an experience of the holy that blows away all of our reasonable doubts.

Just as I finished writing what I thought was the last paragraph in this introduction, at 6:30 p.m., September 29, 2006, the phone rang in our farmhouse in southwest Wisconsin, where Jo and I go to retreat from our busy city lives. It was tragic news. That morning, just five miles up the road, at a local high school, a fifteen-year-old freshman boy had walked in the front doors carrying a shotgun. A custodian wrestled the weapon away from him, and the boy then took out a handgun, turned toward the principal, and shot him three times as he, too, tried to disarm him. The principal died eight hours later. Twenty minutes before this incident, which occurred on the day the school was to celebrate homecoming with a football game and a dance, another student, one of the football players, was killed in an auto accident on the way to school.

My heart breaks for all of those touched by these tragedies. How do you go on after a thing like this? Can one really believe that all will ever be well again in all of those broken lives? What will become of the boy who committed murder? How will his family recover? It is what every person who has made a mess of his or her life wants to know when they come to hear our sermons on Sunday mornings. Is there really a God who cares and acts in our lives to save us?

The four people whose personal stories are shared below and the 35 people whose stories are sprinkled throughout this volume, answer this age old question with the bits and pieces of grace that has saved their lives.

God's Gift

Susan Rosenbaum

In May 1977, my husband, Randy, graduated from college and in September, took a good job in advertising in Pittsburg, Kansas. We had been married six years and had two daughters, Amy, five, and Melissa, four. This job was a dream come true, because I would be able to stay home with the girls and not have to work. We moved to Pittsburg, which was about two hours from our parents, bought a beautiful old home, and began our lives as a family.

After he had been on the job about nine months, I could tell that it was very stressful for Randy. It was obvious that this job was not a good fit for his life. We began talking about options. We talked about him staying with the job until the end of 1978, and then going back to school to get his master's degree in printing, a field he had come to love as he worked with printers in ad layouts. It would be tough financially, but since he had spent five years in the Air Force, he would get GI Bill money while he was in school and we could manage.

As time went on, his stress level continued to mount, and on October 28, he came home and told me he had quit his job, effective October 31. That was when my stress level went up. We had house payments, utilities, food, clothing, and other expenses of a young household. Randy did go out and find a minimum wage job, which barely helped with the major expenses, and I went to our state agency and applied for state assistance. Still, we were barely making ends meet. In November, we joined the United Presbyterian Church and began attending on a regular basis. It was through a Sunday school class that I was reminded of God's care. One of the members had witnessed to the fact that when she was struck with a serious illness, God had let her know in advance, through dreams, that she needed to prepare her daughter for what was to come.

I thought about her story for a while, and the next Saturday, when stress was keeping me awake in the middle of the night, I poured out my heart to God in a moment of despair. Christmas was almost upon us and I was not sure how I was going to make it through until Randy could start school and we would begin to get the GI Bill money. Immediately, a very bright light appeared in the corner of our bedroom, and as I gazed at the light, in spite of its brightness, I suddenly heard a voice that said, "Don't worry, everything is going to be all right." From that moment on, I was filled with a deep peace. I immediately went to sleep, and the next morning, and from that time on, I did not feel any stress about the future. I knew God was taking care of us.

I wish I could say that we had a great Christmas, but to tell you the truth, I don't really remember that Christmas. But I do remember my visit from God. And no matter what has happened in my life since, I am still aware of God's presence leading me on.[36]

A Sense Of Calm
Candy Harvey

My first experience at a book study group was during January, February, and March of 1986. We met in the home of one of our members every two weeks. The book we were reading was *The Road Less Traveled* by M. Scott Peck. It was during one of these sessions that I had my most profound experience of being in the presence of God.

This particular session was during a very painful time in my family's life. We had two small children, we sold our house, our plans to move into a house of our own had to be abandoned, I had had a miscarriage, there was talk of a job transfer for my husband, and I did not want to move. Someone asked me how I was that week and I ended up letting everything go and weeping in despair.

The group was tremendous. Under the leader's guidance, they prayed for me. I was laying face down on the carpet while everyone was gathered round, touching me. There were about thirty of

41

us. We prayed for strength and comfort. I could sense feelings of warmth seep into my body, starting at my toes and working their way up my body. I felt like I was floating and an overwhelming sense of calm enveloped me. It's hard to describe — to put into words with our limited human vocabulary. I don't know how long we were like that — time seemed to stand still. I remember receiving strength and courage and knowing without a doubt that life would be fine — that everything would be okay. I remember feeling a strong sense of being loved. And I knew that I wanted to pass on that love to others — I felt called to new life.[37]

Circle Of Joy
Mary Goldade

In the not too distant past, I was the victim of a crime. The perpetrator was someone I knew and whom I had come to trust. In the long run, I was not hurt physically, but the emotional effects were quite damaging. I struggled with what I now understand to be a common response amongst victims. I blamed myself, wondering what I could have done to elicit such criminal and immoral behavior in a person whose professionalism I trusted. It took several weeks for me to come out of shock enough to realize that I must do everything that I am able to keep the perpetrator from hurting someone else. I did not want another woman to go through what I had. It was then that I realized that I must go to the police.

Never was another more naive about police policy and legal proceedings than me. At the time I thought that the mere act of filing a report with the police would be enough to give the perpetrator a record. So, I filed my report. The officers were kind and understanding, but aside from the actual event I could not remember a more grueling three hours in my life. I told myself to hang on and that the effort would be worth it, because I was taking the step necessary to keep the perpetrator from hurting someone else.

Shortly after filing my statement, I learned that the perpetrator must be charged to have a record and a district attorney must decide whether there is enough evidence to file charges. My heart sank and that old feeling in the pit of my stomach came back —

fear. Given the lack of physical evidence and the "he said/she said" nature of the charge, I feared that charges might not be filed at all. How would the next woman be forewarned if the perpetrator had no record? I worried and obsessed day and night about whether charges would be filed. My circle of friends and family told me that I had done as much as I was able and that I should leave it in God's hands. Easier said than done! But, I did try to focus on my own healing. I looked for a counselor to help me through this time.

As he so often does, God led me to the therapist who was meant to help me. With her guidance, I learned what happened to me was not my fault. We met every week and chiseled away at the emotional effects of the crime. I'd be lying if I said I forgot about the legal proceedings, but I did more praying than worrying in those days of waiting. Finally, five weeks after filing my report, I got word that charges were filed. Hallelujah! Moved by this realization, I spontaneously put my hands together and lifted my face and folded hands to heaven. I said simply, but fully "Thank you, God!" As I did this, I felt light and joy surrounding me. I was suddenly aware of many beings of light encircling me. As I raised my voice in thanksgiving, I heard a joyous song in unison about me. Angels were praising God with me! At that moment my heart and soul were overwhelmed with pure joy. I was bathed in the light and love of the Holy Spirit as the angels and I sang our brief but heartfelt song of joyful thanks. It was truly a breathtaking and awe-inspiring moment.[38]

Larry Winebrenner tells a miracle story that has been handed down in his family for generations. Like many of the miracles described in the scriptures, it sounds too good to be true. Surely there has been some stretching of the truth here, I want to think. But there is also a part of me that knows from personal experience that the seemingly impossible is sometimes, dare I say often, possible in this wonderful world God has given us.

Don't Shoot The Angel

Larry Winebrenner

Joachim Christopher Martens believed in angels, especially the Angel of Peace. He migrated to the United States from Bremen, Germany, to escape war. He found in western Pennsylvania a land just like home. Almost. The farm he bought had shale fields. In order to grow corn, he lifted a piece of shale, dropped a kernel of corn, let the shale down on it and poured a tin can of water on top of it.

To grow hay, he plowed a field atop a hill behind his barn and farmhouse. He sowed the seed, mowed the hay when it had matured, raked it into piles, and loaded it on a hay wagon pulled by two horses — Blackie and Bruce. Pulled the load? He actually guided the wagon down the steep hill and into the barn. By strenuous braking and the holding back by Blackie and Bruce, the wagon barely stopped on the threshing floor of the barn. The hay was then tossed by hand into the haymow in the top of the barn. Once unloaded, the wagon departed through a second door. This time the wagon was pulled up the hill for another load.

Now Chris, as they called Joachim Christopher Martens, had a little two-year-old angel he adored named Flora Blanche. Sometimes he would let her place the corn kernels under the shale pieces. Sometimes he would let her ride on Bruce's back to the stable after Bruce was unhitched from the wagon after a day's work. And sometimes he'd just walk carefully when little Flora Blanche was under his feet as he went about the chores.

He had never bought any of his other children toys. "Waste of money," he said. But he bought Flora Blanche a doll. Her favorite place to play with the doll was in the barn on the threshing floor. She would pretend the doll was tossing hay up into the haymow, or that the doll was riding Bruce to the stable.

Chris had warned Flora Blanche not to play in the barn when he was making hay. "I can't stop the horses until they are completely on the threshing floor," he had explained. But what does a two-year-old understand about horses and threshing floors? So one day, she was playing on the threshing floor just as Chris was hauling back on the brake lever to slow the wagon on its descent down the hill. As the horses guided the wagon into a turn to enter the barn, Chris saw her. He was already pulling on the brake lever with all his might.

"Gott im himmel!" he cried as he yanked on the reins to hold the horses back. But at that moment, Bruce took the bit in his teeth and it was useless to pull on his reins. Chris could visualize the big hoofs kicking the little girl senseless — or worse, the large iron-banded wheels rolling over her like a great buzz saw, cutting her in half. He was crazy with agony. His only thought was to shoot Bruce for taking the bit in his teeth.

Then the miracle happened. As Bruce reached Flora Blanche, he let go of the bit. He reached down. He grabbed her dress in his teeth. He picked her up. He gently put her back down when the wagon stopped. The Martens family ever after claimed Bruce was an angel in disguise. And Chris didn't shoot him.

Larry says, "This is a true story that happened to my grand-mother as a girl. I've heard family members repeat it many times."[39]

---

1. Ruth Marilyn MacDonald was ordained in 1980. She retired recently from the Newport Pastoral Charge, where she shared in ministry with four congregations as well as working in Valley Presbytery. Marilyn and her partner, Leigh Sanford, make their home at 1981 Hwy #2, Milford Station, Nova Scotia B0N 1Y0.

2. Mona Lisa Schulze, *Awakening Intuition* (New York: Random House, 1997), pp. 308-310.

3. Thomas Merton, *Conjectures of a Guilty Bystander* (New York: Doubleday, 1966), pp. 140-141.

4. Caroline Myss, *Why People Don't Heal and How They Can* (New York: Three Rivers Press, 1997), p. 177.

5. Jeff Guin, *The Milwaukee Journal Sentinel*, May 24, 2004.

6. On other occasions the disciples asked Jesus about the meaning of a parable. The gospel writers have included explanations, which are of dubious origin; some scholars say they were later additions to the text. See the Parable of the Weeds and explanation in Matthew 13:24 and 37, and the Parable of The Sower explanation in Mark 4:10-20.

7. Eugene L. Lowry, *Doing Time in the Pulpit: The Relationship Between Narrative and Preaching* (Nashville: Abingdon Press, 1985), pp. 52, 70.

8. Martin Buber quoted in "Sunbeams," *The Sun*, July 1989, p. 40.

9. *Kenosha News*, February 7, 1994.

10. Raymond Moody, *Reunions* (New York: Villard Books, 1993), p. 45.

11. M. Scott Peck, *The Denial of The Soul: Spiritual And Medical Perspectives On Euthanasia And Mortality* (New York: Harmony Books, 1997), pp. 137, 156.

12. Tony Campolo, *Carpe Diem* (Nashville: W Publishing Group, 1994), pp. 140-141.

13. *Ibid*, p. 142.

14. Johnson Oatman Jr., "Count Your Blessings" (1897), *Tabernacle Hymns Number Four* (Chicago: Tabernacle Publishing Company, 1951), p. 50.

15. Renita Weems, *Listening To God: A Minister's Journey Through Silence and Doubt* (New York: Simon & Schuster, 1999), pp. 185-186.

16. Ken Gelhaus retired from parish ministry after forty years of service and returned to Madison with his wife, Joan. After 43 years away, they now enjoy a two-bedroom apartment located about half-way between the homes where they grew up. Ken and Joan have two children and two grandchildren. Ken says his spiritual journey began with Mrs. Peters, "... my kindergarten Sunday school teacher, whose love for wee kids introduced me to Jesus' love for me."

17. *Op cit*, Campolo, p. 144.

18. Phyllis Tickle, *The Shaping of a Life: A Spiritual Landscape* (New York: Doubleday, 2001), pp. 217-218.

19. Jean Callihan is an ordained Presbyterian clergy person who serves as a Marriage and Family Therapist and Independent Substance Abuse Counselor in Eagar, Arizona. She has a Master of Divinity and a Master of Arts in Marriage and Family Therapy from Louisville Presbyterian Theological Seminary. Though born in Florida, Jean lived in the midwest for 43 years and says she is a midwesterner at heart. She now lives at 7,000 feet at the foot of the beautiful White Mountains in Arizona, not far from her two sons, granddaughter, and soon-to-arrive grandson, in California.

20. Karen Steineke, "An Overpowering Light," *Shining Moments: Visions of the Holy in Ordinary Lives*, ed. John E. Sumwalt (Lima, Ohio: CSS Publishing, 2004), p. 179.

21. *The Book of Common Prayer: According to the Use of the Episcopal Church* (New York: The Church Hymnal Corporation and The Seabury Press, 1977), p. 493.

22. Brian Donst, shared on Midrash, Holy Week, 2002. Brian Donst is an ex-Baptist from Winnipeg, Manitoba, who has enjoyed a variety of congregational and university ministries. He serves Fifty United Church in Winona, Ontario. Brian and his wife, Japhia Cowling, share the joys and struggles of three children.

23. Keith R. Eytcheson Sr., "No One is Lost," *Vision Stories: True Accounts of Visions, Angels and Healing Miracles*, ed. John E. Sumwalt (Lima, Ohio: CSS Publishing, 2003), p. 77.

24. Jim B. Tucker, *Life Before Life: A Scientific Investigation of Children's Memories of Previous Lives* (New York: St. Martin's Press, 2005), pp. 195-196.

25. Mark Taylor, Ignaz Semmelweis: "Please Wash Your Hands," *Microbiology and Biotechnology News*, April-June, 1999. http://www.np.edu.sg/lsct/ssm/news/apr_jun99/ignaz.htm.

26. Charles Singer, *A History of Scientific Ideas: From the Dawn of Man to the Twentieth Century* (New York: Dorset Press, 1990), pp. 418-419. (Originally Oxford University Press, 1959.)

27. From notes taken at the "Immunity To Change Workshop" in Beaver Dam, Wisconsin, April 2006. Harvard Professor, Robert Kegan, and Lisa Laskow Lahey are co-authors of the book, *How the Way We Talk Can Change the Way We Work: Seven Languages for Transformation* in which they explain the immunity to change process. Dr Kegan describes the immunity to change

workshop as "an interior aerobics course, an inward-bound program ... a rope activity for the mind."

28. Morton T. Kelsey, *The Other Side of Silence: A Guide To Christian Meditation* (New York: Paulist Press, 1976), pp. 146-147.

29. *Ibid.*

30. Ralph Waldo Emerson, *An Address, Emerson: The Basic Writings Of America's Sage*, Eduard C. Lindeman, editor (New York: A Mentor Book, 1947), p. 175.

31. Reynolds Price, *Letter to a Godchild (Concerning Faith)* (New York: Scribner, 2006), p. 55.

32. *Ibid*, p. 58.

33. This writer prefers to remain anonymous. One of her stories appears at the conclusion of chapter 4, "While It Was Still Dark."

34. *Ibid.*

35. Marcus J. Borg, *The God We Never Knew: Beyond Dogmatic Religion to a More Authentic Contemporary Faith* (San Francisco: Harper, 1997), p. 53.

36. Susan Rosenbaum is pastor of First Presbyterian Church in Columbus, Kansas. She and Randy have been married for 35 years and have two daughters and five grandchildren. Susan loves to read, knit, and do counted cross-stitch.

37. Candy Harvey is the pastor of Lucknow United Church in Lucknow, Ontario. She and her life partner, Stan, have three adult children. Ministry is a second career for Candy, but her first vocation. She was a teacher for many years before making her way back to university to complete her Master of Divinity at Emmanuel College, University of Toronto. lucknowunited@hurontel.on.ca.

38. Mary Goldade resides in the majestic Rocky Mountains with her beloved husband and 47 fish. She's in her element in the forested woodlands and feels God's presence in the snow-capped wonderland where sunrise and sunset gleam in glory. As an environmental scientist, Mary has in the past struggled with how to be true to both science and faith. However, life experiences like the one described in this book have strengthened her spirituality and acceptance in the powerful and immutable mysteries of God.

39. Larry Winebrenner is Professor Emeritus of Miami-Dade Community College, after 33 years of teaching. He served as pastor of churches in Georgia, Florida, Indiana, and Wisconsin, retiring after thirteen years as pastor of York Memorial UMC in Miami. Larry has authored two college textbooks, served as an editor for three newspapers and an academic journal, and contributed articles to several magazines.

Miracle 1

Dreaming Joseph

Now the birth of Jesus the Messiah took place in this way. When his mother Mary had been engaged to Joseph, but before they lived together, she was found to be with child from the Holy Spirit. — Matthew 1:18

Joseph had a problem. What to do about Mary? (God also had a problem. What to do about Joseph, but first things first.)

It was actually more Mary's problem than it was Joseph's. She had the most to lose in this situation. According to the Law of Moses she could have been put to death:

If there is a young woman, a virgin already engaged to be married, and a man meets her in the town and lies with her, you shall bring both of them to the gate of that town and stone them to death....
— Deuteronomy 22:23-24a

This law was not enforced by the rabbis at the time Matthew was writing, but it was still considered adultery, a grave offense which would affect Mary's social standing for the rest of her life.

Imagine how young Mary must have felt. Not more than thirteen or fourteen years old, her life was just beginning. She had been excited about her engagement to Joseph, though she must have wondered if she was ready for the responsibilities of wife and mother. She must have thought, also, about what it would be like to be intimate with Joseph. Surely she had received advice from older girls, perhaps from her own mother — what to expect, how to prepare herself to be a good partner, and now to discover that she is with child. How could it be? She and Joseph had taken long walks together, but always within sight of someone from the family. He had held her hand once when no one was looking, but Mary knew enough about the world to know that babies were not the result of handholding. What was she going to do? Would her family disown her? If she lost Joseph, would she ever have a second chance to be a wife and mother?

Mary is in serious "trouble," as we used to say when a girl became pregnant out of wedlock. In the late 1960s, when I was in high school, there were basically two choices for a girl in trouble. She might be sent away — to a home for wayward girls or to relatives in the next state — or she would "have to" marry the boy. More often than not, she and the offending boy would be given what was called a "shotgun wedding." Theirs was not a match made in heaven, but at the insistence of their families, and to maintain some semblance of propriety, they "made the child legal." Though, of course, everybody knew what was up, or would know as soon as the ninth month rolled around. Sometimes, the boy would flee to the military or simply deny paternity, something one could get away with in the days before DNA testing was available.

A Righteous Man

> *Her husband Joseph, being a righteous man and unwilling to expose her to public disgrace, planned to dismiss her quietly.* — Matthew 1:19

There was no paternity test in Joseph's day. And since an engagement was a legal bond, dissolvable only by divorce or death, Joseph decided to "dismiss her quietly," an allowable legal solution, one that Matthew suggests Joseph preferred because he was a righteous man and did not want to bring Mary to public shame. This also meant she would not be charged with adultery or thought to be a rape victim.

52

Joseph is shown here to be what we would call a "stand-up guy." He was not only going to do the right thing, he was going to do it in the most merciful way possible. He is what the writers of *The Women's Bible Commentary* call a model of "higher righteousness," like Tamar, Rahab, Uriah, and Ruth who "also acted in a manner not expected in the social mores of their time, in order to further divine purposes." Joseph did what was right "... even though his action is neither legally necessary nor socially expected."[1]

We have all known stand-up guys like Joseph, both men and women, who will never run from a bad situation, will always do what is right and suffer any consequence.

Senator John McCain, of Arizona, told a personal story about a righteous man as part of a campaign speech when he was running for president in 2004. The righteous man happened to be a prison guard in a prisoner of war camp where McCain was being held during the Vietnam war. McCain had been placed in isolation and tied in "torture ropes" that grew tighter with each movement. Relief came in the midst of that long night from a most unexpected source. One of the guards came in and loosened the ropes to relieve McCain's pain. Early in the morning he returned and tightened the ropes so the other guards would not know what he had done.

> *He never said a word to the grateful prisoner, but some months later, on a Christmas morning, as the prisoner stood alone in the prison courtyard, the same Good Samaritan walked up to him and stood next to him for a few moments. Then with his sandal, the guard drew a cross in the dirt. The prisoner and guard both stood wordlessly there for a minute or two, venerating the cross, until the guard rubbed it out and walked away.*[2]

Esther Raab, a survivor of the Holocaust, tells about the night before she and "... 300 of her fellow inmates at the Sobibor death camp in Poland mounted a daring escape." She said her mother came to her in a dream. Like so many European Jews, they had been separated during World War II, not knowing each other's fate.

"I said, 'Tomorrow we are escaping,' and she said, 'I know.' And then she took me by the hand, out of the camp, and showed me the barn that she said I should hide in."

It took Esther two weeks to find the barn because she could only move about at night. When she finally found it, she made "... a startling discovery. Her brother, whom she had believed had been shot to death during a Nazi execution of young Jewish men, emerged from a shadowy corner of the building. He had heard her speak a few Yiddish words. The siblings, each thinking the other had died, were incredulous." Esther's brother had been in the barn for nine months and cared for by a farmer who "... regularly brought him bread, milk, and newspapers." She said the man was thrilled to see her, and kept them alive for nine-and-a-half more months, until it was safe for them to emerge. "That man had seven children, and his entire family was in danger if he had been caught helping us," she recently said in a phone interview. "They would have all been killed."[3]

One who is righteous is willing to risk everything to be faithful to God. Matthew foreshadowed the kind of righteousness Jesus would call for when he urged his followers to have righteousness that "... exceeds that of the scribes and Pharisees ..." (Matthew 5:20). Joseph was the epitome of the faithful Jewish man who made the best of a bad situation within the parameters of the law. The child was not his; what else could he do? God was about to show him what else. (As I wrote at the beginning, this was God's problem, too.)

Joseph decided to sleep on it before he did what he had to do, although one wonders how he could sleep at a time like that. Surely it was a fitful sleep as he wrestled unconsciously with what might have been the most important decision of his life. Can you imagine yourself in a situation like this?

A Righteous Joe: The Story Of A Modern Joseph

Mary didn't know what to do. How could she break the news to Joe? They had only been dating for six weeks, but she knew that he loved her. She could see it in his eyes. And she knew that she loved him. He was so gentle and understanding. There weren't many men in the world like Joe.

Mary had met Joe in the emergency room on the very night of the assault, and they had been together every day since, as if it was meant to be. Joe was there waiting for a friend who had twisted an ankle in a softball game. She sat next to him in the waiting room before they took her in to be examined. Mary had been too upset to talk, and Joe hadn't tried to make conversation. He didn't even ask what had happened. He simply looked at her with tenderness and said, "It will be okay. They will take care of you." Even those few words had been enough to create a bond between them. And Joe had come back later, after he took his friend home, to see if she was all right. By then, Mary was able to talk about the rape; the horror she had felt during the attack and the humiliation and anger that were still growing within her. She was grateful for his presence. Somehow it was easier to talk about it with him than with the counselor who had been assigned to her case. Joe had listened quietly for several hours that night, and had called or come to keep her company every night since, gradually coaxing her out of her small apartment into the world again.

Joe had never once tried to touch her, and Mary loved him for that. He seemed to know without her saying it that she couldn't stand to be touched — not yet. Soon, maybe. She had found herself longing for that moment and wondering what it would be like during the last couple of weeks. Mary knew that Joe would wait until she gave him a sign, and she had thought that it might be tonight. But when she let him know what the doctor had told her today, would Joe want to touch her? Was this the end of her hope that their love would lead to marriage and a family? What would Joe do when she told him about the baby?[4]

What Dreams Will Come?

> *But just when he had resolved to do this, an angel of the Lord appeared to him in a dream and said, "Joseph, son of David, do not be afraid to take Mary as*

55

your wife, for the child conceived in her is from the
Holy Spirit. She will bear a son and you are to name
him Jesus, for he will save his people from their sins."
— Matthew 1:20-21

In the midst of this restless sleep, Joseph had a dream. He had *the* dream, one that would change the course of his life. If you or I had such a dream we might dismiss it as "just a dream" and think no more about it. In the ancient Middle East, dreams were thought to be messages from supernatural powers. It was thought the gods communicated their will for humankind through the dreams of priests and kings. When the Pharaoh of Egypt had his dream about the "seven sleek and fat cows ..." and "seven other cows, ugly and thin ..." he knew God was telling him something significant. He called for Joseph, a prisoner who had made a name for himself interpreting dreams, to come and explain the meaning of his dream. Joseph told the Pharaoh that the dream portended the coming of a great famine. He was then released from prison and put in charge of a strategic planning team that would prepare for the coming disaster. Dream interpretation was a handy skill to have in the ancient world (Genesis 41:1-36).

Dream interpretation was also the source of upward mobility for Daniel, a young Hebrew living in exile in Babylon. When the king, Nebuchadnezzar, had a troubling dream about a great statue, he was bothered by it so much that he was unable to sleep. When his own sorcerers and magicians were unable to interpret the dream he called for Daniel, who was able to tell the king what God was revealing in the dream, and, he, like Joseph was promoted to a position of prominence in the kingdom (Daniel 2:31-49).

In the book of Judges we have the story of Gideon, who overheard one of his soldiers telling a dream just before the start of a big battle. The dream was about a cake of barley bread tumbling into the enemy camp and knocking down a tent. Another soldier interpreted the dream as an indication that Gideon's troops would prevail, and Gideon took it as a sign that God would give him the victory, which God did (Judges 7:9-23).

When Solomon succeeded to the throne of his father, David, God came to him in a dream and asked what he could do for him. Solomon asked for, and was given, wisdom (1 Kings 3:5-15).

In Acts, we read of an Italian centurion named Cornelius who was terrified one afternoon when he clearly saw an angel of God. The angel, whom Cornelius later described as wearing "dazzling clothes," told him to send servants to bring a Jewish man named Peter, who was visiting at the home of Simon the tanner in Joppa, to see him. While the servants were on the way, Peter went up onto the roof of Simon's house to pray. He fell into a dreamlike state and had a vision in which he was encouraged to eat foods that, by the laws of Moses, are considered to be unclean. While Peter was trying to sort out the meaning of this strange occurrence, the three servants of Cornelius arrived and convinced him to go back with them to their master's house. Peter went, and told the people gathered in the centurion's home, "... it is unlawful for a Jew to associate with or to visit a Gentile; but God has shown me that I should not call anyone profane or unclean." Peter's direct word from God and the message that Cornelius received from an angel marked the beginning of a profound change in the life of the early church. Jewish followers of Jesus could now visit the homes of Gentiles and eat with them, something no God-fearing Jew would ever have considered before (Acts 10:1-35).

It was then possible for the gospel to be taken into all the world, a theme Matthew emphasizes in the last paragraph of his gospel: "Go therefore and make disciples of all nations ..." (Matthew 28:19a). Also, near the end of Matthew, is an account of Jesus, who, while being tried before Pilate, was almost saved by a dream. Word came from Pilate's wife who had received an urgent message in a dream. She warned her husband, "Have nothing to do with that innocent man for today I have suffered a great deal because of a dream about him" (Matthew 27:19).

Matthew knew his readers assumed that one of the ways God communicates with human beings is through dreams. There are four more accounts of message dreams in Matthew. The wise men, after visiting the Christ Child and Mary, were warned in a dream not to return home the same way they came, but to avoid Herod by taking a different road (Matthew 2:12).

Joseph then had a series of warning dreams of his own: "... an angel of the Lord appeared ... and said, 'Get up, take the child and his mother, and flee to Egypt, and remain there until I tell you: for Herod is about to search for the child to destroy him' " (Matthew 2:13). After Herod died, the angel returned, telling Joseph to "... take the child and his mother, and go to the land of Israel, for those who were seeking the child's life are dead" (Matthew 2:19-20). Joseph took the family to Israel, but then was warned in another dream that Herod's son, Archelaus was ruling in Judea, so they went to Galilee instead (Matthew 2:22). Like the patriarch Joseph, of Genesis, this righteous Joseph got a lot of mileage out of his dreams.

There are many examples of people receiving communications in dreams in the first centuries of the church. Morton Kelsey points out that "... every major Father in the early church, from Justin Martyr to Irenaeus, from Clement and Tertullian to Origen and Cyprian, believed that dreams were a means of revelation. The same view was held by Athanasius ... Ambrose, Augustine, all the Doctors of the church, both East and West, considered the dream a source of revelation, as the Eastern tradition still does." This is no longer true in the Western church. Scholars of the enlightenment, which began with Descartes in the seventeenth century, dismiss dreams as irrational, as Kelsey adds, "... even though [Descartes'] insights came in two famous dreams ... As Protestant thinking came to accept this framework ... it rejected any idea of communication with God or the spiritual world."[5]

Still, evidence of messages in dreams abound in modern times. Abraham Lincoln told his wife, and his friend, Ward H. Lamon, of a dream he had not long before he was assassinated in April of 1865. He had been working late and not long after he had gone to bed he dreamed that he heard someone sobbing in a nearby room. Lincoln said he followed the sound to the East Room where he saw a corpse on a catafalque, which was guarded by soldiers, and large group of mourners looking on sorrowfully.

"Who is dead?" I demanded of one of the soldiers. "The president," was his answer. "He was killed by an assassin." Then came a loud burst of grief from the crowd, which awoke me from my dream. I slept no more that night; and although it was only a dream, I have been strangely annoyed by it ever since.[6]

President Harry Truman told about a comforting dream he had at the time his mother died.

... Mary Jane called to say Mama had pneumonia and might not live through the day. The president ordered his plane, the "Sacred Cow" made ready ... Somewhere over Ohio, dozing on a cot in his stateroom, he dreamt Mama came to him and said, "Good-bye, Harry. Be a good boy." He later wrote, "When Dr. Graham came into the room on the Sacred Cow, I knew what he would say." She had died at 11:30 that morning.[7]

King Abdullah of Jordan receives messages of affirmation and comfort from his father, the late King Hussein, in dreams:

"I'm not a person who's really into spirituality, but I have had a couple of dreams that have been so unique," the King said. "One of the times his majesty came to me was the day I went to the Baqa camp, the Palestinian camp. I went just to tell Hamas, 'Oh yeah, you think you have support here? Well, I have support here, too.' That night I had a dream that H.M. stepped off an airplane — we were in Tanzania or something, I don't know why, you know how dreams are — and he just came and gave me a big hug and said, 'I'm so proud of you.' "[8]

Angels Speak In Dreams

Renita Weems writes in her book, *Listening for God*, about a strange night vision she experienced in her bedroom at the age of seventeen. "Two people appeared and sat on the empty bed across the room, whispering to each other and noisily thumbing through the pages of a book. They never looked at her, but communicated with her all the while they were there." Weems ran downstairs and woke her stepmother. "She heard me out ... and without appearing the least bit surprised or flabbergasted by the dream, assured me that the people in my dream were probably angels coming to tell me something." Weems believes that "while some dreams are forgotten the moment we awake ... the ones we remember, whether laughing or trembling, are kernels of truth, pinches of revelation, whispers of God's voice."[9]

Laura Wassink received a message from an angel when she was a young girl, ten or eleven years of age:

> *I was sleeping in my bed when in the early morning hours something woke me up. I had a full-length mirror on the wall next to my bed, and when I looked at it, I saw an angel standing at the foot of my bed. However, when I looked at the foot of my bed, she was not visible. Then slowly I saw her walk around my bed toward my head. I was terrified. When she neared the head she became visible to me and I can, even thirty years later, see her in my mind. She was short, I'm guessing probably five feet tall, with long brown hair to her waist. We communicated by telepathy. She pointed to a picture I had of Jesus in my room, and told me that he loved me very much, but wanted me to pray more. I looked at the picture and the smile appeared bigger. Then she said, "Do not be afraid." I nodded but could not speak. I was awestruck at the fact that we were communicating in that manner. Then she smiled at me and then just disappeared. I laid there for a while contemplating what she said.[10]*

Sometimes the message is simply the presence of an angel. While we were planning his father's funeral in 1993, my cousin, Daniel Sumwalt, told me about flying to see his mother just before she died several years before. He had fallen asleep on the plane from Wisconsin to Florida. He saw his mother's room in a dream and he saw someone lift his mother's feet. God or an angel was at the foot of the bed. Then the angel took her, and when he woke he knew that she had died. He asked to see her body when he arrived at the hospital. The room was just as he had seen it in the dream. His sister told him that the nurse had come in and elevated his mother's legs just before she died.[11]

Sometimes the message in the dream is the presence or touch of a deceased loved one. In their book, *Dreaming Beyond Death: A Guide to Pre-Death Dreams and Visions*, Kelly Bulkeley and Patricia Bulkeley give examples of visitation dreams. A 32-year-old teacher named Kim went to visit a friend who was dying of cancer and felt deep regret after his death because she forgot to hold his hand one last time before he died. The night he passed, she had a dream. "I am lying in my bed when I see Keith at my bedside and feel the warmth of his skin as he slowly reaches for my hand. He stands close to me and holds my hand gently, but firmly, for a long time. This feeling of his hand is so real, too real to be a dream ... I never experienced in dreams feelings that felt so real." The authors add that when she awoke, "... the touch of Keith was still in her hand."[12]

I visited with John McLaughlin, a member of our congregation in suburban Milwaukee, in the spring of 2005, a few weeks after the death of his wife, Mary. He told me he was sitting beside her bed at St. Joseph's Hospital, half sleeping, half awake, when he saw three angels come through the window on a beam of light. One stood at the foot of the bed and one on each side. The one at the foot seemed to be saying prayers and then made an upward sign with his hand. John watched as Mary's spirit came out of her body and ascended up through the window with the three angels. When he approached the bed, Mary was not breathing and there was no pulse. He pushed the buzzer for the nurse who came immediately and confirmed that she had passed. John said to me, "It was so vivid. I want you to tell people about what I saw."[13]

All My Stories Are True

> *All this took place to fulfill what had been spoken by the Lord through the prophet: "Look, the virgin shall conceive and bear a son, and they shall name him*

Emmanuel" which means "God is with us." When Jo-
seph awoke from his sleep, he did as the angel of the
Lord had commanded him; he took her as his wife, but
had no marital relations with her until she had borne a
son; and he named him Jesus.

— Matthew 1:22-25

I have been writing and telling stories for over 25 years. Often people come to me after I have told a story in a sermon and say, "Was that a true story?" My standard response has become, "All of my stories are true, and some of them really happened." Fred Craddock puts it this way, "Happens all the time."

When I tell a story, I hope that, as my listeners and I live in that world for a while, we will come out transformed, as Jesus' hearers were when he told the parables. I seek to tell modern stories in my sermons that will help the congregation experience stories from the scriptures, like Joseph's dream of the angel, more fully. Hearing a story can be a dream-like experience, which, as Morton Kelsey writes, sometimes "... show us parts of ourselves that we do not want to see." The listener enters a meditative, dream state where one is "not only more open to the depth of one's self, but also beyond the world of psychoid realities where one is able to come into contact with the realm of God...."[14]

Almost every year I write a Christmas story to send with the Christmas cards to our family and friends. In 1998, I wrote a story inspired by Matthew's account of Joseph's dream. It was also inspired by a certain obsession that overtakes my wife, Jo, every year just before Christmas.

www.ChristmasHouse
John Sumwalt

Joe and Marilyn Naazerman were living the busy, successful, and very comfortable suburban life when Joe had his famous dream. They were in their late fifties, looking forward to retirement and very much enjoying their empty nest years now that they had the Christmas House and all of the fun and hoopla it had brought into their lives. But I'm getting ahead of myself.

The story really begins several years before Joe's big dream. It was the year their youngest son, Jimmy, went away to college. Marilyn fell into a deep depression that wouldn't go away. The therapist said it was not uncommon for a woman in her stage of life; and after a time, with the help of Prozac and weekly therapy sessions, Marilyn began to feel like herself again. The Christmas House helped, too.

Joe and Marilyn had bought a big, old Victorian house just after they were married. It had nineteen rooms, including five bathrooms, seven bedrooms, and a three-story tower that was their pride and joy. For years and years, the Naazermans had spent every spare minute renovating their dream house. The last major phase, the completion of the tower rooms, including authentic Victorian wallpaper, had been finished in time for Jimmy's graduation party.

"Perhaps you need a new project," the therapist had suggested to Marilyn. And that was when she decided to put up the Christmas lights. It was a fairly modest display that first year, a few strings of white lights around the tall arborvitae shrubs on each corner of the house, an eight-foot blue spruce with blue lights on the balcony over the porch, a large balsam wreath on the front door with a lighted red bow, and mounted high above the tower roof, on a wire frame etched with soft yellow twinkling lights, a five-foot-high star. Marilyn received many positive comments from her neighbors and friends, especially about the star.

The next year, Marilyn hired two high school boys from her Sunday school class to help make a few additions to this modest display of lights. They started the day after Labor Day. That was Joe's first clue that something extraordinary was going on. When the electrician appeared to install an additional circuit breaker, and when he stumbled over the four-foot-high pile of stringed lights in the garage, Joe knew that Marilyn was indeed planning something big. But he didn't say anything. It was a relief to see her so happy again. Joe decided he would do what he could to help. He booted up the computer and did a web search. A site called www.christmaslights caught Joe's eye. It was just what he was looking for, a treasure trove of plans for light displays and specific instructions for design and installation. Joe downloaded the whole website and printed it out. When he showed it to Marilyn she was delighted with all of the ideas, and glad to welcome his help.

They set to work. Their goal was to have it all completed and to have a grand lighting ceremony on Saint Nicholas Day, December 6. It was also Marilyn's birthday. They just made it. Joe was putting the finishing touches on the star when the reporter from the television station arrived with a camera crew. The reporter interviewed Joe and Marilyn as their neighbors and friends began to fill up the yard. There were well over a hundred people gathered, with necks craned upward, when Marilyn flipped the master switch at precisely 7 p.m.

At first the crowd was silent, and then a crescendo of oohs swooped up over the house and filled the night air. It was a dazzling sight! The carefully crafted light sculptures were stunningly beautiful, "like a great painting," one of their friends said, "a true work of art." There were no garish plastic Santas with sleighs full of toys, no reindeer named Rudolph with blinking red noses, no impish elves wrapping presents to beat the clock, no snowmen with carrot noses and stovepipe hats; this was the real Christmas story, the authorized version, come to life in lights.

Forty feet above the chimney, on the western side of the roof, was an angel with gold-tipped wings and arms outstretched. The angel, hovering over the house with no visible means of support, appeared to be over ten feet high and was surrounded by a host of smaller angels, also with wings unfurled. Below them, on the edge of the roof, was a small flock of sheep and awestruck shepherds, hands shading their faces as they peered into the night sky at this unlikely invasion of heavenly host.

On the eastern side of the house, high above the tower, was the star, three times as high and wide as it had been before. The star's soft yellow lights twinkled and glowed as it lighted the way for the travelers below. Wise men on camels traversed from afar over the peak of the roof, bearing gifts that shimmered and glistened in a golden light. To the rear of the camels, lower on the roof and cast in a harsher light, was King Herod waving angrily to helmeted soldiers with spears and swords.

And beneath the star, on the balcony over the porch where the blue spruce had been the year before, was the silhouette of a simple stable. There were cattle nearby and the donkey, all gazing toward a manger where the babe was swaddled in what can only be described as a heavenly light. Mary and Joseph beamed over the child, and across the way an innkeeper looked on curiously from the doorway of his inn.

The crowd on the lawn below stood quietly for a long time, looking up at this wondrous sight. And then suddenly all the lights went out and music could be heard coming from speakers somewhere in one of the second floor windows. It was a recording of a church choir, singing "Angels We Have Heard On High." When they came to "sweetly singing o'er the plains," the angel and the heavenly host reappeared. Then came "shepherds, why this jubilee," and once again the shepherds lit up the night. The crowd joined in, singing along as each scene appeared in turn: "Come to Bethlehem and see," "We three kings of Orient are," "Away in a manger, no crib for a bed," and "Silent night, holy night, all is calm, all is bright...."

When the last note of "sleep in heavenly peace" had dissipated in the night air, the crowd began to applaud, quietly at first, and then wildly, cheering at the tops of their voices. This was a light show like they had never seen before: a human creation that pointed dramatically at the creator come to join the created, in the flesh.

Word of the Naazermans' unusual light display spread like wildfire. People came in droves. Television, radio, and newspaper reporters descended like a plague; the police department had to hire extra officers to maintain order at what everyone, by then, was calling simply the "Christmas House."

This went on for several Christmas seasons. Each year the light display was a little bigger and better than the year before. Recorded music was replaced with live choirs, as every choral group in the city vied for an opportunity to sing at the Christmas House. Joe developed a website — www.ChristmasHouse — where visitors could take a virtual tour of the light show. One Christmas Eve, the *Today* show did a live remote broadcast from the Naazermans' balcony. Al Roker, in the days when he was still in his portly incarnation, stood by the manger and did a special Christmas weather report predicting partly cloudy skies with intermittent showers of "peace on earth and mercy mild." Joe rigged the lights so it appeared that Al had angel wings.

It was the following year, on the night of December 5, that the angel appeared to Joe in a dream — not the angel he had attached to the roof but the real thing, or so it seemed to Joe as he sat straight up in bed, trembling for over an hour, pondering what the angel had said: "Joe, do not be afraid of what is about to happen in your life. A child will come to Marilyn, and you must care for him, for the child is a gift to you from God."

The next morning, Joe said nothing to Marilyn about his disturbing dream, attributing it to the stress of preparing for another busy Christmas season. That afternoon, Joe took off work early to get ready for the annual premiere of the Christmas House light display. He was surprised to find Marilyn still in her housecoat, sitting at the kitchen table, looking like she had looked during her months of depression. She told him that her stomach had been upset that morning, so she had stayed home from work; she said it felt like a mild case of the flu. And then she dropped the bombshell.

"Joe, your friend, Greg Hoster, down at social services called this morning." Joe knew Greg from Rotary Club. They worked together in the food tent at the fair every year, and they both served on the finance committee at church.

"Greg said they have a newborn baby boy who they haven't been able to place in a foster home. He asked if we would consider taking care of him for a few weeks. I told him this was the busiest time of the year for us, and he said he knew that, but all of their foster parents already have their quota of children and everyone else he has asked said no. I told him I would talk to you and get back to him this afternoon." Joe took a deep breath, then he wrapped his arms around Marilyn and said, "Call Greg and tell him 'Yes.'" And then he told her about the dream.

They picked the baby up at the hospital at about 5 p.m. Joe had called the radio and television stations, asking them to make an announcement postponing the opening of the Christmas House light display. They put little Manuel in a hastily organized nursery in the second floor tower room. It had been Marilyn's sewing room, and it was her favorite room in the house because of the way the morning sunlight streamed in through its floor-to-ceiling windows.

Joe called their grown children and all of their friends to tell them the news. Greetings and gifts flowed in from far and wide. The lights above the Naazermans' Christmas House never did get turned on that Christmas season, but the light in their nursery never ceased to shine. Little Manuel had turned their lives upside-down and stolen their hearts. Joe saw a glow in Marilyn's eyes that he hadn't seen since their children were young, and he couldn't remember ever being happier himself.

In February, when the call came from social services saying they had found a young couple who wanted to adopt Manuel, Joe looked at Marilyn and said, "Why don't we adopt him?" Marilyn gave him one of her best "you've got to be kidding me" looks and said, "Joe, you are 59 years old, and I'm 57. We'll be almost eighty by the time Manuel graduates from high school!" So Joe and Marilyn said good-bye to their little gift from God. It was one of the hardest things they had ever had to do, though the young couple who adopted Manuel promised to send pictures and made them promise to come and visit.

Many more babies visited the Naazerman nursery in the years that followed, and Joe and Marilyn took them all into their hearts and cared for them until room was found in other hearts.

One Christmas Eve, following the candlelight service at church, Joe and Marilyn walked to the parking lot with Greg Hoster and his wife, Jan. Joe said to Greg, "I have always wondered how it was you happened to call us about Manuel that day. Anyone else would have thought we were the last people in the world to take in a newborn."

"Well," Greg said, as he dusted the snow off the windshield of his car, "I guess I figured that anybody with a fifteen-foot star shining over their house was just asking for a baby."

---

1. Carol A. Newsom and Sharon H. Runge, editors, *The Women's Bible Commentary*, (Louisville: Westminster/John Knox Press, 1992), pp. 253-254.

2. From a speech delivered by Senator John McCain in Virginia Beach on February 28, 2000, just prior to the Virginia presidential primary. http://archives.theconnection.org/archive/category/politics/mccainspeech.shtml.

3. Damien Jaques, " 'Esther' Keeps Alive Painful Memory of Camp, Escape," *Milwaukee Journal-Sentinel*, September 15, 2004.

4. John E. Sumwalt, *Lectionary Stories: Forty Tellable Tales For Cycle A* (Lima, Ohio: CSS Publishing Company, 1992), pp. 20-21.

5. Morton Kelsey, *The Other Side of Silence: A Guide to Christian Meditation* (New York: Paulist Press, 1976), pp. 167-168.

6. Web Garrison, *The Lincoln We Never Knew* (Nashville: Rutledge Hill Press, 1993), pp. 251-252.

7. David McCullough, *Truman* (New York: Simon & Schuster, 1992), p. 571.

8. *New York Times* magazine, February 6, 2000.

9. Renita J. Weems, *Listening for God: A Minister's Journey Through Silence and Doubt* (New York: Simon & Schuster, 1999), pp. 98-99.

10. Laura Wassink is a member of the Praise Fellowship Church in Sheboygan, Wisconsin, where she works for the American Orthodontics Company. She is the mother of three grown children. Laura and her husband, Don, enjoy going to the local Christian coffee house to meet other Christians and love having bonfires in their backyard.

11. John Sumwalt, journal entry 3-15-93, a dream related to me by my first cousin, Daniel Sumwalt, who lives in Allenton, Wisconsin.

12. Kelly Bulkeley and Patricia Bulkeley, *Dreaming Beyond Death: A Guide to Pre-Death Dreams and Visions* (Boston: Beacon Press, 2005), p. 19.

13. John and Mary McLaughlin were married for 51 years. Mary Todd was born September 12, 1934, in Butler County, Pennsylvania. A caring Christian woman, Mary was in worship with her family every Sunday in the 8 a.m. chapel service at Wauwatosa Avenue United Methodist Church in suburban Milwaukee.

14. *Op cit*, Morton Kelsey.

Miracle 2

Now I See

As he walked along, he saw a man blind from birth. His disciples asked him, "Rabbi, who sinned, this man or his parents, that he was born blind?" Jesus answered, "Neither this man or his parents sinned; he was born blind so that God's works might be revealed in him. We must work the works of him who sent me while it is still day; night is coming when no one can work. As long as I am in the world, I am the light of the world." When he had said this, he spat on the ground and made mud with the saliva and spread the mud on the man's eyes, saying to him, "Go, wash in the pool of Siloam" (which means Sent). Then he went and washed and came back able to see. — John 9:1-7

I went to my optometrist a few years ago because I was having difficulty reading the small print on medicine bottles and on other such essentials. The doctor increased the power of my bifocals by two increments — and suddenly I was able to read medicine bottles again, and the back of cereal boxes and soup cans. I was greatly relieved, but my relief was nothing compared to that of this man born blind. His whole experience of the world was changed dramatically from that moment on. Everything he had known before would now have new meaning. He had previously known the world only through touch and sound. Now, suddenly, he would come to know a whole different dimension of reality, and those around him would benefit from this rare perspective he would bring to everything he saw.

When I was a boy growing up on the farm, we used to listen to the radio every night in the barn while milking the cows. One of my father's favorite programs was a religious broadcast with one of those old-fashioned gospel preachers. This evangelist, whose name I don't recall, was not only a good preacher, he had a compelling personal story. He had been blinded by an accident when he was a child. I remember wondering what it must have been like to live life as a blind person. One evening he announced to the radio audience that it had become possible for him to have an operation that might restore his sight. He asked for our prayers and I imagine that thousands of people prayed for his sight to be restored. Then came the day he announced that the operation had been a success. He was able to see for the first time in many years. His voice was filled with joy as he told about what it was like to see after all those years of blindness.

Susan Ivany tells about the moment a whole new world was opened for her ten-year-old son when he put on prescription glasses for the first time.

> We were sitting in the living room one evening, watching television, when my son asked me what time it was. There was a clock on the VCR, which was right in front of us below the television, so I said, "See for yourself; it's on the VCR." He gave me a strange look and said, "No one can see those little numbers, Mom; you have to get close up." Oops. It seems he had been moving closer to the front of the classroom at school for some time. His teacher hadn't noticed his squinting and neither had his parents. By the end of that week, the optometrist brought my son's new prescription glasses out for him to try for the first time. The office has a wonderful view of the harbor; the optometrist turned my son toward the window, placed the glasses on him, and said, "This is my favorite part of the job." As we looked on, the veil was quite literally lifted. The expression on my son's face was exquisite. He was speechless as a whole new world opened up to him....[1]

Sheila Hock is a British housewife who had been blind for thirty years, and had never seen the face of her husband, until one day it became possible for an eye operation that might restore her sight. When they took off the bandages, this woman who had never seen before said,

> *It was like an electric shock, as if something hit me ... I looked at the pavement and it was moving and the lamp-posts and the trees were moving so fast that I wanted to shout stop ... I never knew the world was so beautiful. I had a picture in my mind of what I thought my husband looked like because I had felt his features, but he was a lot better looking than I thought and I was pleased about it.*[2]

R. Buckminster Fuller, the great twentieth-century inventor and thinker who gave the world the geodesic dome, and a new synergetic geometry, which revolutionized mathematical thinking, was blind for the first four years of his life. His eyes were crossed and unfocused so that he could see only "masses of color with no distinct outlines." He recognized family members by voice and by the size of their blurry shapes. He was thought to be a hopelessly clumsy child until the day he was given eyeglasses. Fuller said, "For the first time I saw leaves on a tree, small birds, and lovely butterflies; I saw the stars and the shapes of clouds and people's faces. It was a time of utter joy as though all those things had been created just for me ... I was filled with wonder at the beauty of the world and I have never lost my delight in it."[3]

Fuller reflected later in life that his years of blindness "proved to be a blessing in disguise." When he put on his glasses he saw everything differently than he would have if he had never been blind. Tony Campolo, in his book, *Carpe Diem*, writes: "[Fuller] ... contended that society had trained him to view the world in a taken-for-granted fashion. But the hold society had on him had been broken by his blindness." His time of blindness had forced him to rely on other ways of knowing the world and he had developed an extraordinary creative imagination. Campolo writes: "Fuller's visual re-engagement with the world was accomplished by a sense of awe and new passion for discovery that others seldom know ... his excitement for life was intensified beyond anything that would have been possible had he always been able to see."[4]

How happy the family and friends and everyone in the community of the man born blind must have been when Jesus healed him that day.

Not so, you say? How could that be? There is more to this story than meets the eye.

Getting Beyond Stereotypes

The neighbors and those who had seen him before as a beggar began to ask, "Is this not the man who used to sit and beg?" Some were saying, "It is he." Others were saying, "No, but it is someone like him." He kept saying, "I am the man." But they kept asking him, "Then how were your eyes opened?" He answered, "The man called Jesus made mud, spread it on my eyes, and said to me, 'Go to Siloam and wash.' Then I went and washed and received my sight." They said to him, "Where is he?" He said, "I do not know." They brought to the Pharisees the man who had formerly been blind. Now it was a Sabbath day when Jesus made the mud and opened his eyes. Then the Pharisees also began to ask him how he had received his sight. He said to them, "He put mud on my eyes. Then I washed, and now I see." Some of the Pharisees said, "This man is not from God, for he does not observe the Sabbath." But others said, "How can a man who is a sinner perform such signs?" And they were divided. So they said again to the blind man, "What do you say about him? It was your eyes he opened." He said, "He is a prophet." The Jews did not believe that he had been blind and had received his sight until they called the parents of the man who had received his sight and asked them, "Is this your son, who you say was born blind? How then does he now see?" His parents answered, "We know that this is our son, and that he was born blind; but we do not know how it is he now sees, nor do we know who

72

opened his eyes. Ask him, he is of age. He will speak for himself." His parents said this because they were afraid of the Jews; for the Jews had already agreed that anyone who confessed Jesus to be the Messiah would be put out of the synagogue. Therefore his parents said, "He is of age; ask him." So for the second time they called the man who had been blind, and they said to him, "Give glory to God! We know that this man is a sinner." He answered, "I do not know whether he is a sinner. One thing I do know, that though I was blind, now I see."   — John 9:8-25

J. Robert Stimmel tells the story of an incident in the life of a seminary classmate that he says has helped to shape his own ministry.

> *Many of the details have slipped my memory. It took place on a bridge, but I can't recall the name of the bridge. I don't think I ever knew the name of the town. Those details don't really matter. It is a true story.*
>
> *My classmate was walking one night, on the bridge, in the misty early twilight of evening. It was the moment of evening when it is dark enough to see the outlines and shadows; yet a bit past the time for easy recognition. As he walked along the bridge, he came upon a woman standing there at the side of the bridge, leaning against the railing. There was some strange fear and anticipation in the night air; my friend said he knew what she was going to do.*
>
> *He looked at her, standing there beside the railing, hesitant, apprehensive, tentative. She looked at him, uncertain, skeptical, bewildered.*
>
> *He said, "I looked at her; she looked at me; and I looked away. When I looked back again, I was alone on the bridge."*
>
> *It must have been only a split second, an infinitesimal moment in history, hardly more time than it takes to blink, yet he was alone on the bridge, and her life was gone because he did not look, and he did not see.*[5]

Not seeing can have devastating results. How often have you kicked yourself because you didn't see something that, in retrospect, you realize should have been very clear? They say, "Hindsight is twenty-twenty." They also say, "If it had teeth, it would have bitten you." This was one of my family's favorite sayings, which popped out every time I was looking for something but couldn't see it, though it was, as they also used to say, "right there under my nose."

I have a guilty pleasure. I read murder mysteries, usually before I go to bed. I find them relaxing. Don't ask me what that says about my personality or character; I prefer not to know. I read all kinds of these potboilers, good ones and bad ones. I don't particularly try to guess whodunit; I just enjoy the ride.

My favorite series was written by Rex Stout, who cranked out 73 Nero Wolf mysteries between 1934 and 1975, the year he died at the age of 89. I have read thirty or forty of them and I am always looking for one I haven't read. Recently, my sister Ruth, who is a bookseller, gave me a volume I had not seen before, and when I opened it I was thrilled to discover that it was the very first book in the series.

The plot revolves around the murder of a prominent university president on a golf course. Nero Wolf, the eccentric genius, who never leaves his house, and who weighs one-seventh of a ton, is an epicure with a full-time cook who prepares "world class meals" three times daily. Wolf, who also has a live-in gardener who cares for 6,000 orchids in the plant rooms on the third floor of his old brownstone townhouse on West 35th Street in Manhattan, has his legman, Archie Goodwin, round up four caddies who were present at the scene of the murder. He then begins a marathon interview session with these four young men with this statement:

> *Mr. Goodwin has heard two of your stereotypes; I fancy*
> *the other two are practically identical. A stereotype is*
> *something fixed, something that harbors no intention*
> *of changing. I don't expect you boys to change your*
> *stories of what happened on the first tee; what I ask is*
> *that you forget all your arguments and discussions, all*

your recitals to families and friends, all the pictures
that words have printed on your brains, and return to
the scene itself.

Wolf then takes them through the events surrounding the murder, moment by moment, and sure enough, discovers the critical clue, something previously over looked, which leads to the identity of the killer. This is what I like about mystery novels; unlike the mysteries in my own life, everything is always neatly resolved.[6]

There is so much that we overlook in life because it is not what we expect it to be; we have no reference point, no experience that enables us to bring it into focus. Some things can only be seen with the guidance of someone who helps us to look in a different way than we have ever looked before. This is what Jesus tries to do with his disciples over and over again, and often unsuccessfully. In this case they could not look beyond the commonly accepted world view that this man was blind because someone had sinned, "this man or his parents" (John 9:2a). Jesus tries to broaden their view by getting them to look from a different perspective. "Neither this man nor his parents sinned; he was born blind so that God's works might be revealed in him" (John 9:3).

Jesus then shows them what he means by healing the blind man. He applies the saliva and mud, sends the treated man off to wash in the pool of Siloam, which John makes a point of telling us "means Sent" (John 9:7a). He goes and washes and comes back able to see. End of story? Hardly.

John goes on to describe what we might call a three-ring circus of responses from everyone in the neighborhood. No one can see beyond the stereotype that sickness can only mean that someone has sinned.

The neighbors, who presumably have seen him every day since he was a child, are incredulous. "Is this not the man who used to sit and beg?" He kept telling them, "Yes, it's me." And they could only respond, "Then, how were your eyes opened?" (John 9:8-10). It was just not possible for them to believe that little blind Sammy who had grown up to be Samuel the beggar could now see. It is usually the people closest to us who have the greatest difficulty accepting dramatic changes in our lives. Ask a friend who is a recovering alcoholic what makes it most difficult to stay on the road to recovery, and likely she will tell you, old friends who still insist on treating her in the same way: "Oh, come on, one little drink won't hurt."

The Pharisees are only concerned that Jesus has done this healing work on the sabbath, thus making him a lawbreaker: "How could a man who is a sinner perform such signs?" They ask the formerly blind man what he believes about Jesus and when he tells them, "He is a prophet," they pass the buck to other religious authorities who, in their official capacities, do what most officials are prone to do to protect their positions: They stall by insisting on an investigation. They would not accept that "... he had been blind and had received his sight until they called the parents...." The blind man's parents will only confirm that he is indeed their son, but will say nothing else, John says, because they feared the religious authorities would cast all of them out of the synagogue, something they knew happened to anyone "who confessed Jesus to be the Messiah." It is safer to say only what is "politically correct." "... We know this is our son, and that he was born blind; but we do not know how it is he now sees, nor do we know who opened his eyes. Ask him ..." (John 9:18-23).

"Here we go 'round the mulberry bush." Everyone is dancing around the truth. No one can see or will accept what is plainly true, as the blind man states matter of factly, "I do not know whether he is a sinner. One thing I do know, that though I was blind, now I see" (John 9:25).

Rachel Naomi Remen cites Talmudic teaching to explain this kind of social and personal blindness in her book, *Kitchen Table Wisdom*:

> *We do not see things as they are. We see them as we are.*
> *A belief is like a pair of sunglasses. When we wear a*
> *belief and look at life through it, it is difficult to con-*
> *vince ourselves that what we see is not what is real ...*
> *Knowing what is real requires that we remember that*

we are wearing sunglasses, and take them off. One of
the great moments in life is when we recognize we have
them on in the first place.[7]

Former first lady, Betty Ford, wrote about the day her family confronted her about her alcohol and drug addictions in a carefully planned intervention aided by Captain Joe Pursch, a navy doctor who was the head of the Alcohol and Drug Rehabilitation Service at the Long Beach Naval Hospital. One after another, they told her how she had let them down and finally convinced her that without treatment she would surely die. She agreed to sign herself into the rehabilitation hospital. When they took her up to what she assumed would be a private room, she was shocked to discover she would be sharing a room with three other women:

> *I balked. I was not going to sign in ... Captain Pursch*
> *was used to this sort of thing, and perfectly able to*
> *handle it. "If you insist on a private room," he said, "I*
> *will have all these ladies move out."*
> *The former first lady of the land, who had lived in*
> *the White House with servants to care for her every*
> *need and secret service agents to protect her round the*
> *clock, relented. "No, no, I won't have that ..." and an*
> *hour later I was settled in with three roommates.*[8]

That was the beginning of Mrs. Ford's healing, but her eyes were not fully open yet; the worst was still to come. She believed she was only addicted to medications: "Now these doctors wanted me to admit I was also an alcoholic." Mrs. Ford's response was tears and more tears, and when the president strongly encouraged her to come to grips with what she had to do, she tells of "... sobbing so hard I couldn't get my breath. My nose and ears were closed off ... my head felt like a balloon. I was gasping, my mouth wide open, sure my air was going to be cut off. I hope I never have to cry like that again. It was scary, but once it was over, I felt a great relief." Mrs. Ford issued a statement to the press saying she was addicted to alcohol as well as the medications she was taking for her arthritis. Betty Ford was beginning to see.[9]

By telling her story, Betty Ford has helped millions of people to open their eyes to their own addictions. At the Betty Ford Center, which Mrs. Ford cofounded with Leonard Firestone in 1982 in Rancho Mirage, California, everyone has three roommates.

Like Betty Ford, this man born blind was able to see, when given the opportunity, despite the unpleasantness of the spit and mud and the hostile responses of everyone around him. It is as the psalmist writes: "The Lord opens the eyes of the blind" (Psalm 146:8). But there are some who seem to be beyond even God's help, as we shall see.

How Could They Be So Blind?

> They said to him, "What did he do to you? How did he open your eyes?" He answered them, "I have told you already, and you would not listen. Why do you want to hear it again? Do you also want to become his disciples?" Then they reviled him, saying, "You are his disciple, but we are disciples of Moses. We know that God has spoken to Moses, but as for this man, we do not know where he comes from." The man answered, "Here is an astonishing thing! You do not know where he comes from, and yet he opened my eyes. We know that God does not listen to sinners, but he does listen to one who worships him and obeys his will. Never since the world began has it been heard that anyone opened the eyes of a person born blind. If this man were not from God, he could do nothing." They answered him, "You were born entirely in sins, and are you trying to teach us?" And they drove him out. — John 9:26-34

"The prophet Isaiah wrote about a servant God would send to '... lead the blind by a road they do not know ...' " (Isaiah 42:16a). Jesus had certainly led the religious authorities here down an unfamiliar road: "I came into this world for judgment so that those who do not see may see, and those who do see may become blind" (John 9:39).

78

After these authorities have judged the man born blind, denying the credibility of his witness to his own healing by telling them,
"... God does not listen to sinners ..." but only "... to one who wor-
ships him and obeys his will," they drove him out (John 9:31-34).
John goes on, heaping irony upon irony as Jesus gives the formerly
blind man an opportunity to do what the willfully blind authorities
refuse to do, asking him, "Do you believe in the Son of Man?" His
response is what John hopes will be the response of everyone who
reads his gospel, "... 'Lord, I believe.' And he worshiped him" (John
9:35-38).

Those who were the acknowledged spiritual guides of the community are shown not only to have relinquished their authority,
arrogantly denying the truth of a healing in that "a blind man could
see," but also "nail the lid on their own coffins" as we might say,
giving Jesus one of the all time great set up lines: "Surely we are
not blind, are we?" Well, duhhh, Jesus says to them, "If you were
blind you would not have sin. But now that you say, 'We see,' your
sin remains" (John 9:40b-41). Is it really possible that anyone could
be so blind?

During World War II, there was a Navy pharmacist's mate who
performed a successful appendectomy on a fellow sailor in a submarine beneath enemy waters. The seaman, who would have otherwise died, survived — but like the Pharisees and religious authorities who chastised Jesus for working on the sabbath, the naval medical officers were very angry that this lowly seaman had dared to go
beyond navy regulations; never mind that he had saved someone's
life. The Navy never officially recognized the pharmacist's mate
for his heroism until two months before his death in April of 2005.
Associated Press reporter, Steve Hartsoe, wrote about this remarkable feat performed by a young seaman on the *USS Seadragon* 120
feet below the surface of the Pacific Ocean over sixty years ago.

> *Lipes, then 22, relied on makeshift instruments — bent*
> *spoons for retractors and alcohol from torpedoes for*
> *sterilization. He and an assistant wore pajamas rather*
> *than operating room gowns ... The surgical environ-*
> *ment was less than ideal: The patient, Darrel Dean*

Rector, was too tall to lay on the makeshift operating table, so a nearby cabinet was opened and Lipes put the patient's feet in the drawer. The table was bolted to the floor, so Lipes had to stand with his knees bent throughout the operation. After nearly two hours, Lipes removed a swollen five-inch appendix that had several inches of blackened tissue.[10]

What was even more remarkable than the successful submarine surgery, was the reaction Lipes received from the Navy medical community. One doctor reminded him that he was not authorized to perform surgery and said it would have been better if he had let Darrel Rector die. Another physician actually tried to hit him. Others in the medical community, according to a National Public Radio report, spread rumors that the surgery had never taken place, that it was a lie.[11]

Wheeler Lipes told about this most puzzling response from Navy authorities in a statement he gave to the Naval Historical Center.

After we submitted our report, there was a great deal of consternation in the Bureau of Medicine and Surgery. Everyone did then exactly what they would probably do now. They reacted to a situation they knew absolutely nothing about. There was an old warrant officer I knew back at BUMED (US Navy Bureau of Medicine and Surgery) who was on duty the night the message came in about the operation. He told me later how much trouble I had caused him. There were many doctors back there who were very upset about what I had done.[12]

How could they have been so blind?

Sometimes the blindness to the healing God has made possible, is more subtle, more what is not said than what is said. Verna Windrem tells how she was healed as the result of a dream and what did not happen after she told her doctor and others about her healing. God's call to minister came late in life for Verna Windrem.

80

Only A Dream?

Verna Windrem

I am a grandmother who went back to school in 1983. I was commissioned in 1987, as a Diaconal Minister, in the United Church of Canada. This designation is part of the Order of Ministry in our denomination and the job I was received into was as the sole minister to a three-point charge.

Healing ministry has always interested me, but I had little time to investigate it. It was like a rollercoaster took off in our lives while I was still in studies. My husband was diagnosed with Non-Hodgkin's Lymphoma. After that, the disease would return again and again, causing much suffering through both the illness and the treatments of radiation and chemotherapy. Mind you, there was lots of prayer that went up for him, and again and again, he returned to health.

In 1993, the cancer returned again. We were preparing to move to another pastorate and, as he wasn't well, it fell to me to do most of the packing. Books! How could I have stacked up so many? Box after box was marked and I carried them to the basement out of the way.

After the move, everything needed doing again, in reverse. Along with this hard work came the challenge of a new job in a four-point charge. There was much to be done. In the process, my back became very painful. Hoping for help, I went to a chiropractor who told me to expect healing to take a long, long time. I prayed. Nothing changed.

One night, I had a dream. All I remember was that the setting seemed to be at a prayer meeting where people were praying for one another. A man and a woman stepped up behind me as I sat in a chair. They laid their hands on my shoulders and began to pray. I felt as if a bolt of lightning was going through me, powerful but not painful. It zapped my spine and I woke knowing my back was healed. It was that fast!

Now, eleven years later, I am retired and we have moved back to our farm home. My husband and I have toted those same books; we have worked on renovating the house and moved gardens. I give thanks to God that I am well, and so is my husband! I have not shared this event in my life often, but when I do, people seldom make a comment. I did tell our family doctor and he didn't comment either. After all, perhaps it was only a dream. But God and I know better![13]

How could they have been so blind?

Sometimes healing comes when our illness enables us to see in a different way. The formerly blind man may have had an advantage on the religious authorities. Perhaps the suffering he endured each day because of his blindness helped him to open his heart not only to the healing Jesus offered, but also to the new life he would have with Christ. "He said, 'Lord, I believe.' And he worshiped him" (John 9:38).

Vanessa Bruce Ingold came to Christ as a result of healing that occurred after a devastating accident in which every long bone in her body (a total of 111) was broken, except for one.

Hope In The Midst Of Pain
Vanessa Bruce Ingold

Two weeks after my 23rd birthday, I awoke to a foggy, winter morning in southern California. Having cried myself to sleep, I felt foggy, too. Yet, dressed for aerobics, I began my usual bicycle route to the gym. Since there was no bicycle lane, I pedaled alongside the parking lane of the four-lane business district roadway. If it weren't illegal, I would have ridden against traffic instead. Ahead of me was a car in the parking lane. Just before I drew up beside it, the driver opened the door. I swerved. Traffic noise seemed to intensify as I veered into the left turn lane for on-coming traffic. Simultaneously, a Ford Ranger truck entered. I was trapped! Scenes from my life flashed before my eyes, while my mind raced. Will I be able to walk? Am I going to die? Will I go to heaven? Then the truck hit me.

Following the truck's piercing screech was the sound of a two-car collision. Debbie, the owner of a pet shop, ran to the sidewalk.

Instead of two cars, she saw the truck next to my smashed bicycle. I lay in a pool of blood. Debbie called 911.

"She looks like a doll whose legs and arms are turned all the wrong way, the lower part of her left leg is like a balloon!"

Employees from other nearby shops encircled me. Debbie joined and directed traffic. The man who had opened the car door fled. Police questioned the truck driver. His truck, having left a brief skid mark, was damaged in the front and had to be towed.

Paramedics rushed me to Long Beach Memorial Hospital. All four tires of the truck had run over me. I was screaming and crying hysterically and was in and out of shock. Wheeling me into the emergency room, they yelled, "Trauma code yellow!" In one of my lucid moments, I said, "Call my friend, Ray," and mumbled his phone number. A nurse called Ray. He gave the phone number of the hair salon where I worked. The salon owner provided my emergency contacts, then the nurse phoned my out-of-state family.

A heart surgeon, Dr. McConnell, entered. His eyes widened as he saw tire tracks going across my chest. My heart rate was 147, as if I was doing high-impact aerobics. After evaluating, he said, "We've got to get her into surgery, now." During surgery, I had sixteen blood transfusions. They found gross, unstable blood in my abdomen; my liver was severely lacerated, my heart's papillary muscle was ruptured, and my mitral valve was ripped.

Every long bone in my body was broken except one, totaling 111. My lower left leg had the largest open wound, from which a fragment of the tibia — the bone that extends from the knee to the ankle — was sticking out of a six-inch longitudinal laceration. Plus, many short, flat, and irregular bones were fractured, including knees, wrists, ankles, ribs, left clavicle, pelvis, and the C7 section of my cervical spine. A cervical collar was placed around my neck.

At 7:30 p.m., my family members arrived. Dr. McConnell told them, "Her mitral valve is hanging like a thread, but we're trying to prolong replacing it because of the multitude of injuries and blood loss." Relatives were allowed to see me. They and the nurses laughed as I told a funny childhood story about my brother terrorizing me by putting my beloved stuffed animal in the freezer. Laughter was interrupted. I had a heart attack. "Now our only hope is to replace her mitral valve," Doctor McConnell explained. Immediately a priest was sent to read me my "last rites." He asked if I understood. With closed eyes, I nodded.

After a ten-hour open-heart surgery, my chest couldn't be closed, because of severe pulmonary edema, coupled with edema of my heart. Thus, it was left open three days, covered with an Esmarch bandage. Paralyzing drugs kept me from moving. After it was closed, I awoke with Dad at my bedside. I knew it must be bad if Dad was there. My parents had divorced when I was in the first grade. We were not a close-knit family.

My broken bones prevented me from wiping my tears. I was too weak, anyway. I remembered having prayed the night before the accident, "Please change me, God." Now I asked, "Why'd you let this happen, God? Am I being punished for my out-of-control party life?" With tears on my face, I sensed him reply, "It will all work together for good." At least it can't get any worse, I thought; this is the worst thing that has ever happened to me!

But, gangrene of my forefeet worsened. Still, oxygen therapy had to be postponed until excess fluid that had accumulated in my chest was drained. With my legs elevated, I could see my black toes.

Two weeks after my chest was closed, I was brought to hyperbarics twice daily, where I was transferred into a single person oxygen chamber that was seven feet long and 27 inches wide. Each time, I was kept for one-and-a-half hours, with hopes to save my feet and legs. Two weeks passed, and I was told, "We'll be amputating all ten of your toes." Again, I nodded my head.

During almost four months in the Intensive Care Unit, my ventilator alarm sounded because I lacked oxygen, a blood infection nearly killed me, and because of constant fever, ice packages surrounded me.

Nevertheless, I witnessed God's love. My Christian trauma nurse visited me during her off-hours. And a Christian family who met my family while I was having heart surgery, frequently visited me. Trying to wean me off of the ventilator was a battle. Oxygen couldn't be reduced for long, because I panted. "We're worried she'll be dependent on it forever," I heard doctors say.

After nearly four months of dependence, a doctor was changing my tracheal tube. When she pulled it out and quickly tried to replace it, she couldn't insert the new tube. "The incision in your neck has closed!" Finally, I was independently breathing. An oxygen tank was placed next to my bed, but I never needed it. "Now you can begin rehab," a nurse said.

I frowned, "Rehab?" I breathily, hoarsely whined. "I thought as soon as I was off the ventilator I'd be able to leave."

After a day in rehab, I questioned doctors. "You mean I broke over 111 bones, had seventeen surgeries, and over 100 blood transfusions?" Wow, it really was a miracle I was alive! I began to see God's purpose for my life.

After a six-month hospital stay, on a clear, sunshiny day, with a cast on my left leg, accompanied by two friends from whom I would be renting a room, I cheerfully left the hospital. Six months later, a friend with whom I had worked at the hair salon invited me to church. Many there had been praying for me. The assistant pastor and his wife had visited me while I was in ICU, where they had anointed me with oil, while praying for my healing, as stated in the book of James. Now I sat in the front row at church next to them. After worship and Bible study, the teaching pastor said, "Whoever wants to receive Jesus Christ as Lord and Savior tonight come to the front." I stood and closed my eyes as he led in prayer.

The following Sunday, the pastor read from Romans, chapter 8, "And we know that all things work together for good to those who love God, to those who are the called according to his purpose." Wow, that's the scripture of my life! What the enemy had tried to use for evil, God was using for good. The accident had drawn my family together. Broken relationships were being re-built. Trauma was bringing healing. A few weeks later, I visited my orthopedic surgeon, Dr. Peek. For ten months I had been in a cast. Hoping my tibia had finally hardened, he once again shaved the cast off. Still soft, my tibia actually bent. While he plastered a new cast onto my leg, I said, "I'm going up to the mountains today for our church retreat. I'll just pray the whole weekend for God to heal it." The following Wednesday, Dr. Peek announced, "Amazing — your tibia has hardened." He never replaced the cast.

Eight years later, I participated in a two-day bicycle trip to San Diego, a 110-mile ride, with a church group. I rode thirty minutes behind, and was last to finish the ride. Although I'm not as fast, my hope will last! Since then, I've had nine more surgeries. Yet, in the midst of pain, God has blessed me. Now life is especially more pleasurable since I have a cycling partner, my best friend and loving husband, Greg.[14]

---

1. Susan Ivany, *AHA!* magazine, Wood Lakes Books, Winfield, British Columbia, Jan/Feb/March, 2003. Susan Ivany is an ordained pastor with the United Church of Canada. She and her partner, Peter, live in Thunder Bay, Ontario. Their sons, Derek and David, are embarking on their own careers and continue to make their parents exceedingly proud. In addition, Susan and Peter are owned and operated by two very spoiled cats. Susan loves to write, and has a profound respect for the power of words to transform lives.

2. William J. Bausch, *Telling Stories, Compelling Stories* (Mystic, Connecticut: Twenty-third Publications, 1991), p. 11.

3. Alden Hatch, *Buckminster Fuller: At Home In The Universe* (New York: Crown Publishers, 1974), p. 11.

4. Tony Campolo, *Carpe Diem* (Nashville: W Publishing Group, 1994), pp. 16-17.

5. J. Robert Stimmel retired after 35 years of ordained ministry in both parish and connectional ministries in The United Methodist Church. Now living on the central coast of California, Bob works full-time running his own tax preparation business, which also offers payroll and bookkeeping services. He finds it spiritually beneficial that his office features a view of the local pier and the Pacific Ocean. He continues his church involvement by serving as treasurer of his local church, which is engaged in a seven million dollar building project. Occasionally Bob preaches, writes, and contributes to preaching publications.

6. Rex Stout, *Fer-De-Lance: A Nero Wolfe Mystery* (New York: Bantam Books, 1983), pp. 168-169. (Originally published in 1934.)

7. Rachel Naomi Remen, *Kitchen Table Wisdom: Stories That Heal* (New York: Riverhead Books, 1996), p. 77.

8. Betty Ford, *The Times of My Life* (New York: Harper Collins, 1978), pp. 281-285.

9. *Ibid.*

10. Steve Hartsoe, Associated Press, *The North Carolina News*, February 21, 2005.

11. National Public Radio, February 19, 2005.

12. From recollections of Pharmacist's Mate Wheeler Lipes collected for the Naval Historical Center. http://www.history.navy.mil/faqs/faq87-3a.htm.

13. Verna Windrem, the daughter of a United Church pastor, grew up in the village of Omemee, Ontario, where she attended elementary and high schools and married Earle Windrem, a farmer from the Cavan area. They have two sons, David and Verne, and grandchildren ranging in age from 10 to 23. In 1983, Verna went back to school through the Centre for Christian Studies in Toronto and the University of Toronto — as a grandmother, with lots of support and help from family. In 1987, she became Diaconal Minister, and served three rural churches in Cold Springs Charge, near Cobourg, Ontario. In 1993, she transferred to Warsaw, Ontario, and served four country churches for twelve years. Verna and Earle retired on their farm near Cavan in 2004, where they live with a lovely little schnoodle named Millie.

14. Vanessa Bruce Ingold says people often tell her, "You're a walking miracle!" She and her husband, Greg, live in Fullerton, California, and attend Capo Beach Calvary Chapel. Jcnessa@aol.com.

Miracle 3

Healing Tears

When we came up out of the tomb of Lazarus, the other half of our touring group, who were waiting their turn to go down, greeted us with shhhh's and whispers of "be quiet, a funeral procession is coming." My wife, Jo, and I were on a tour of Israel in 1989, and our guide had brought our group to the place at Bethany where tourists are shown what the home of Mary and Martha and Lazarus might have looked like, and then we were taken down into a tomb, supposedly like the one where Lazarus was buried. We went down many steps, deep below the street.

The entrance to the tomb is located midway up a small hill and, sure enough, when we looked down the narrow street to the foot of the hill, where everyone was pointing, we could see them coming, several burly men in front carrying the open bier on their shoulders. There were about eighty men and boys following behind waving palm branches. We could see the outline of the body wrapped in a black cloth. We stood reverently trying not to gawk, aware of the irony that our pilgrimage to venerate an ancient grave and revel in a sacred old story of death and resurrection should be interrupted by this stream of life carrying death straight at us.

In this story of death and resurrection from John's gospel, death comes straight at us. We are transported with Jesus to the door of the tomb, where we encounter the finality and the stench of death, and then strangely, a transforming power and glory like we have never seen before — and a question Jesus asks the church in every age.

A Certain Man Was Ill

> *Now a certain man was ill, Lazarus of Bethany, the village of Mary and her sister, Martha. Mary was the one who anointed Jesus with perfume and wiped his feet with her hair; her brother Lazarus was ill. So the sisters sent a message to Jesus, "Lord, he whom you love is ill." But when Jesus heard it, he said, "This illness does not lead to death; rather it is for God's glory, so that the Son of God may be glorified through it." Accordingly, though Jesus loved Martha and her sister and Lazarus, after having heard that Lazarus was ill, he stayed two days longer in the place where he was.*
>
> *Then after this he said to the disciples, "Let us go to Judea again." The disciples said to him, "Rabbi, the Jews were just now trying to stone you, and are you going there again?" Jesus answered, "Are there not twelve hours of daylight? Those who walk during the day do not stumble, because they see the light of this world. But those who walk at night stumble, because the light is not in them." After saying this, he told them, "Our friend Lazarus has fallen asleep, but I am going there to awaken him." The disciples said to him, "Lord, if he has fallen asleep, he will be all right." Jesus, however, had been speaking about his death, but they thought that he was referring merely to sleep. Then Jesus told them plainly, "Lazarus is dead. For your sake I am glad I was not there, so that you may believe. But let us go to him." Thomas, who was called the Twin, said to his fellow disciples, "Let us also go, that we may die with him."*   — John 11:1-16

This is a story for all time. It begins in the tried and true fashion of all good "once upon a time" tales with a rhythmic line, like "There once was a man...." or "Long ago and far away...." The formula is also apparent in some of the parables of Jesus: "A farmer went out to sow ..." (Matthew 13:36), and the familiar opening of the Good Samaritan, "A man was going down ..." (Luke 10:30). The rhythm of the words pulls us in: Ta da da, ta da, ta what?

"Now a certain man was...?" John, the writer/storyteller of this gospel has us in the first breath. Before the name of the man is mentioned we know his story is universal. This is an every man, every woman drama, drawn deep from the well of human experience, my story, your story. We hold our breath waiting for the inevitable.

"Now a certain man was ..." wait, wait, wait ... here it comes ... "was ill." Now we are hooked completely. We want the rest of the story, all of it. We want to know everything. Who is ill? Why? Where is he from? Why should we care about him? Who else is involved with this man? Give us all of it. Don't leave out a word.

The gospel writer sets the scene:

> *... Lazarus of Bethany, the village of Mary and her sister Martha. Mary was the one who anointed the Lord with perfume and wiped his feet with her hair....*
> — John 11:2a

Oh, that Mary. There are so many Marys; it is difficult to remember which one is which. Mary, the anointer, the one who prepared Jesus for his death, the one who was listening when Judas complained about wasting expensive perfume when it could have been sold and the money given to the poor, the Mary who heard Jesus say to Judas:

> *Leave her alone ... It was intended she should save this perfume for the day of my burial. You will always have the poor among you, but you will not always have me.*
> — John 12:7-8

That Mary.

The gospel writer, in setting the scene for Lazarus' death, is also foreshadowing Jesus' own imminent demise. This is, on the surface, a story about death: the death we all fear, the one death we all have to die and would avoid if we could. Everyone has an appointment with death.

W. Somerset Maugham wrote about this dreaded rendezvous in the retelling of an old folktale about a merchant in Baghdad who sent his servant to the marketplace to do some shopping. The servant came running back babbling about an encounter with Death, saying to his master:

> *"I was jostled by a woman in the crowd and when I turned I saw it was Death that jostled me. She looked at me and made a threatening gesture; now lend me your horse, and I will ride away from this city and avoid my fate. I will go to Samara and there death will not find me." The merchant lent him his horse, and the servant mounted it ... and as fast as the horse could gallop he went. Then the merchant went down to the marketplace and he saw Death and said, "Why did you make a threatening gesture to my servant when you saw him this morning?" "That was not a threatening gesture," Death said. "It was only a start of surprise. I was astonished to see him in Baghdad, for I had an appointment with him tonight in Samara."[1]*

We all die. Even those who have been raised from the dead will eventually die again, as did Jairus' young daughter whose resuscitation we read of in Mark 5. So also did the only son of the widow of Nain (Luke 7), and the son of the widow at Zarephath raised by the prophet Elijah (1 Kings 17), and the son of the Shunammite woman raised by the prophet Elisha (2 Kings 4). There is no getting around death, though we continue to look for ways to postpone it.

There is a well-traveled joke that still pops out at water coolers now and again:

> *Three friends were discussing death and one of them asked, "What would you like people to say about you at your funeral?"*
>
> *The first one of the friends said, "I would like them to say, 'He was a great humanitarian who cared about his community.'"*
>
> *"He was a great husband and father, who was an example for many to follow," said another.*

92

The third friend said, "I would like them to say, 'Look, he's moving.'"

When asked what he would want to be done in the event of his death, Woody Allen quipped, "I would like several of my closest friends to gather around my body and do everything they can to bring me back to life." On another occasion Allen said, "I'm not afraid to die, I just don't want to be there when it happens."

Was Jesus avoiding death when he delayed going to Bethany for two days after receiving word that Lazarus was deathly ill? What are we to make of his little proclamation? "This illness does not lead to death; rather it is for God's glory; so that the Son of God may be glorified through it" (John 11:4).

More is going on here than meets the eye. There is something the disciples are unable to see and understand. Look deeper, John is saying to his readers who are just as blind to the ways of God as the disciples. Pay attention. Jesus is telling you how God's purposes are being worked out in this event. The glory of God is about to be revealed. Something that has not been known about God, at least not known by this generation, will now be made known.

The disciples are about to begin their last road trip with Jesus. They hesitate, warning Jesus that the last time they were in Judea the religious authorities tried to have him stoned. What they don't get is that this is the point. "It's okay," Jesus says, "those who walk during the day do not stumble, because they see the light of the world." What?

Jesus has now turned his face toward Jerusalem. He looks off into the distance, perhaps seeing beyond Bethany to what awaits him on a distant hill. Thomas says, "Let us also go that we may die with him." Thomas doesn't really know what he is saying, at least not yet. His time, too, will come.

If this were a musical this is the point that someone would break into song, perhaps a riff by that old jazz singer, Ezekiel, the dry-bones prophet:

> *Prophesy to these bones and say to them: O dry bones,*
> *hear the word of the Lord. Thus says the Lord God to*

93

*these bones: I will cause breath to enter you, and you
shall live ... And you shall know that I am the Lord,
when I open your graves, O my people. I will put my
spirit within you and you shall live....*
                                    — Ezekiel 37:4b-5a, 13-14a

Jesus Wept

*When Jesus arrived, he found that Lazarus had already
been in the tomb four days. Now Bethany was near
Jerusalem, some two miles away, and many of the Jews
had come to Martha and Mary to console them about
their brother. When Martha heard that Jesus was coming, she went and met him, while Mary stayed at home.
Martha said to Jesus, "Lord, if you had been here, my
brother would not have died. But even now I know that
God will give you whatever you ask of him." Jesus said
to her, "Your brother will rise again." Martha said to
him, "I know that he will rise again in the resurrection
on the last day." Jesus said to her, "I am the resurrection and the life. Those who believe in me, even though
they die, will live, and everyone who lives and believes
in me will never die. Do you believe this?" She said to
him, "Yes, Lord, I believe that you are the Messiah, the
Son of God, the one coming into the world."*

*When she had said this, she went back and called
her sister Mary, and told her privately, "The Teacher is
here and is calling for you." And when she heard it, she
got up quickly and went to him. Now Jesus had not yet
come to the village, but was still at the place where
Martha had met him. The Jews who were with her in
the house, consoling her, saw Mary get up quickly and
go out. They followed her because they thought that
she was going to the tomb to weep there. When Mary
came where Jesus was and saw him, she knelt at his
feet and said to him, "Lord, if you had been here, my
brother would not have died." When Jesus saw her
weeping, and the Jews who came with her also weeping, he was greatly disturbed in spirit and deeply moved.*

He said, "Where have you laid him?" They said to him,
"Lord, come and see." Jesus began to weep. So the Jews
said, "See how he loved him!" But some of them said,
"Could not he who opened the eyes of the blind man
have kept this man from dying?" — John 11:17-37

Lazarus was one of Jesus' best friends. Jesus often stayed in the home of Lazarus and his sisters, Mary and Martha. Their home and their friendship were a haven for Jesus, a resting place away from the continual demands of the crowds that followed him wherever he went. It is no small blessing to have friends like this.

When Mary and Martha sent word of Lazarus' illness they said simply, "Lord, he whom you love is ill." When you hear that about someone you love, you go. And Jesus went, not immediately, for reasons that were a mystery to his disciples, but two days later, at great risk to his own life. He went, arriving, it seems, too late. John tells us, "Lazarus had already been in the tomb for four days."

The first thing Martha said to him was, "Lord, if you had been here, my brother would not have died." Then, when he greets the other sister, Mary, the first thing she says to him is, "Lord, if you had been here, my brother would not have died."

There is great frustration underlying these two statements. Have you ever felt the brunt of someone's anger, the pointed finger of blame at the time of a death? It happens often to law enforcement officials, emergency medical personnel, nurses, doctors, funeral directors, and pastors, whoever is on the scene when death comes to call.

Those in the death biz understand that these projections of anger are a normal response when a loved one is taken. Death feels like an assault. We want to fight back. We want to blame someone. Somebody must be responsible for our pain. Even God and the dear departed are not spared the irrational mourner's wrath. Many a widow and widower has shaken an angry fist at God, or hurled the picture of the beloved spouse against a wall, wailing, "How could you leave me? How dare you?"

How often have we screamed that in the face of death — or wanted to?

Death at any age, but especially the death of the very young, feels unjust. How could a good God permit it? — is a universal plea. Martha and Mary spoke the angry truth to Jesus that day: "Lord, if you had been here my brother would not have died."

Jesus understood their need to vent. He looked behind the anger to their tears and fears. When Jesus saw Mary weeping, and those who were with her weeping, he was deeply moved and said, "Where have you laid him?" They took him to the tomb. And when he came to the place where Lazarus' body was resting, the gospel writer described what happened by stating simply, "Jesus wept." He didn't say Jesus wept uncontrollably or unreservedly. He didn't have to.

There was Jesus, as vulnerable as we all are when we go to the funeral home to view the body of one we love. In that first moment of comprehension that the one we love is gone, there is nothing to do but weep, if you are able to weep. Sometimes our grief is so deep that tears will not come. The body shuts down; the spirit goes into shock.

People express concern if you are unable to cry at appropriate times. "You need to cry," they say. "Just let go, get it all out." Tears are healing, even when it seems they will never stop. The psalmist wrote: "Weeping may linger for the night, but joy comes with the morning" (Psalm 30:5b).

Sometimes it feels like morning will never come. When Abraham Lincoln was assassinated, his secretary of war, Edwin Stanton, who had vigorously maligned him during the first election campaign, but had come to love the president dearly after working closely with him during the war, could not stop weeping. Doris Kearns Goodwin wrote in *Team of Rivals: The Political Genius of Abraham Lincoln*, "Stanton's grief was uncontrollable ... at the mention of Lincoln's name he would break down and weep bitterly."[2]

As wrenching as it can be, weeping is the best way of coping with overwhelming emotion. It is unfortunate that our culture has not encouraged weeping, particularly among men. Many men, and some women, are taught that it is a sign of weakness to weep, that public displays of emotion are unseemly.

Tears are the safety valve for the body — and the soul. When King David heard of the death of his wayward son, Absalom, he wept. He went to his bedroom and wailed. "O my son Absalom, my son, my son Absalom! Would I had died instead of you. O Absalom, my son, my son!" (2 Samuel 18:33).

When was the last time you heard someone express grief so profoundly? Keening for the dead is not heard much in suburban North America. Jesus mourned unabashedly for his friend, Lazarus. He shed tears publicly in a way that is not often observed in Western culture. We are taught to keep grief private. Big boys don't cry. Nice girls don't fall apart in front of their friends and relatives. We find it embarrassing when someone makes a public display of raw emotion.

John Warren Steen, editor of *International Christian Digest*, wrote, "I have been to only one funeral in which people wailed and screamed. It was on a mountainside in Kentucky, among people who were poor and uneducated. In contrast, I have attended many a funeral in which no tear was shed. Middle-class, educated people try to maintain their composure because it is expected of them." Steen said, "Crying in our society is considered a symptom of instability." And yet, he asked, "What about the stability of the psalmist, who wrote 'Every night I flood my bed with tears; I drench my couch with my weeping'?" (Psalm 6:6).[3]

Be thankful if you cry easily and often. There is no merit in holding back tears. "Big boys don't cry" is a lie that has brought many a man to an early grave.

My favorite scene in the movie, *A League of Their Own*, is when one of the women players begins to cry during a game. The crusty old manager, played by Tom Hanks throws up his arms and says, "There's no crying in baseball!"[4]

Many tears flowed when they buried slugger Ken Caminiti on a cloudy day in October of 2004. A veteran of fifteen years in the big leagues, Caminiti was the unanimous choice for the National League's most valuable player (MVP) in 1996, batting .326, with 40 home runs and 130 runs batted in. He led the San Diego Padres to the World Series, and just six years later admitted to using steroids throughout that MVP season. Dead at 41. There is crying in baseball. There *is* crying in everything. Tears are a sign of life.[5]

Did you ever feel like you needed to cry, but for some reason you couldn't or wouldn't let yourself? Then some little thing sets you off. Someone says something, you hear a certain song on the radio or sing a favorite hymn at church, and suddenly the dam bursts. I cry every time I hear "Rock Of Ages," because I'll never forget hearing it sung at my grandfather's funeral when I was ten years old. It was a time in my life when I cried and cried and thought I would never stop.

We are embarrassed when we lose control like this, saying things, like: "I don't know what came over me." But we feel better for it. Whatever it was that we were holding in that needed to come out, came out in the tears. The ancient Greeks called this catharsis.

Early one morning in the spring of 2004, I was walking with our dog, Eli, along a creek that runs through our 25 acres of farmland. Something drew me toward a gurgling sound that comes from water flowing rapidly over rocks. As I drew near, I found myself weeping. I had no idea where the tears came from, or why. Somehow the flowing water had released something inside of me that needed to come out: some sadness or sorrow I had not known was there.

When Violet Anderson, a woman from our congregation in suburban Milwaukee, died a few years ago, her nephew told the story of her son's tragic death at the age of sixteen in an auto accident. He said his aunt told how she had cried every day for a year. She cried so much her tear ducts dried up. The doctor prescribed a special ointment to restore her tears. Then one morning, Violet awoke to see her son, Edward, standing at the foot of her bed. He said, "Mom, you've got to stop this crying. I am where I am and I am happy where I am and nothing is going to change it." From that moment on, Violet was better. She didn't need to cry anymore.[6]

Tears express what cannot be put into words. We are moved to tears on those occasions when we cannot speak. Lucille Ball portrayed this so well in the old *I Love Lucy* shows. She and Ethel would do something outrageous that turned into a disaster. Then

Ricky would come in and say, "Lucyyyyyy! You've got some 'splainin' to do." And Lucy would begin to wail. The tears said it all.

In her powerful book, *Ashes Transformed: Healing from Trauma*, Tilda Norberg shares the story of Rodney Miller, a United Methodist pastor in Tamaqua, Pennsylvania, who awoke about two hours before the attack on the World Trade Center on September 11, 2001, and began to weep for no apparent reason. He felt deep grief, but had no idea why. Rodney yielded to the sadness and allowed himself to cry for as long as the tears would come.

> *Later that day Rodney was stunned and horrified as he watched the disaster on television. At the same time, he felt an instant sense of recognition and peace that linked his inexplicable tears to the crashing planes and falling buildings. A certainty that he had been given a gift of profound mystery, that of crying the tears of Christ, enveloped him. Rodney now believes that Christ embraced this new cross before it happened, that Jesus wept over New York just as he wept over Jerusalem.*[7]

Tears can be healing in so many ways. Weeping is one of the characteristics of the abundant life.

Milwaukee Journal Sentinel columnist, William Janz, wrote about his oldest son's first day of school:

> *His first day without us. Scott had his nametag on a string around his neck. "Don't come out," he said. He asked us to kiss him inside the house, so nobody would see. Then we stood in the living room, where he couldn't see us, and we watched him going into the garage. "I hope he isn't going to drive to school," I said. He took a small, red metal child's chair, carried it down the driveway, unfolded the chair, sat down, and waited for the school bus. His mother and I held each other, tears running down our faces. And we watched the boy on his little red chair, as he waited for the rest of his life to begin.*[8]

Music often evokes healing tears. Internationally renowned cellist, Yo-Yo Ma, tells about a time in his youth when he was trying to break with his father's strict orthodox beliefs about music. He told his father, "If you want me to be really obedient I can do that, but it means absolutely not finding my own voice. If you want me to be a good musician, it means I have to go deeply into myself to find out." He got his chance in 1971, when he was fifteen and away from home for the first time at Meadow Mount music camp in upstate New York. Wendy Rose, now a violinist with the Toronto Symphony, was a fellow camper. She recalls a moment when Yo-Yo did begin to find his own voice. "I heard Yo-Yo playing the Franck sonata, and I burst into tears. The sheer beauty of his playing was totally overwhelming. I just couldn't stop crying."[9]

In his book, *Visions: The Soul's Path to the Sacred*, Eddie Ensley tells of a vision he had when he was thirteen years old. Eddie had been brain-damaged at birth and was not able to do many ordinary tasks, like dressing himself or writing his name. "... the part of the brain that processed visual-spatial information wasn't working right." He suffered great abuse because of his disability. Teachers called him lazy and careless; his peers teased him mercilessly. Music was a refuge, and one day while listening to Schubert's *Unfinished Symphony* Eddie's head started spinning:

> *I became aware of a light, a light I saw not with my eyes but with my heart. That light filled the room, and in the light I saw a gentle, somewhat bluish figure surrounded by a white brightness ... The light was all warmth. And the warmth of the light spoke to me, but without words. I asked the light, "Who are you?" "I am the one who dries the tears of little boys ... I am the one from whom people hide their faces." "They hide their faces from me, too," I responded, speaking to the light not with words but with the communication of the heart. "I know, that's why I came. I am here to cradle you."*[10]

Tears open a portal that allows the Spirit to come in and do its healing work.

Jesus wept at the tomb of Lazarus as we weep at the graves of those we love. If he had not, he could not have done what he did next.

Something Rotten In Bethany

> *Then Jesus, again greatly disturbed, came to the tomb. It was a cave, and a stone was lying against it. Jesus said, "Take away the stone." Martha, the sister of the dead man, said to him, "Lord, already there is a stench because he has been dead four days." Jesus said to her, "Did I not tell you that if you believed, you would see the glory of God?" So they took away the stone. And Jesus looked upward and said, "Father, I thank you for having heard me. I knew that you always hear me, but I have said this for the sake of the crowd standing here, so that they may believe that you sent me." When he had said this, he cried with a loud voice, "Lazarus, come out!" The dead man came out, his hands and feet bound with strips of cloth, and his face wrapped in a cloth. Jesus said to them, "Unbind him, and let him go." Many of the Jews therefore, who had come with Mary and had seen what Jesus did, believed in him.*
> — John 11:38-44

Something stinks in this passage and it's not just the corpse of Lazarus. Jesus comes to the tomb, "greatly disturbed" (John 11:38a). He is affected by the grief of Mary and the others. John doesn't want us to miss this. He repeats what was written in the previous paragraph. John wants us to feel what Jesus is feeling: "... he was greatly disturbed in spirit and deeply moved" (John 11:33b).

Jesus is truly grieved by the passing of his dear friend, and by the anguish expressed by those who were closest to Lazarus. But that is not all John wants us to see here. There is something else, another level of meaning, and it has to do with what Martha said to Jesus at the end of that exchange when she greeted him upon his arrival. First she is indignant that he hasn't come in time to save her brother. Then she and Jesus have this conversation about resurrection. Jesus tells her that Lazarus will rise again. She acknowledges that she knows "... he will rise again on the last day." Jesus tells her, "I am the resurrection and the life. Those who believe in me, even though they die, will live, and everyone who lives and believes in me will never die. Do you believe this?" (John 11:20-26).

"Do you believe this?" This is the question John wants his readers to answer in the affirmative, as Martha does: "Yes, Lord, I believe you are the Messiah, the Son of God, the one coming into the world" (John 11:27). The difficulty is being able to hold onto this belief when faced with the harsh reality of death. Martha acts out the ambivalence that most of us experience. We move easily from faith to doubt and back again.

When Jesus gives the word to move the stone, Martha blurts out, "Lord, already there is a stench because he has been dead four days." This is the fearful Martha of "Lord, if you had been here, my brother would not have died" (John 11:21). Jesus' response to Martha's stinky comment is, "Did I not tell you that if you believed, you would see the glory of God?" It is almost as if John writes this in bold print. Something is rotten in Bethany, and John is about to tell us why it is essential that we know what it is.

In his magnificent novel, *The Last Temptation of Christ*, Nikos Kazantzakis describes, in graphic images, the intensity of that moment when Jesus arrives at the tomb with Mary and Martha.

> *Then suddenly while he stood there trembling all over, he uttered a wild cry, a strange cry, something from another world. The archangels must shout in the same way when they are angry.... "Lazarus," he cried, "come out!" And all at once we hear the earth in the tomb stir and crack. The tombstone begins to move; someone is gradually pushing it up. Fear and trembling ... Never in my life have I feared death as much as I feared that resurrection.*[11]

This is like that moment in the storm on the Sea of Galilee when the disciples, scared to death, are at the same time annoyed with Jesus because he doesn't share their fear. He's asleep. "How could he sleep at a time like this?" They wake him with their whining, "Don't you care that we are about to die?" Jesus shushes the sea, "Peace! Be still!" The disciples are shocked, more afraid of what they have just seen Jesus do than of the life-threatening storm (Mark 4:39b-41).

When Jesus raised Lazarus, the fear in the air must have been palpable. Suddenly everything everyone knew about life and death was obsolete. There is no ambivalence after seeing something earth-shaking. See it, believe it, and more importantly, John fairly shouts here, believe in the one who did it! John says they did. The stink was gone.

Then comes the gospel writer's unspoken (unwritten) question for us, "Do you believe?"

When I was collecting stories for the first book in the three volume Vision series I edited for CSS Publishing, I came to the text about Jesus raising a little girl from the dead (Mark 5:21-43). Each vision story was to give insight into one of the texts in Cycle B. I didn't know where I was going to find a contemporary story about someone raising the dead. Does that still happen? I didn't know. I didn't think I would ever find a story for a raising the dead text: something symbolic maybe, but not the real thing.

Then, while sitting at a picnic table and eating potato salad at a reception after an outdoor wedding in a beautiful garden, someone told me about a preacher he had known who had once raised someone from the dead. The preacher was now dead, but my potato-salad-eating friend thought his widow was living in a retirement community not far away. I managed to find Jean Hodge and she agreed to an interview.

Overcome With Amazement
Jean Hodge, as told to John Sumwalt

Pastor Tom Hodge was about to leave his office to go home for supper when he received word that one of his members was in the hospital and was not expected to live. He called his wife, Jean, to tell her he was going to be late, and set out for the hospital. When

103

he arrived, he found the man's family crying and embracing each other in the corridor outside the room. The doctor had just announced to them that their loved one had died.

Pastor Hodge asked if he could go into the room. There were several more members of the family gathered around the bed. He said to them, "Any of you who don't know the Lord, you leave this room." Then he went over to the bed, laid his hands on the man, and prayed. The man opened his eyes and looked up. The family was elated and the hospital staff was amazed.

The man lived for about a week before he became ill again. This time the Lord took him home for good. "But in that week of extra life," Mrs. Hodge said, "he received the Lord as his personal Savior. And many who witnessed this miracle also gave their lives to Christ."[12]

1. W. Somerset Maugham, *Appointment in Samara, John Ohara, Appointment In Samara* (New York: Random House, 1934), p. 5. *Scheppey* (a play, 1933), William Heinemann, London, 1933.

2. Doris Kearns Goodwin, *Team of Rivals: The Political Genius of Abraham Lincoln* (New York: Simon & Schuster, 2005), p. 743.

3. John Warren Steen, editor, *International Christian Digest*.

4. *A League of Their Own*, dir. Penny Marshall, with Tom Hanks, Geena Davis, Madonna, Rosie O'Donnell, and Lori Petty, Columbia Pictures, 1992.

5. "Caminiti Comes Clean: Ex-MVP Says He Won Award While Using Steroids," *Sports Illustrated*, May 28, 2002, http://sportsillustrated.cnn.com/si_online/special_report/steroids/.

6. Violet Anderson was a longtime member of Wauwatosa Avenue United Methodist Church in Wauwatosa, Wisconsin.

7. Tilda Norberg, *Ashes Transformed: Healing from Trauma* (Nashville: Upper Room Books, 2002), pp 130-131.

8. William Janz, *Milwaukee Journal Sentinel*, April 2, 1995.

9. Gerri Hershey, "We Are the World," *Parade* magazine, January 30, 2005.

10. Eddie Ensley, *Visions: The Soul's Path to the Sacred* (Chicago: Loyola Press, 2000), pp. 26-27.

11. Nikos Kazantzakis, *The Last Temptation of Christ*, (New York: Simon & Schuster, 1960), p. 362.

12. John E. Sumwalt, editor, *Vision Stories: True Accounts of Visions, Angels, and Healing Miracles* (Lima, Ohio: CSS Publishing, 2002), pp. 118-119. Tom Hodge served Assembly of God churches for over fifty years in West Bend, Hartford, and Mather, Wisconsin, and in Ishpeming, Michigan. He died in 1998. His wife, Mrs. Jean Hodge, is over ninety years of age and lives in a retirement home near West Bend. Jean tells how her husband has sometimes appeared to her in bed at night. She said, "One night he came to me, put his hand on my shoulder, and when I went to put my hand on his hand, his hand slipped away. I just couldn't get over it because he was right there, and he smiled at me. He was comforting me. I felt so elated. It was just so wonderful. I know he is with the Lord."

Miracle 4

While It Was Still Dark

March 7, 1961, was by all appearances an ordinary day. My brothers and I were sledding under the yard light just after dusk on the small hill between the house and the barn. Mom and our little sister were in the kitchen fixing supper. We could tell something was wrong the moment Dad got out of the car. His shoulders sagged and there was no light in his eyes. "Daddy's gone," was all he said, referring to his father, his voice breaking and his eyes filling with tears, as he passed us on the way to the house. Two words, and my whole world collapsed. Death had come home for the first time in my life. I had seen cows die, had buried favorite dogs and cats and attended the funerals of relatives and neighbors, but I had never lost someone I couldn't imagine living without. Grandpa had just retired — "I'll have time to take you fishing now," he had said.

I'll never forget that awful day or the grief that overwhelmed all of us in the week that followed. I had never seen my strong dad so vulnerable, and would not see him like that again until I sat with him as he lay dying 37 years later.

Mary Magdalene's world collapsed when Jesus took his last breath on the cross. Her beloved teacher and friend was "gone."

The Thick Darkness

> *Early on the first day of the week, while it was still dark, Mary Magdalene came to the tomb and saw that the stone had been removed from the tomb. So she ran and went to Simon Peter and the other disciple, the one*

whom Jesus loved, and said to them, "They have taken
the Lord out of the tomb, and we do not know where
they have laid him." — John 20:1-2

Mary must have been reeling as she made her way to the tomb that Sunday morning. She had suffered with Jesus through his painful death, the helpless agony of one who can only watch and wait for the suffering of a loved one to end. Jesus' death, when his life was finally "finished," must have come as a relief, followed by the deeper pain of the finality of his absence.

A young physician once said to me that after watching his father, also a physician, suffer greatly before he died, he had come to believe his father's suffering, as excruciating as it was for him to bear, and for their family to watch, had served a purpose. It made his father ready and glad to leave this world with all its pains and sorrows, and it helped his family to let him go, knowing he would have no more pain.

Many of us know this to be true from painful experience. Still we let our loved ones go reluctantly, fearing they are lost to us forever, wondering how we can possibly live without them, not wanting to live without them. Our hearts ache for years. We are tempted to despair. We feel sorry for ourselves, we are angry with our loved ones for leaving, angry at God for taking them, and angry with everyone else for going on with their lives as if nothing has happened.

"It's not fair!" we want to scream. This is not what we signed up for. When we gave birth to our little ones, we thought we could protect them from everything! When we said, "until death do us part," we thought it would never happen.

When my father-in-law died at 93, he was in so infirm and in so much pain that we gave thanks for his release. But the pain of his absence is no less than if he had passed at a young age. Death wounds us deeply — and frightens us like nothing else. We all walk the hard path Mary walked as she made her way to the tomb, "... on the first day of the week while it was still dark" (John 20:1).

John wants us to take note of the darkness here just as he does when he tells how Nicodemus "came to Jesus by night" (John 3:2;

108

19:39), and when he describes the evening the disciples "saw Jesus walking on the sea ... It was now dark" (John 6:17, 19b). Like a movie director setting a scene for dramatic effect, John shows Mary in the situation Jesus warns we may all find ourselves, "If you walk in darkness you do not know where you are going" (John 12:35b).

This is a culmination of the light and darkness theme that runs throughout John's narrative, "The light shines in the darkness and the darkness did not overcome it" (John 1:5), "... people have loved darkness rather than light" (John 3:19), "whoever follows me will never walk in darkness ..." (John 8:12a), "... night is coming when no one can work" (John 9:4b), "... those who walk at night stumble, because the light is not in them" (John 11:10b), "Walk while you have the light, so that the darkness may not overtake you" (John 12:35a), "I have come as a light into the world so that everyone who believes in me should not remain in darkness" (John 12:46).

We who live in this world know more about darkness than light. Though we stumble along, we cling to the darkness because it feels safer than the light we do not know. Mary represents all of us as she walks alone, fearfully, through the dark, forgetting for the moment that the darkness will not, indeed cannot, "overcome" the light.

Why does Mary decide to go the tomb "... while it is still dark"? Why not wait until first light? Does she want to keep her grief private? Is she afraid to go in the light of day for fear she, too, might be arrested and killed? The text raises more questions than it answers.

Why doesn't Mary wait for others to join her? John is the only gospel that has Mary going to the tomb alone. In the synoptics she is shown in the company of other women, "... the other Mary" in Matthew 28:1; "Mary the mother of James and Salome," in Mark 16:1; and "Joanna, Mary the mother of James, and the other women" in Luke 24:10.

John describes a solitary woman walking through the dark, as we all walk alone when we mourn the death of a loved one. It is not so much that we love "darkness rather than light" (John 3:19), though there are times we clearly do, or that the "light" is not in us (John 11:10b). It is simply that we are blinded by fear and grief.

109

When death comes, darkness takes hold of us for a while. There is something about the dark that is terrifying, that calls up in us the deepest kind of archetypal dread. When children whine about being afraid of the dark and wail about monsters under the bed, they are in touch with a cellular memory of the "beginning" when "... the earth was a formless void and darkness covered the face of the deep" (Genesis 1:2).

There is also something about the dark that is comforting, indeed, enlightening. This is one of the paradoxes we experience as we come to know the one who was "In the beginning ..." (before there was light) through whom all things "came into being ..." (John 1:1-3). God is in the darkness as well as the light. It was in darkness that God approached the Hebrews fleeing slavery in Egypt:

Moses brought the people out of the camp to meet God. "... Mount Sinai was wrapped in smoke, because the Lord had descended on it in fire; the smoke went up like the smoke of a kiln, while the whole mountain shook violently. As the blast of the trumpet grew louder and louder, Moses would speak and God would answer him in thunder ... The Lord summoned Moses to the top of the mountain and Moses went up" (Exodus 19:18-20). "When all the people witnessed the thunder and lightning, the sound of the trumpet and the mountain smoking, they were afraid and trembled and stood at a distance, and said to Moses, 'You speak to us, and we will listen; but do not let God speak to us or we will die' " (Exodus 20:18-19).

We are afraid to speak when God comes too close. Like the disciples in the boat, on that dark night during the storm, we are "terrified" at the first sight of "Jesus walking on the sea and coming near ..." (John 6:16-19). Like the Hebrews standing at a distance at the foot of the mountain, fearing for their lives as God's voice peals out in thunder, we are terrified when God comes near. And like them, we are even more terrified by what Moses does next. "... Moses drew near to the thick darkness where God was" (Exodus 20:21b).

In his book, *Losing Moses On The Freeway: The 10 Commandments in America*, Chris Hedges writes about finding God in the "thick darkness" in Roxbury, one of the poorest ghettos in

Boston. Hedges, a journalist and war correspondent for many years, served a church in Roxbury and worked with inner-city youth there while attending Harvard Divinity School. The seminary administration did not approve: "They had given me a full scholarship, but not, in the words of a dean, to 'be a social worker.' "[1]

In Roxbury, Hedges encountered hopeless poverty, despair, and hardened government bureaucrats "that regarded the poor as vermin," he writes. "I spent my first few weeks in despair." One day, a ten-year-old boy came to the manse where Hedges lived behind the church, and asked him to come help his mother. He went with the boy to his apartment building:

> ... climbed the stairs that smelled of urine and pushed open a metal door ... The woman was lying on a couch. Her arm was raw with blood and her flesh torn from rat bites. She had fallen drunk on her floor and become a meal for rodents. The wounds were unattended. She did not respond ... I found dishtowels in the kitchen, which was filled with dirty plates and filth, and wrapped them around the bites. I lifted her onto the couch and left her breathing heavily and smelling of alcohol.[2]

Despite some good he was able to do in Roxbury, Hedges left feeling like a failure. Despair led to hatred and violence. He discovered a shadow side of himself he did not like: "... my own complicity in oppression, my own sinfulness, how evil lurked within me, how when I was afraid I could turn on the weak and the powerless." And, Hedges discovered something else, "The darkness I found in Roxbury is my darkness, our darkness ... It is knowledge of this darkness that alone makes faith possible ... It is in this fear, this darkness that I found God, even as I thought I was fleeing God."[3]

Rachel Naomi Remen found something redemptive in darkness while working with cancer patients at the University of California-San Francisco School of Medicine, where she developed a psychological approach to dealing with life-threatening illness. One patient described his cancer as "this black hole in the middle of my life that keeps pulling me in." Remen asked him what was in the hole. "Just darkness," he told her. She suggested he explore the darkness with his imagination. He agreed to go into the darkness and reported, "The darkness is very soft ... gentle ... It supports me. I have no needs here ... *(sighs)*. I am tired. I am at rest ... I can open up in the darkness. Life is everywhere."[4]

Another patient was experiencing rage at the cancer inside of him, which he described as "unending darkness." Remen invited him to "close his eyes and allow himself to experience it." He, too, was surprised by the comfort he found. "It holds me. I am held in darkness. Wrapped in darkness. The darkness is ... soft ... almost tender *(sighs)*. It's safe here."[5]

Joan Borysenko found, in her work with cancer and AIDS patients, that healing sometimes begins in darkness, or because of darkness. Answering questions about the soul and the higher self in an interview for a book edited by Rex Hauck, she was asked about darkness. "... we love the stories of light, but we like to repress the darkness ... I think Jung had a great quote; he said, 'You don't get enlightened by imagining figures of light. Essentially the way to enlightenment is to go back out through the darkness.' "[6]

Light comes, Borysenko discovered, when her patients were going through a dark night of the soul.

> *Suddenly the bottom of life had dropped out from under them, and when that happens, you come face-to-face with the big questions: Who am I; what is the meaning of life ... Usually it isn't until we get to that really dark moment that we ask these big questions.*[7]

The anonymous fourteenth-century English spiritual director who wrote *The Cloud of Unknowing* knew about finding God in the dark, saying, "The Divine darkness is the unapproachable light in which God is said to dwell." He warned novice contemplatives:

> *... in the beginning it is usual to feel nothing but a kind of darkness about your mind, or as it were, a cloud of unknowing ... Try as you might this darkness and this cloud will remain between you and your God. You will feel frustrated, for your mind will be unable to grasp*

him ... But learn to be at home in this darkness. Return
to it as often as you can, letting your spirit cry out to
him whom you love. For if, in this life, you hope to feel
and see God as he is in himself it must be within this
darkness and this cloud.[8]

We cannot find the light, or be found by light, until we have known darkness. Jesus is "... the light of the world" because he has known, and is known, in both darkness and light (John 8:12b).

The Case For Resurrection

So she ran and went to Simon Peter and the other dis-
ciple, the one whom Jesus loved, and said to them, "They
have taken the Lord out of the tomb, and we do not
know where they have laid him." Then Peter and the
other disciple set out and went toward the tomb. The
two were running together, but the other disciple out-
ran Peter and reached the tomb first. He bent down to
look in and saw the linen wrappings lying there, but he
did not go in. Then Simon Peter came, following him,
and went into the tomb. He saw the linen wrappings
lying there, and the cloth that had been on Jesus' head,
not lying with the linen wrappings, but rolled up in a
place by itself. Then the other disciple who reached the
tomb first, also went in, and he saw and believed; for
as yet they did not understand the scripture, that he
must rise from the dead. Then the disciples returned to
their homes.   — John 20:2-10

The gospel writer sets a tone of urgency in this scene by moving quickly from one action to another. The moment Mary finds the stone has been removed, we see her *running* away from the tomb to "... Simon Peter and the other disciple ..." breathlessly *exclaiming*, "They have taken the Lord out of the tomb, and we don't know where they have laid him." Then we see the two disciples *running* to the tomb. "The other disciple," as John always refers to him, *outruns* Peter and arrives first. He "*bends*," "*looks*," and "*sees*" linen wrappings. Then "Simon Peter came, *following*

113

him, and *went* into the tomb and he *saw*...." The other disciple "also *went in*, and he *saw* and *believed*" (John 20:2-8). We have thirteen actions described in just seven sentences; not quite a Clint Eastwood, knock 'em down, shoot 'em up action sequence, but a lot of action, nevertheless.

When Michael Williams, editor of *The Storyteller's Companion to the Bible*, teaches storytelling seminars, he tells his students to pay special attention to four things as they tell a story: actions, setting, characters, and objects. John certainly knows how to show action.

John also knows how to show a setting that grabs our attention. What could be more dramatic than the setting of an empty tomb with the door open? Who rolled away the stone? Where is the body? What does it all mean? Inquiring minds want to know.

Character development has already been done in previous scenes. Peter is shown a number of times, representing the ambivalence of the disciples (and perhaps the early Jewish church) who express belief one minute and doubt or obstinate blindness the next. Peter expresses belief (John's hope for everyone who hears his gospel) early on, during the calling of the disciples, when Jesus changes his name from Simon, son of John, to Cephas (rock or Peter), and later, when he confesses to Jesus, "You are the Holy One of God" (John 1:40-42; 6:67-69). This is in contrast to Jesus' brothers and the temple police, the chief priests and the Pharisees who do not believe (John 7:5, 45-52). When Jesus is about to wash his feet, Peter says, "You will never wash my feet," but relents, asking for his head and hands also to be washed when Jesus tells him "Unless I wash you, you have no share with me" (John 13:8-9).

John shows the dark side of Peter when he shows him raising his sword to protect Jesus at the time of his arrest, and in the courtyard of the high priest when the "rock" denies Jesus three times (John 13:36-38; 18:10-11, 16-27). It is likely John intends for followers of Jesus in the early church to see themselves reflected in Peter's unfaithfulness and ineptitude.

"The disciple whom Jesus loved" appears twice before the empty tomb scene. He is shown reclining next to Jesus, an intimate relationship (also John's hope for all who read his gospel), with

Peter who directs him to ask Jesus whom he is speaking about when he says "one of you will betray me." We also see him at the foot of the cross with the three Marys when Jesus asks him to care for his mother, a sign of Jesus' love for him and confidence that he will remain faithful (John 13:23-26; 19:26).

Mary's deep love for Jesus is seen in her presence with Jesus' mother, and his aunt, Mary, wife of Clopas, at the crucifixion (John 11:33; 12:3; 19:25). This is a faithful disciple who loves Jesus.

There is an abundance of objects interwoven in this series of actions, along with clues to their significance, no doubt a direct response to resurrection bashers who were aggressively casting doubts on the church's witness. If it is true that the devil is in the details, John may be doing a little creative bedeviling here: what Jesus calls being "wise as serpents and innocent as doves" (Matthew 10:16b). A modern defense attorney couldn't have done better. Each object is presented in a way that builds the case for resurrection. John is looking for conviction: believers who will act on their belief that Jesus is alive, as Mary does when she announces to the disciples, "I have seen the Lord ..." (John 20:18).

John begins with the stone, which has been removed, hard evidence that something extraordinary has happened. Who removed it, we wonder? First century readers would have known that stones of the size needed to close the entrance to a tomb could not be moved easily. The tomb is mentioned no less than seven times in these eighteen verses. It is as if John, our defense attorney, keeps holding it up to the jury. Don't miss this; it's empty. The body is gone. Then we have defense exhibits three and four, "the linen wrappings" and "the cloth that had been on Jesus' head, not lying with the wrappings but rolled up in a place by itself" (John 20:5-7). John piles on the evidence. "See," he seems to say, "the body was not stolen. Tomb robbers would not have taken time to remove the linen wrappings or the head cloth."

John's comment about Peter seeing all of this evidence, but saying nothing about any conclusions Peter might have drawn, and "the other disciple," who "saw and believed," and then his statement, "for as yet they did not understand the scripture, that he must be raised from the dead" is more problematic, not the smooth summation we might have expected from a renowned gospel defender (John 20:8-9). What is it that "the other disciple, the one whom Jesus loved," believed? Confusion reigns. Everyone is still in the dark.

Seeing Jesus

> *But Mary stood weeping outside the tomb. As she wept, she bent over to look into the tomb; and she saw two angels in white, sitting where the body of Jesus had been lying, one at the head and the other at the feet. They said to her, "Woman, why are you weeping?" She said to them, "They have taken away my Lord, and I do not know where they have laid him." When she had said this, she turned around and saw Jesus standing there, but she did not know that it was Jesus. Jesus said to her, "Woman, why are you weeping? Whom are you looking for?" Supposing him to be the gardener, she said to him, "Sir, if you have carried him away, tell me where you have laid him, and I will take him away." Jesus said to her, "Mary!" She turned and said to him in Hebrew, "Rabbouni!" (which means Teacher). Jesus said to her, "Do not hold on to me, because I have not yet ascended to the Father. But go to my brothers and say to them, 'I am ascending to my Father and your Father, to my God and your God.'" Mary Magdalene went and announced to the disciples, "I have seen the Lord"; and she told them that he had said these things to her.* — John 20:11-18

I memorized all of the eighteen verses in this story and recited them on an Easter Sunday, before preaching on this text, some years ago. Committing the words to memory was not as difficult as I feared, though I don't have time to do that every week. Deciding how to say the words, with what inflection and emphasis, was the hard part. The exchange between the risen Jesus and Mary was particularly vexing, especially that pivotal moment when she still thinks he is the gardener and he says her name, "Mary!"

I must have repeated verse 16 about 100 times, trying to imagine how Jesus would have said her name and how Mary would have heard it. Surely it must have sounded familiar, natural, like he said it every day. There is nothing sweeter than the sound of your own name on the lips of one who loves you. And this must have been the way Mary responded, reflexively, without thinking, repeating "Rabbouni!" in the familiar way she had addressed Jesus so many times before.

What John describes so well here is what we have come to call an "aha" event, a gasp of recognition. When Bill Miller, Frank Sinatra's pianist and "closest musical adviser," died in July of 2006 at the age of 91, Frank Sinatra Jr. said, "Bill Miller was the greatest accompanist that any popular singer ever had ... There was no one who had his touch, no one who had his taste." Frank Sr. "... who did not read music, relied on Miller to articulate his wishes to his arrangers." Several months after Sinatra's death in 1995, his son performed a tribute to his father. Bill Miller, who had played for his dad for almost forty years, was brought out "... onto a dark stage unannounced and sat down at the piano. When he began playing the introduction to the haunting 'One For My Baby,' the audience let out a gasp," the Junior Sinatra said. "They were all Sinatra fans and they recognized Bill immediately."[9]

Seeing Bud
Tyler Pease

I was at work when I received a shocking call from Lisa. She told me that Tom and Lee's dad had died. I thought I hadn't heard her correctly, that someone else in the family had passed away. My marriage to Lee had ended a year earlier, but I had remained close to her father. He was a dear friend to me and we cared for each other.

We all knew that Bud had health problems and that he was suffering from a degenerative muscle disease, but he had been doing somewhat better. I had visited Bud about a month earlier and we had a great visit. I had planned to make another visit in August. I felt shock, sorrow, and emptiness that I was not able to say good-bye.

117

Bud was raised in large by his grandparents in a time when people did not always tell you that they loved you or cared; you just knew it even though it was unspoken. He was much like that; you could see how deeply he loved his family by the way his eyes sparkled when they were around and the smile he had on his face as he sucked on his pipe. Bud was not a church-goer. I'm not sure if something had driven him away from the church, or if he had just gotten out of the habit of going. We had spoken a few times about faith and I felt he believed in God, but again, he grew up being told those are topics you just don't discuss.

Family members flew in from different parts of the country for the funeral. Most of us were having a very difficult time dealing with our loss and the grief that came so quickly and unexpectedly. I left the funeral unsure of Bud's faith and praying that he did believe. Several weeks passed by, and I found myself feeling like a major chapter in my life had just had the last page ripped out and was unfinished. Feeling depressed was becoming my daily norm; I wasn't sleeping well.

It was the third week after the funeral when I went to bed, exhausted, hoping I would sleep. I had a dream that I was in Bud's shop, where we normally spent our visits. He was a paint contractor and the shop was where he spent much of his time, working and socializing with the many good friends who stopped by often to discuss local events.

I saw Bud. He had on the dark red and black flannel shirt that he frequently wore, unbuttoned, a white T-shirt underneath, and his khaki colored pants. He was standing behind the sawhorse with some woodwork in front of him with a beautiful smile on his face. It was the same grin I had seen often when he was enjoying his family.

I told him I was so sorry that I hadn't had the chance to say good-bye and that I loved him; and then tried to reach out to hug him, but I could not. I don't remember if he spoke out loud, but it didn't matter; I felt his love and I knew that everything was okay. There was an overwhelming sense of calmness, peace, and reassurance. Then I awoke, weeping, not just from letting the sorrow go, but also from finding the peace I had been searching for. It was a flood of emotion, and I said a prayer of thanks to God and slept soundly for the remainder of the night.[10]

I Heard Dad's Voice
Donna Mrozinski

My father was a UCC pastor, and upon retirement from his last church in southern Illinois, he and Mom settled into the first home of their own in Manitowoc, Wisconsin. There were some happy years, and as their health issues mounted in number, the relationship between Dad and I became more open and stronger than it had ever been. About the same time as Dad was diagnosed with lung cancer, Mom started to "not be Mom," which we naively thought was part of her aging process. By the time we were told there was at best a year left for Dad, Mom was having huge mood swings, wandering away, forgetting many basic everyday things, such as how to set the table for lunch, and becoming increasingly paranoid. At the time we didn't know that now well-known word ... Alzheimer's.

Because Mom refused to consider an assisted living situation, we did our best to keep Dad and Mom in their own precious little house. Dad asked me to give him my word that I would care for Mom after he was no longer with us. When we had time alone, we talked about everything under the sun, leaving nothing to chance as to how he felt about things. One horrible June morning he called me saying he felt like he was drowning — and he was! His lungs had collapsed and were filling with fluid. After two weeks in the hospital, and two weeks with Mom staying in my home, I was told to make arrangements in a nursing home for both of them. He still had a drain tube in his lung and was very weak; Mom had run away from us trying to find Dad. Going against everything in my heart that said, "No," I had to do it: the hardest decision of my entire life.

Seven months later, Dad was once again in the hospital, this time with a cracked rib from a fall. He spent his ninetieth birthday there. That evening, over a Pepsi, we talked. He told me what I should have him wear to be buried in. He realized he could no longer be strong for Mom. I told him I would be so lost without

119

him. He said he knew where he was going, and was so curious to see what it would be like, but was not afraid. I asked him to let me know if he could. It was a strange but beautiful time we had that evening.

One week later Dad passed to his peaceful reward. A few days after the funeral, the children had all returned to their homes and the house was quiet as I began the morning. The sun was shining and with a cup of fresh coffee in hand, I was walking to my "prayer corner" at a window looking out on the backyard. Without thinking, I said out loud, "Well, Dad, is it as wonderful there as you had hoped it would be?" I could feel the warmth of a hand lightly touching the top of my hair as he said, "It is." He always was able to say so much with a few words. That was in February 1998, and I can still hear him as if it were yesterday. This "happening" gave me great comfort, and I shared it with many others as a comfort to them.

Then in June, on Father's Day, after participating in some special music during our church service, then relaxing into the sermon, a flood of overwhelming grief hit me and I was unable to control some really hard crying! As I stuffed tissues into my mouth and face, I heard Dad's voice a second — and last — time, saying "It is good!" as if he was telling me, "Okay, stop crying for me, this is great!" I never heard his voice again. Occasionally, I would see him in a dream, giving a smile or a wave.

Then, after a hard, long journey into the no-man's-land of Alzheimer's, I was keeping vigil at my mother's deathbed in April 2001. I must have nodded off for a while, and saw Dad sitting in his armchair, just staring into the distance with a very solemn look on his face. During that night she murmured his name, as if she might have seen him. Later that morning, she joined him. As I thought about all this a bit later, I realized he had been sitting there waiting for her.[11]

What would it be like to hear your name spoken by someone you knew to be dead? Through the fog of sorrow and the drowning darkness of death, Mary heard her beloved teacher speak her name.

It was like one of those dreams where something startling occurs and we wake up shaking. In one shocking moment of recognition Mary knew Jesus was alive, though it would take years for her, and the church, to assimilate this new reality.

There is no more intimate or dramatic scene in all of scripture. John is showing us the instant everything changed in Mary's life and in the lives of all humankind for all time to come. The church may have been born on Pentecost, but the conception of the new body of Christ occurred in that split second Mary ceased relating to Jesus as someone dead and gone — and began a new relationship that would never end. Her response to this transformation is the essence of the gospel. John writes: "Mary Magdalene went and announced to the disciples, 'I have seen the Lord ...' " (John 20:18).

John wants the readers of his gospel to experience both the emotional and intellectual impact of the paradigmatic shift that occurs as one who knew Jesus best began to respond to this startling new reality. His account of the resurrection has the same effect as Jesus' parables. You cannot enter into the story and come out the same person you were when you went in. Just hearing this "good news" of Mary's encounter with the living Christ can be transforming, life changing for the hearer as it was for Mary.

After the debut of his 1988 film, *Paris By Night*, David Hare wrote:

> *People walk around thinking they know what they believe about things, but ... they rarely examine the reasons for their beliefs ... when they are confronted with a real work of art then they discover that they don't believe what they thought they believed all along.*[12]

John's gospel is a powerful new art form that he and the synoptic writers created, of necessity, to carry the message of a new age in which Jesus would show himself again and again.

> *When it was evening on that day, the first day of the week, and the doors of the house where the disciples*

had met were locked for fear of the Jews, Jesus came
and stood among them and said, "Peace be with you."
                    — John 20:19; Luke 24:36-43; 1 Corinthians 15:5

A week later his disciples were again in the house, and
Thomas was with them. Although the doors were shut,
Jesus came and stood among them.... — John 20:26a

... Jesus showed himself again to the disciples by the
Sea of Tiberius; and he showed himself in this way ...
Just after daybreak Jesus stood on the beach; but the
disciples did not know it was Jesus. Jesus said to them,
"... Come and have breakfast." Now none of the dis-
ciples dared to ask him, "Who are you?" because they
knew it was the Lord.   — John 21:1-12

John's concluding words foreshadow the many more occasions
to come when Jesus would show himself in this world: "... there
are also many other things that Jesus did; if everyone of them were
written down, I suppose the world itself could not contain the books
that would be written" (John 21:25).

In her book, *Ashes Transformed*, Tilda Norberg tells about the
death of her parents in a plane crash when she was sixteen years
old. She was waiting at the airport to meet them on an Easter Sunday, after worship, and witnessed the horrific, fiery crash that killed
all 47 passengers instantly. In the midst of the shock and the pan-
demonium all around her, Tilda experienced an unforgettable, comforting presence:

Then I saw Jesus. He stood directly in front of me and
gazed at me with great love. I don't mean I saw him
with my mind's eye, as I have many times since. I saw
him with physical eyes, perceiving him in the same way
I see my dog curled up at my feet. His clothing glowed,
and I knew that I was seeing his resurrected body. Jesus
spoke to me, and I heard seven words with physical
ears. "Don't be afraid; I am always with you." He re-
peated these words many times as if to make sure that I

understood and would be certain for the rest of my life
that he had indeed spoken to me.[13]

I received a phone call from Paul Tulppo a few weeks after doing a vision program at his church in a neighboring Milwaukee suburb. He told of seeing Jesus while in the company of two friends when he was a child in Detroit:

> *Back in 1946, when I was eight years old, I was return-*
> *ing from a day in the woods on the far west side of*
> *Detroit with my friend, Jim, who was my age, and his*
> *brother, Anthony, who was two years older. As we*
> *headed toward home, the brothers suggested that we*
> *stop at their church so they could show me, a non-Catho-*
> *lic, how they blessed themselves with holy water when*
> *they entered the church.*
>
> *I followed them into their church, we all put our*
> *fingers into the holy water, and they crossed themselves.*
> *Then we knelt in the very last pew. When we looked up,*
> *we saw the Lord Jesus Christ standing on the altar,*
> *about 25 feet away. His arms were outstretched and*
> *there was a beautiful glow completely surrounding him.*
> *The three of us were in complete awe. We jumped to*
> *our feet and ran out of the church, and we didn't stop*
> *running until we reached home and told our mothers*
> *what we had seen.*[14]

Paul told me his vision of Jesus was still a source of comfort and hope 67 years later. He said, "I remember that vision as though it happened five minutes ago." An encounter with Jesus is life-changing and can also be deeply disturbing.

The *Glasgow Sunday Herald*, a small Scottish newsweekly, ran a story in January of 2006 about a woman named Naomi Wolf who was overwhelmed one day by the presence of a divine being she concluded was Jesus:

> *It wasn't this crazy theological thing. It was just this*
> *figure who was just the most perfected human being —*
> *full of light and love. It was complete joy and happiness*

and there were tears running down my face ... But the
visitation wasn't entirely euphoric. When I came out of
it, I was absolutely horrified because I'm Jewish.[15]

Naomi Wolf is a well-known American feminist author. It occurred to her that other liberal feminists would think she had lost her mind. Nonetheless, Ms. Wolf now has full faith in a higher power:

I don't want to be co-opted as the poster child for any
religion or any agenda ... There are a lot of people out
there just waiting for some little Jewish feminist to cross
over. I don't claim to get where this being fits into the
scheme of things but I absolutely believe in divine provi-
dence now, absolutely believe God totally cares about
every single one of us intimately.[16]

Belief in life after death is outside the officially sanctioned concept of reality. Those who dare to speak of their encounters with the holy do so because, like the disciples, they can't help themselves. The news is too good not to tell. Once you have caught a glimpse of the eternal, you are never the same.

Phyllis Tickle, known for her devotional books, tells about a transforming near-death experience after a miscarriage, in her autobiography, *The Shaping of a Life.*

I was up in the corner of the room just above my bed ...
something or someone had caused me to move to my
right; and there in the spot where there should have
been only more ceiling, there was only light ... it radi-
ated out in sweetness from a marvelous tunnel that was
green like summer grass ... and the light at the other
end was sending out the blessing of that place, and it
said, "Come."[17]

Tickle tells how she was "irrevocably changed by this event, living for decades after with no fear of death, viewing it as a 'state to be anticipated, hoped for....' " Still, since that year, 1955, when she was a young bride, she has developed some doubts, perhaps like those the disciples must have had as time separated them from the events surrounding the resurrection. Tickle writes, "... although I am increasingly convinced I experienced a physiological event that I interpreted simplistically for years, I am not to this day sure enough of that conclusion to go on record as saying so without some caveats ... There is in those brief encounters, all the sureness of acceptance and sustaining, unending being that the soul has ever longed toward...."[18]

Joan Borysenko wrote of a remarkable dream/vision experience she and her son shared at the time of her mother's death. It happened about three in the morning as they were praying.

I was a pregnant mother giving birth to a baby, but I was also simultaneously the baby ... I was coming out through a dark tunnel, and I came out into an experience of ineffable light ... my entire life with my mother made sense, and it seemed perfect that she had birthed me into this world, and it seemed that I had just birthed her soul back out of the world ... When I opened my eyes, the room was literally filled with light ... my son weeping, tears just pouring from his eyes ... looked at me and he said, "Can you see the light in the room? ... It's Grandma; she's holding open the door to eternity for us so that we can have a glimpse."[19]

In this portrait of Mary and the risen Christ, John is "holding open the door to eternity for us so we can have a glimpse." His masterfully crafted words reach out over the centuries, drawing us toward "the true light," which the darkness can never overcome (John 1:9a, 5).

My Nightingale Song
Alice Rippen

In 1993, I met my "first love." We were very close, and absolute best friends. We always assumed that we would marry someday, but we were very young. Five years after our relationship

125

began, George decided to pursue a career dream in New York, while I stayed behind in Arizona. For the next two years, we were involved in a long-distance relationship; however, it became clear that he was never going to return to Arizona, and being a small-town girl myself, I had absolutely no desire to move to New York. I was very close with my family, and could not imagine being that far away from home. Neither of us could change, so we determined that, in spite of our great love for one another, perhaps we weren't "meant to be" after all. We decided to try our best to maintain our friendship, as neither of us could imagine life without the other.

Time passed, and we both dated other people. George called one evening and told me that he was miserable without me, and that he was actually physically sick over the ending of our relationship. He mentioned a few symptoms he was having, and what he said concerned me. I urged him to see a doctor. A couple of weeks later he called and said that he had been diagnosed with an extremely rare and fatal form of cancer. I was stunned and devastated. I immediately made plans to fly to New York. I went to the clinic with him where he was to receive treatment. The doctors there were honest with us, and told us that his chances of being cured were practically nil, that history has shown this to be a fatal form of cancer. He was only 22.

I had to return to Arizona because I had a job and an apartment here. George had given me his two cats to take care of when he went to New York and, of course, they needed me as well. For the next five months, I flew to New York as often as I could, while George dealt with treatments, and the side effects of chemo. I did everything I could to take care of him, and keep him comfortable. He lovingly called me his Florence Nightingale.

On my last trip out, George was in the hospital, and the doctors had said that he would not go home. He was very, very sick. His body was so ravaged from the cancer and the chemo. We begged his doctor to release him for one afternoon and night, so that we could spend that last time together. His primary doctor agreed to sign him out, but was very reluctant to do so. He wanted a private conference with me. He was very kind, but explained to me what could happen while I was with George. He explained that George was on very toxic chemo in an effort to control the tumor growth, and that this chemo was very hard on the heart and other major organs. I think he wanted to be sure I understood that George could pass away in my presence, and wanted to know if I would I be able to handle it if that were to happen. I assured him that I was prepared for anything, and I was. I honestly don't know where I found the strength, but I knew I could handle it. That last time together was just too important for me to let that fear get in the way.

We went to my hotel, where we stayed up all night talking, inasmuch as he was able. He confided that he was very confused, as there had been people from nearly every denomination coming to his hospital room and trying to "convert" or "save" him. He was not raised in a church, and had no idea what any form of religion was all about, and now he was looking to me for answers. This was something we had never discussed before. I was raised in the Lutheran church, but had kind of slid away from the whole issue of religion. Not that I didn't believe, but I was busy with my life, and my career, and I just didn't give it much thought anymore. But all my dormant beliefs sprang back to life that night, and the words poured from me. I still don't know where they all came from, but I know I spoke with absolute conviction. It surprised us both. He had so many questions, questions I didn't even know I had the answers to, but I did. By daybreak, he understood, and accepted Christ. He had no doubt.

He had such peace from that time on. He told me that when he passed, he would try to find a way to let me know that he was, indeed, with Jesus. I didn't believe that this was possible; I believed that when a person died, all earthly bonds were cut, and they were exclusively with God from that moment on. I told him I would be watching for a sign, but secretly, I didn't have high hopes. Maybe that is why I didn't recognize it for what it was when it came.

We said our last good-byes, and I returned home to Arizona. Since I was so upset that I could barely function, I had temporarily moved back in with my parents. They had always sheltered me, and this was no exception. I had never had to deal with anything even remotely like this in my life, and I felt like it was the end of the world. Nothing made sense anymore. I prayed, but I could never get back that feeling that I had in the hotel room that night: the feeling of being enveloped by God. I felt physically cold and abandoned. My teeth chattered all the time, and I ached all over. Every time the phone rang, I nearly fainted. Nothing I say could ever adequately describe the utter devastation I felt. I could not imagine life without my best friend. Worst of all, I knew I had made my last trip to New York; I would not see him again. I had to return home or lose my job. My employer had been very understanding, but business was business. George asked that I not return to New York again. He did not want me there when he passed. He felt that I had been through enough, and he had this newfound peace and didn't really need me anymore. Selfishly, I was glad. The strength that I had felt that night at the hotel had deserted me, along with the conviction that I could handle anything that happened. Now I wondered how I would be able to go on.

We spoke on the phone a time or two, as he was able, but neither of us had much to say, we had already said it all. We were both exhausted: he physically, me mentally and emotionally.

I awoke from a sound sleep one night when George's cats jumped off my bed and onto the windowsill. It was a dreadfully hot night in August, and my parents' air conditioning had chosen the day before to break down, so I was sleeping with my windows and drapes open, trying to catch any breeze. The cats both rubbed their faces on the window screen, and made the same tiny noises of affection they sometimes made to me, sort of a chirping sound with purring. I tried to raise up to see what had caught their attention, but strangely, I seemed to be paralyzed. I could raise my head slightly, but that was all. In the meantime, the cats were almost in a frenzy, rubbing on the window screen. I began to panic — why couldn't I move? There was a feeling of pressure in the room, I could hear it as well as feel it. It was like diving suddenly into very deep water. That pressure was keeping me pressed flat against my bed.

For some reason, I turned my head to look at my bedside clock. It was 3:32 a.m. I noticed that the room was beginning to fill with light, and it was coming through the window. The light became very bright, and I have a vivid recollection of seeing dust motes floating in the air. I forgot to pay attention to what the cats were doing, I was so mesmerized by this light. I was in total disbelief. What was it? I had crazy fleeting thoughts: UFO's, nuclear attack, or maybe I had died, but why? Or was I just dreaming? I had never had a dream like this. I panicked, and struggled to get out of the bed, but I couldn't. It was as if a huge hand was pressing me down, and I felt that my ears would pop if the pressure in the room continued to increase.

As I lay there trying to make myself wake up from this bizarre dream, a bird began to sing. I had never heard a bird that sounded like this. The notes were clear and bright, but not shrill. And it was loud. For some reason, I stopped being afraid, but I still didn't understand what was happening. The bird sang and sang. It occurred to me that the cats might tear through the screen to get at that bird, and it sounded so close I was afraid they might be able to get to it and kill it. But they were lying on the windowsill, content. I couldn't believe that they weren't reacting to any of this. The air pressure alone should have been enough to send them running. This was such a surreal experience, and it seemed to go on forever. I raised my head to look at the clock again. It was 3:33 a.m; — only a minute had passed. I don't have any recollection at all as to what happened after that. I don't know if the light faded away or went out abruptly; I don't know when the bird stopped singing, I don't know when the pressure in the room returned to normal, either. As unbelievable as it seems, I must have fallen asleep in the middle of this experience.

The next morning, the cats were asleep on my bed as if nothing had happened. The night before was so vivid in my mind (and is to this day), but I just had to chalk it up to a stress-induced dream. When I went into the kitchen for breakfast, my mom was sitting at the table with her usual cup of coffee, but without her customary newspaper. It appeared she had been waiting for me. She gave me a look that I couldn't quite read, and said, "You know that phone call will be coming today, don't you?" It felt like the floor fell out from under me. She had witnessed everything I had. Her bedroom windows were on the same side of the house as mine. I said, "It wasn't a dream, was it?"

129

"No," she said. "I saw the light, and I heard a bird singing. I haven't heard a nightingale sing since I was a little girl. I didn't think there were any around here." A nightingale. That's how George chose to show his Florence Nightingale that he was okay, and he even gave me a witness, so I would know it wasn't a dream. When I did get the phone call, I was told George passed away at 6:32 a.m. New York time: 3:32 a.m. by my bedside clock.[20]

---

1. Chris Hedges, *Losing Moses On The Freeway: The 10 Commandments in America* (New York: Free Press, 2005), p. 28.

2. *Ibid*, pp. 17-18.

3. *Ibid*, pp. 36-37.

4. Rachel Naomi Remen, *Kitchen Table Wisdom: Stories That Heal* (New York: Riverhead Books, 1996), p. 310.

5. *Ibid*, p. 311.

6. Rex Hauck, editor, *Angels: The Mysterious Messengers*, "Joan Borysenko, Ph.D." (New York: Ballantine Books, 1994), p. 61.

7. *Ibid*.

8. William Johnston, editor, *The Cloud of Unknowing* (New York: Doubleday, 1973), pp. 48-49.

9. Elaine Woo, *The Milwaukee Journal Sentinel*, July 20, 2006. (Originally in *Los Angeles Times.)*

10. Tyler Pease is a member of Wauwatosa Avenue United Methodist Church in Wauwatosa, Wisconsin, where he is active in the church praise choir, "Agape." He is a native Wisconsinite who grew up in a small town, and is the proud father of one daughter, Sarah. Tyler is a sales engineer in the packaging industry and enjoys volunteering for both non-profit professional and academic organizations as well as being involved in faith-based groups. tosa@tds.net.

11. Donna Mrozinski is a member of Wesley United Methodist church in Manitowoc, Wisconsin, where she and her husband raised four children. She

is retired from the County Department of Social Services and enjoys her seven grandchildren and two great-grandchildren. Donna says, "As the years have gone by, there has been one truth learned over and over again. It is to listen. Many of God's answers come as just a whisper."

12. David Hare, "Paris By Night," *Chicago Tribune*, August 13, 1988.

13. Tilda Norberg, *Ashes Transformed: Healing from Trauma, 43 Stories of Faith* (Nashville: Upper Room Books, 2002), p. 18.

14. John E. Sumwalt, editor, *Vision Stories: True Accounts Of Visions, Angels, And Healing Miracles* (Lima, Ohio: CSS Publishing, 2002), p. 166.

15. Torcuil Crichton, *Glasgow Sunday Herald*, January 22, 2006, http://www.sundayherald.com/53687.

16. *Ibid.*

17. Phyllis Tickle, *The Shaping of a Life: A Spiritual Landscape* (New York: Doubleday, 2001), pp. 210-211.

18. *Ibid*, pp. 217-218.

19. *Op cit,* Rex Hauck, pp. 57-58.

20. The writer of this personal story, "My Nightingale Song," prefers to remain anonymous. Alice Rippen is a pseudonym. Her name, the other names, and the locations in the story have been changed at her request.

Miracle 5

The Best Send Off Ever

In the summer of 2004, I had the joy of traveling with Rosmarie Trapp on a five-day, whirlwind storytelling tour of southern Wisconsin. Rosmarie is the firstborn child of the Captain and Maria, of the famed von Trapp Family Singers of *Sound of Music* fame. She has seven older and two younger siblings, five of whom are still living. The von Trapps escaped from Austria when the Nazis came in 1938. Rosmarie said her parents had a vision like Abraham to go to a new land that God would show them; a decision, she said, that saved their lives. She was nine years old when they arrived in "Amerika" and settled on a farm in Stowe, Vermont, where the von Trapp Family Lodge is still located today. They slept in a haymow in a barn the first summer while their home was being built.

The von Trapp Family Singers offered concerts all over the world in the 1940s and '50s. "Tiny one-horse towns and big cities, we went everywhere — every state in the US (except Alaska), Canada, Mexico, South America, and New Zealand," Rosmarie said. When we passed Kohler, Wisconsin, on our way from a book signing in Plymouth to a church event in Sheboygan, she exclaimed, "Oh, we played here in the 1940s." She remembered touring the factory where the popular Kohler tubs, sinks, and other bathroom accessories were made.

I opened each program with vision stories from the three books in the Vision series (Rosmarie has a personal story in each one), and after I had warmed up the crowd, Rosmarie would come out and tell the stories behind the story of *The Sound of Music*; what really happened and what was just "Hollywood." She said it was

133

true that the captain had a whistle, but he was not a soldier and did not teach the children to march. He had a whistle because he had been a submarine captain — it was the only way to get the sailors' attention over the noisy engines. She told about appearing briefly as an extra with her mother and a niece in one scene of the movie as Julie Andrews sang "I Have Confidence" under an arch. It was shot in Salzburg, their former home. After ten takes, she was glad that that was the beginning and the end of her movie career.

Wherever we went, Rosmarie witnessed to her faith, played guitar, and led people in singing favorite songs from *The Sound of Music*: "Do-Re-Mi," "My Favorite Things," "Edelweiss," "Climb Every Mountain," and "The Hills Are Alive with the Sound of Music." The tunes are still ringing in my head. Rosmarie always invited the children to come up and sing with her. At one event, there was a developmentally disabled girl who was singing loudly and off-key. Rosmarie invited her up on stage and had her sit by her side and sing with her during the rest of the performance.

I heard new stories each time Rosmarie spoke. On the last night, she told about a sister who was always late. They used to tease her, telling her that she would be late for her own funeral. When she died, her body was sent, by mistake, to Waterbury, Connecticut, instead of Waterbury, Vermont. They had to start the funeral without her, and when the casket arrived about halfway through the service, everyone had a good laugh. "It was the best funeral we ever had," Rosmarie said.[1]

That's one way to make a memorable exit. The disciples would not have called Jesus' departure, the "best ascension we ever had," because they had never had one before. But it had to have been one of the most defining moments of their lives. And, of all of their many experiences with Jesus, raising the dead, healing the sick, feeding 5,000, and his many resurrection appearances, it may have been the most difficult to explain. What could the angels have meant when they said, "This Jesus, who has been taken up from you into heaven, will come again in the same way as you saw him go into heaven"? (Acts 1:11b).

What Goes Up ...

Then he said to them, "These are my words that I spoke to you while I was still with you — that everything written about me in the law of Moses, the prophets and the psalms must be fulfilled." Then he opened their minds to understand the scriptures, and he said to them, "Thus it is written, that the Messiah is to suffer and to rise from the dead on the third day, and that repentance and forgiveness of sins is to be proclaimed in his name to all nations, beginning from Jerusalem. You are witnesses of these things. And see, I am sending upon you what my Father promised; so stay here in the city until you have been clothed with power from on high."

Then he led them out as far as Bethany, and, lifting up his hands, he blessed them. While he was blessing them, he withdrew from them and was carried up into heaven. — Luke 24:44-51

In the first book, Theophilus, I wrote about all that Jesus did and taught from the beginning until the day when he was taken up to heaven, after giving instructions through the Holy Spirit to the apostles whom he had chosen. After his suffering he presented himself alive to them by many convincing proofs, appearing to them during forty days and speaking about the kingdom of God. While staying with them, he ordered them not to leave Jerusalem, but to wait there for the promise of the Father. "This," he said, "is what you have heard from me; for John baptized with water, but you will be baptized with the Holy Spirit not many days from now."

So when they had come together, they asked him, "Lord, is this the time when you will restore the kingdom to Israel?" He replied, "It is not for you to know the times or periods that the Father has set by his own authority. But you will receive power when the Holy Spirit has come upon you; and you will be my witnesses in Jerusalem, in all Judea and Samaria, and to the ends

of the earth." When he had said this, as they were watch-
ing, he was lifted up, and a cloud took him out of their
sight. — Acts 1:1-9

What goes up here is Jesus. What comes down — and when, and how — is the story we have lived with for 2,000 years.

The season of Eastertide ends every year with this incredible account of Jesus being "carried up into heaven" as the disciples watched. How does one describe such an occurrence or understand it? If you or I were to show up at the coffee shop and announce that we had witnessed such a thing no one would believe us.

Is the response any different when these scriptures are read in worship? It would be interesting to ask several thousand average Jo-and-Joe-pew-sitters what they think about this event and then do some statistical analysis of the results. Would a majority of Christians say they believe what they say when they say that line in the Apostles' Creed, "... he ascended into heaven and sitteth at the right hand of God the Father almighty, from thence he shall come to judge the quick and the dead"? (Is that the coming down part?)

I expect most followers of Jesus would say they believe this, but I also suspect that, if pressed, they would admit that they haven't thought much about it at all. Unlike the resurrection, which gets much bigger play because churches are full on Easter, the ascension gets little attention. This may be, in part, because we have almost no framework for comprehending such an event. After all, how many ascensions have there been in the history of the world? Not many, at least not many that have been recorded. There is, of course, Elijah's dramatic whirlwind and chariots of fire ascension documented in 2 Kings.

The day came when Elijah was to be taken "up to heaven by a whirlwind." The great prophet tells his understudy, Elisha, to remain in Gilgal while he goes ahead to Bethel for the big send off. But Elisha refuses, saying, "As the Lord lives, and as you yourself live, I will not leave you."

When they arrive at Bethel, they are greeted by a delegation from the local Junior Prophets Association (JPs) who ask Elisha if he is aware of what is about to happen. He says yes and bids them

136

to "keep silent." Again Elijah tells Elisha to stay put because God is now sending him to Jericho. And, again Elisha talks back to his mentor, Nothing doing — "As the Lord lives and as you yourself live, I will not leave you."

So they went on to Jericho, and as at Bethel, the local JPs met them and asked Elisha the same question their Bethel brothers had asked. Did he know that this was the day God would take his master away from him? Elisha says, "I know, I know, keep quiet!" Once more Elijah announces another destination, this time God is sending him to the Jordan, and as before he wants Elisha to remain behind, and again his stubborn protégé says, "As the Lord lives, and as you yourself live, I will not leave you."

So they went on together and this time no less than fifty of the JPs tagged along. When they came to the Jordan the parade came to a full and final stop. The JPs watched from a safe distance as Elijah "took his mantle, rolled it up, and struck the water; the water was parted to the one side and to the other, until the two of them crossed on dry ground." The Hebrew storyteller doesn't say, but we might assume that this little repeat of Exodus history was not lost on the boys in the JPs. Surely they knew they were about to witness something monumental.

> *When they had crossed, Elijah said to Elisha, "Tell me what I may do for you, before I am taken from you." Elisha said, "Please let me inherit a double share of your spirit." He responded, "You have asked a hard thing; yet, if you see me as I am being taken from you; it will be granted you; if not, it will not." As they continued walking and talking, a chariot of fire and horses of fire separated the two of them, and Elijah ascended in a whirlwind to heaven. Elisha kept watching and crying out, "Father, father! The chariots of Israel and its horsemen!" But when he could no longer see him, he grasped his own clothes and tore them in two pieces.*
> — 2 Kings 2:9-12

Elisha did indeed inherit a double portion of Elijah's spirit. And his first Elijah-like act of power was another Exodus redux.

He took the mantle of the great prophet, struck the waters of the Jordan and walked across on dry ground. There can be no doubt that he is now in the big leagues, a sure pick to be nominated to the prophets hall of fame.

The fifty big-eyed JPs who had watched all of this were now humming "Swing Low, Sweet Chariot." They could hum a little of the tune but they still couldn't sing with the big boys. They wanted to send a search party out looking for Elijah, just in case he landed on some mountain or ended up in a ditch. Elisha was against it, but they pestered him and pestered him until he began to worry. What if they were right? He didn't want to be the one to leave poor old Lige hanging out there in a tree somewhere, so he said, "Okay, already, go look if you have to!" All fifty of them looked high and low for three days and could find no sign of the great prophet anywhere. When they reported back, Elisha gave them that major prophet look of exasperation and said, "Didn't I tell you?" (2 Kings 2:13-18).

Elisha's own death occurred in quite a different way than his master's. Like Elijah, he performed many wonders and miracles throughout his lifetime, but died as most other humans die and was buried in the ground. Some time later, a man was being buried on the same plot of land when suddenly a band of marauders appeared. The mourners quickly threw the body into Elisha's grave, and, "as soon as the man touched the bones of Elisha, he came to life and stood on his feet" (2 Kings 13:14-21).

Elijah passed on his power through his mantle. Elisha's power was present and still potent even in his dried-up bones. Jesus would bestow power on those who came after him in another way.

The disciples were clearly in the "Elisha seat" at the ascension of Jesus, though they were about to receive the mantle without having to ask. Jesus tells them to stay put in Jerusalem, where in a few days they would be "baptized by the Holy Spirit," "clothed with power from on high," and become "... witnesses in Jerusalem, in all Judea and Samaria, and to the ends of the earth" (Luke 24:49b; Acts 1:4-8).

Then, like Elisha, the disciples gaze in wonder at a miraculous, metaphysical event involving the movement of a human being from one dimension to another, similar to what some of them had witnessed at the transfiguration. They are left standing, looking up with their mouths open, not quite comprehending what they have just seen. What do you do after you see something like that? What words do you employ to describe a phenomenon unlike anything you or anyone else on earth has ever seen, and who would they tell? Who would believe it? And, what do we do with this story in the twenty-first century?

Very likely we will do nothing with it until we come to believe something extraordinary really happened on that day: that ascensions, though exceedingly rare, are possible in the natural order of things, and that the ascension of Jesus, like all of his miracles and his resurrection, are not supernatural, but extraordinary natural events that open our eyes to a dimension of reality that we have heretofore been unable to see or participate in. This is not to say that Jesus has created a new reality, but rather that he has prompted us to wake up and see what has always been there. This can be compared to a swimmer who, coming upon a land-bound people who have no knowledge of the sea, takes them to the shore so that they can look out at the great expanse of water all around. He dives in, invites them to follow, and then teaches them to swim. In Jesus' case, he teaches his followers to swim into the powerful and empowering presence of God, to pray, heal the sick, open the eyes of the blind, and raise the dead.

Phyllis Tickle once asked her pastor, "What do you think happens when we pray?" Earl King, a retired Presbyterian missionary who had served with his wife for 35 years in what was then called the Belgium Congo, replied, "I guess the answer is, 'What is the Mount of Transfiguration?' " Phyllis then asked, "You mean we are transformed?" King said, "Good heavens, no ... What I mean is that prayer is a place, and Peter and James and John just happened to catch Jesus while he was in it." And then as an afterthought he added, "You can't go there as long as you don't recognize that the spirit works because it is spirit."[2]

This is the power that is given to us through the Holy Spirit: an apprehension of the divine energy all around us, and the ability to

139

use it in partnership with God. The problem is, many of us who have grown up in this scientific age assume ascensions like those attributed to Elijah and Jesus are physically impossible. We look for metaphorical explanations.

Then there are those of us on the other extreme who believe every event described in the Bible literally happened: that miracles like the ascension were possible for Jesus because, as the Son of God, he had super powers not available to the rest of us. And probably the greatest number of us don't think very much about these miracle stories at all. We put our everyday living in one compartment and our religious beliefs and practices in another. The two worlds seldom intersect until we are beset by tragedy, face the prospect of our own deaths, or have a direct encounter with the divine.

About a year into my first full-time pastoral appointment, I had an opportunity to hear Elizabeth Kübler-Ross speak at the University of Wisconsin in Madison. I was a great fan of her early death and dying books. It was a thrill to be in the same room with her and to hear her talk about her work. She told a number of stories about patients who described near-death experiences. My eyes were opened to a part of our world I had never known before, had never really believed existed, though I was a student of the scriptures that are filled with stories of such encounters with the holy. It was a life-changing experience that would lead me, twenty years later, to a new calling to tell and interpret vision stories in the Bible by comparing them to the visions of ordinary people today.

I began to pay more attention to bereaved church members who told about experiencing the presence of deceased loved ones. I had previously dismissed these kinds of reports as wishful thinking: normal delusions that sometimes occur in the grieving process.

Jack Kaufman, the lay leader of our congregation, a physician, and professor of Pulminary Medicine at The Medical College of Wisconsin in Wauwatosa, wrote about a guided meditation he experienced in one of our Lenten classes in March of 2005.

Aunt Anna's Smile

Jack Kaufman

Kathryn Rambo, our meditation guide, placed us in a familiar peaceful location.

Where was I? I was on the bank of the Chagrin River, in Ohio, a spot I passed numerous times in my own meditative way on a Sunday whenever I would return to med school. Once on that bank, in the shadow of St. Christopher's-by-the-River Episcopal Church in Gates Mills, Ohio, my younger brother and I went fishing. During the guided meditation, my brother was gone; I was alone.

For years, when I drove past that church and gazed on the golden cross atop the steeple, I prayed for my Aunt Anna. Anna, an Orthodox Jew, had been afflicted with arthritis at a relatively young age. I observed her sufferings in a day before effective medical and surgical techniques. But why that cross? I pleaded with God to alleviate Anna's pain.

She had reared seven daughters until she finally had a son, a man who was to be a bomber pilot on a B-17 in World War II. Anna was a tough woman who, despite the rigors of raising a large family, was able to withstand the pain and discomfort of her arthritis. I always thought she would die from the suffering, but it made her stronger. And yet, I prayed for her each time I saw that cross.

During the guided meditation, I saw Aunt Anna. She questioned me as to why I believed in Jesus. "Aunt Anna," I said, "I have prayed for you for years through Jesus."

"You have abandoned your Jewish faith," she replied.

"I have been no different than those early Jews, including Paul, who did not necessarily give up on Hebrew commandments of mercy and justice, but also felt that Jesus was God incarnate."

However, she then looked upon me in pleasure and satisfaction. From the time I began praying for Anna to the time of her death, 23 years elapsed. Her arthritis was controlled, her pains alleviated. "I prayed for you, Aunt Anna. Please don't criticize me."

She continued to look at me. Finally, she said I had made a good decision. Perhaps, not one she would have made.

By the end of the meditation, Anna smiled down on me. I felt she spoke to me from heaven, a place I longed for her final abode, free from the pain and suffering that I had petitioned from the cross at St. Christopher's.[3]

Spirits come and go, and are sometimes present with loved ones on earth.

Della Reese wrote about both the visitation of a loved one and being outside of her own body after crashing through a glass patio door at her home in Hollywood in the early 1970s. The shattered glass cut deeply into her stomach and just as the glass on top of the door was about to fall down on her head, her mother, who she said, "... had died in 1949 ... reached around from behind me, taking hold of my head and shoulders, and lifted me onto my feet and told me to sit down in my chair." Della knew it was her mother because "... it was her smell only, that wonderful-smelling mixture of Ponds cold cream, vanilla, and spices ... Mama spoke to me, her scent still all around, telling me what to say to Dumpsey (her daughter) to show her how to make a tourniquet for my leg. And then Mama was gone."

Later, in the emergency room, Della describes what she called "... a definite out-of-body experience." She found herself "... sitting above a large medical cabinet, listening to them discuss me as if I wasn't there." They needed an adult relative to sign a release form so they could operate. It made Della angry. She didn't want to die because of some "damn papers." So she came down, and she wrote, "... came back to my body, looked up, saying, 'Give me the papers, I'll sign them myself.' " Della said, "Their eyes bulged as if they were seeing a ghost."[4]

Millions of people have had out-of-body and near-death experiences — and have told about what they have seen.

My cousin, Francis McDonough, tells of an out-of-body experience he had when he was in grade school in Lime Ridge, Wisconsin, in the 1950s.

> *When I was in the third grade at Lime Ridge School, I got very sick and was shaking with the chills. I walked outside and went next door to Grandma McDonough's*

house. She took me in and laid me down in the living room on a parlor bed, covered me up, and then left. I remember floating over to the big stove and being above it to keep warm. Then Grandma came back in with some more blankets. I was watching her as she leaned over me on the couch. It was then that I became aware of a little old man, all white hair and a big mustache, on the side of the room motioning for me to go down by my grandma. I found out later that the little old man was my great-grandfather, but that he had been dead for quite a while. I never told my grandma.[5]

Most people in our society take these accounts about as seriously as ghost stories told around a campfire, no matter how credible the source might be. We find it difficult to integrate out-of-body and visitation experiences, even when they are reported by people we love and trust. We believe them, but put the idea into that compartment that rarely affects our everyday life in the "real world." We don't know what to do with views of reality that are radically different from the accepted scientific worldview by which most of us live.

The apostle Paul also addresses this issue in a dialogue about resurrection with doubtful Christians in the Corinthian church, saying, "If there is a physical body, there is also a spiritual body ..." (1 Corinthians 15:35-51).

It is not as difficult to believe that we have both a physical and a spiritual body as it is to comprehend that a person who has died and left the physical body behind can come back, seemingly appear out of thin air as Jesus did, and pass through walls that feel solid to the touch (Luke 24:36-43; John 20:19-23).

Psychologist Raymond Moody tells about a woman who came to him after her son died from cancer. She missed him terribly. Dr. Moody writes:

One day I received an incredible call from her. A few days after her visit to my clinic, she awoke from a deep sleep ... There, standing in her room, was her son. As she sat up in the bed to look at him, she could see that

143

the ravages of cancer were gone. He now looked vi-
brant and happy as he had before his disease ... The
woman was in a state of ecstasy. She stood up and faced
her son and began carrying on a conversation. "I
couldn't believe it was him ... so I asked if I could touch
him...." Her son stepped forward and hugged her. Then
the woman said he lifted her right off the ground and
over his head.[6]

If this is true, and I believe it is because I have talked to people whose word I trust who have had this kind of experience; it is indeed possible that Jesus was lifted up into heaven, just as it is written in scripture, and that he can and does come back in the same way.

Will Come Down

While he was going and they were gazing up toward
heaven, suddenly two men in white robes stood by them.
They said, "Men of Galilee, why do you stand looking
up toward heaven? This Jesus who has been taken up
from you into heaven, will come in the same way as you
saw him go into heaven."   — Acts 1:10-11

I have come to believe, after hearing many testimonies, that Jesus does come back in the same way he went into heaven, just as the messengers told his disciples that day.

Bill Penaz of Milwaukee tells of a vision he had at a Lenten service at his church in 1965.

I found myself focusing on the cross on the altar about
fifteen feet away. The cross was about fifteen inches
high and made of wood. Although I was not thinking of
anything in particular, I kept my eyes focused on that
cross, and suddenly it disappeared and I saw Jesus in
all of his glory! I saw him standing there in a white,
white robe, the whitest thing I have ever seen. His beard
was black and he had flowing black hair. His body was

144

outlined in the most beautiful color of gold I have ever seen.[7]

While I was studying a commentary on Acts and writing an outline for this chapter, a friend, Mike Rother, who is an active member of the Episcopal church, stopped in my office. He is intuitive and often shows up at some opportune time when I need his assistance, usually before I know I need it. I told him what I was working on and we talked about the ascension. I read him a few verses of the text and asked him if he thought it possible that anyone could leave the earth in this way. This prompted him to relate the following personal experience.

> *It was October, 2004, in San Francisco. I was accustomed, as part of my spiritual practice, to meditate frequently. One night I made my way toward the Hartford Street Zen Center for 6 p.m. Zazen, or* Silent Practice. *I felt very much at home there, and was as frequent a participant as my schedule permitted. On the evening in question, after entering the Zendo, or* Temple Area, *I observed that my forearms seemed "luminous" as I made my way to my chair. The visiting priest and a monk in residence bowed slightly in my direction acknowledging my presence, but something they observed in my regard caused a less than detached response and they conversed in brief sentences which somehow seemed to be about me. After a slight reverence to the altar, I took my place and began my meditation. I very quickly entered an interior place of intense illumination and time/space seemed to meld into something else. I had the distinct feeling, as the bell sounded signaling the end of Zazen, that I had returned from a long trip. Yet only five minutes seemed to have passed. Again, I observed a luminous quality to my physical self. Somewhat uncomfortable with more undue attention from the priest and resident monk, I proceeded to exit quickly before the start of the evening service.*
>
> *The following day, as I made a necessary trip to Walgreens near the Zen Center, I was warmly greeted*

by the resident monk, who cautiously approached and said, "Mike, may I speak with you please?" Of course, I responded, "Yes!"

"You have caused some discussion and sensation around the Zendo lately, and I feel drawn to share with you what was observed last evening by myself and Roshi (the priest). You had an unusual luminous quality about you as you entered the Zendo. Your physicality, in relation to this luminous quality, could only be described as 'fading.' After meditation started, upon impulse I opened my eyes, and even though I could initially hear your breathing, you had vanished. Upon the end of Zazen, I opened my eyes quickly and observed that you had indeed returned to us, but your physical outline seemed 'out of focus.' " Noticing that I was growing uncomfortable, he graciously said good-bye, and offered an "ear" if I wished to discuss it further. As he embraced me as a brother, he said softly, "Don't worry, your secret is safe with us."[8]

1. Rosmarie Trapp is a member of the Community of The Crucified One, 104 E. 11th Avenue, Homestead, Pennsylvania 15120. She lives in an apartment in one of the church's mission houses in Vermont, where she is involved in children's Bible classes and prison ministries. Her family's story was told in the well-known movie, *The Sound of Music*. Rosmarie is the firstborn child of Captain and Maria von Trapp. Three of her personal stories are included in the three-volume *Vision Stories* series edited by John Sumwalt, CSS Publishing, 2002, 2003, and 2004.

2. Phyllis Tickle, *The Shaping of a Life: A Spiritual Landscape* (New York: Doubleday, 2001), p. 374.

3. Jack Kaufman is Professor of Pulminary Medicine at The Medical College of Wisconsin in Wauwatosa. While editor of the Medical College publication, *The Grapevine*, a monthly collection of essays, commentary, and poetry, Dr. Kaufman wrote over 140 articles on the art of medicine and society. He has published more than fifty scientific articles in refereed medical journals, and

has written medical textbook chapters on asthma, smoke inhalation, and carbon monoxide poisoning. Dr. Kaufman has taught adult Sunday school and Disciple Bible Study classes at Wauwatosa Avenue United Methodist Church since 1976 and has served as the lay leader since 2004.

4. Della Reese, Franklin Lett, Mim Eichler, *Angels Along The Way: My Life With Help From Above* (New York: Berkley Boulevard Books, 1997), pp. 220-221.

5. My cousin, Francis McDonough, lives in Lime Ridge, Wisconsin. The old man he saw in his out-of-body experience may have been our ancestor, Edward John Long, who came to America from Tipperary, Ireland, in 1850.

6. Raymond Moody, *Reunions* (New York: Villard Books, 1993), pp. 206-208.

7. Bill Penaz, "I Saw the Lord," *Sharing Visions: Divine Revelations, Angels and Holy Coincidences*, ed., John E. Sumwalt (Lima, Ohio: CSS Publishing Company, 2003), p. 65. (See also "Maundy Thursday Visions," pp. 107-108, and "Visions of Christ," pp. 211-215.) Bill Penaz lives in Milwaukee, Wisconsin, and is a longtime member of Loving Shepherd Evangelical Lutheran Church.

8. Mike James Rother is "an actualized old soul" who is active in the Anglican Communion. He lives in Milwaukee and will soon be returning to his "beloved San Francisco Bay area to resume a spirit-infused life of service dedicated to transformation and healing."

Miracle 6

Pentecost Diaries

The last time I spoke to Ken was on the phone a few weeks before he died. He told me he was "winding down." The emphysema he had battled for years, the result of a cigarette habit augmented during his service as a fighter pilot in the South Pacific in World War II, was about to bring him down for good, something the Japanese fighters had not been able to do despite many attempts. No more near misses and buzzing the control tower in triumph on the way home to beer and bed. This was a straight-on hit from which there was no recovery. I told Ken I loved him and made him promise he would come to me after he passed. He said he would and he did.

My dear friend and mentor, Kendall Anderson, crossed over in the fall of 2005 after 85 years of raising hell, loving a family, grieving a son shot down in Vietnam, preaching the gospel, and aggravating a host of cherished friends with bad jokes and an incisive wit. I flew up to St. Cloud for his funeral and burial at the Fort Schnelling National Cemetery overlooking the Mississippi River in St. Paul. Ken's body was lowered into the earth beside the grave of his son, helicopter pilot Lieutenant Curt Anderson, a casualty of the Vietnam War.

I had the honor of telling some of the stories I know of Ken's life in a brief eulogy at the funeral. One story I didn't tell, and couldn't because it hadn't happened yet, was the account of a reunion that occurred about two weeks later, on Tuesday, November 29, at about 11 p.m., just after I went to bed. It was something like the experience I described in the introduction and only the second time something like this has happened in my life.

I looked up toward the ceiling and saw a pulsating ball of energy about eighteen inches above my head. Vivid colors: blues, brownish yellows, and a rich lavender, came and went in waves that flashed before my eyes. I reached up and touched the energy. It turned a greenish white and was palpable, almost thick to the touch. I knew I was in the presence of a spirit and I knew it was Ken. I said, "Hi, Ken," in my mind and talked to him like we have talked in person and on the phone many times before, telling him how much I missed him and that I would continue to pray for him. I could discern no response other than a feeling of pure joy that filled my soul. I could see him grinning in my mind's eye.

The vision lasted for several minutes. It has given me great comfort and assurance of the wondrous, eternal blessings that await all of us on the other side. I know Ken is alive. I know I will be with him again. This "knowing" is unlike other kinds of knowing I have experienced in my life. It is an inward kind of assurance that permeates body and soul, more than a warm or peaceful feeling, though it is that, too. I live with new confidence in this physical world because I have had a taste of a spiritual dimension that, until that moment, had only been a belief in an idea I could discuss, but to which I could not give witness. I have been touched by someone I love who is in what Morton Kelsey calls "another realm of reality."

Skeptics routinely scoff at this kind of anecdotal evidence, saying it means nothing because it is completely subjective and cannot be measured or proven in any way acceptable in our scientific age. Kelsey puts the burden of proof on the scoffers.

> ... there is no good reason to doubt the reality of the spiritual ... world with which the soul has much in common and with which it can interact directly. As for "knowing" there is no spiritual world nor any spiritual substantiality to the soul, it rests upon the doubter to prove this ... when so many in all ages have maintained that, when the conditions are right, they touched a reality which made everything within this physical world seem pale by comparison.[1]

Jesus was certainly in touch with this spiritual realm and sought continually to bring his followers into an awareness of it through his parables. He often described objects and situations in the physical world that could be compared to this other realm of reality:

> *What is the kingdom of God like? And to what should I compare it? It is like a mustard seed that one took and sowed in a garden; it grew and became a tree, and the birds of the air made nests in its branches ... It is like yeast that a woman took and mixed in with three measures of flour until all of it was leavened.*
> — Luke 13:18-19, 21

Jesus not only made comparisons to explain what this other realm was like, his parables drew people into that world where they were given a vicarious taste of this different reality. Then Jesus would ask them to make a decision: live in and participate in what God was doing, or reject it. The Pharisees were invited to rejoice with a shepherd who had found a lost sheep, and a father who welcomed home a lost son. Jesus must have looked directly at them as he concluded this story of the prodigal. The elder son had not strayed like his brother. Like the Pharisees, he was tempted to turn his back on the grace-filled world that was breaking into their comfortable way of "knowing." Speaking of the elder son, Jesus says, "Son, you are always with me, and all that is mine is yours. But we had to celebrate and rejoice, because this brother of yours was dead and has come to life; he was lost and has been found" (Luke 15:31-32).

Luke gives us this Pentecost story in Acts for similar reasons. He describes an extraordinary event in the lives of thousands of people who have been "clothed with power from on high ... baptized by the Holy Spirit," introduced to a common Spirit language, and are now living in this new realm of reality. The story is a prototype for the new life with Christ for the thousands who have already been embraced by the Spirit, and an invitation to those hearing the story for the first time. Like the parables of Jesus, the Pentecost story is transforming. The power released in the telling compels Luke's first-century audience to say, "Yes" or "No," to what

151

God has done in Jesus, and is now continuing through the Holy Spirit (Luke 24:49b; Acts 1:5b; 2:4).

Wind Blown

> *When the day of Pentecost had come, they were all together in one place. And suddenly from heaven there came a sound like the rush of a violent wind, and it filled the entire house where they were sitting.*
> — Acts 2:1-2

What came blowing in the Pentecost wind was indeed both upsetting and transforming. Leonard Sweet spoke about the "wind-blown life" in an address I was privileged to hear at The American Baptist Assembly in Green Lake, Wisconsin, in May of 2004. "The modern heresy is the belief that the most powerful forces in the universe are physical, material." For Sweet, this is tantamount to saying "the tree moves the wind. Spiritual leaders must understand the power of the wind to move all things, and must live a spirit blown life. Mastery of the spirit is the essence of spiritual leadership. Someone who is living a wind blown life is unpredictable."[2]

This unpredictability is disconcerting to church leaders, who prefer approved doctrines and stayed canonical teachings to fresh reports of the Spirit's movement. But the "wind" is relentless. It will move the tree; God will move and work in our lives in spite of our determined resistance, until we are fully awake to all that we are created to be.

In *The Land Remembers*, his award-winning book about growing up in the hill country of southwest Wisconsin, Ben Logan tells about the Protestant and Roman Catholic children in the one-room rural school he attended, arguing endlessly about religion. One day, Tom Withers, a boy who was something of an "earth child" before the term had been invented, in tune with the ways of nature and absent from their one-room hall of academia more than he was present because he couldn't stand to be indoors, interrupted their little religious war and commanded every one to meet him at a certain spot on the hillside after school. They all came and watched in wonder as Tom:

... climbed up onto a rock, raised his arms above his head and looked straight up.... His mouth opened and the sound roared out: "They Ain't No God!... Strike Me Down Dead If They's A God!" Tom yelled.... We waited. Then a little whirlwind came along the hillside, rattling the dead oak leaves, seeming to attack one tree at a time. It took hold of the tree where we stood, thrashed with it, filling the woods with sound. Then it moved on. Tom lowered his arms. He looked at us, baring his teeth in a smile, jumped from the rock, and ran along the hillside out of sight.... We didn't talk much about religion in school after that.[3]

The psalmist sang, "The voice of the Lord shakes the wilderness ... The voice of the Lord causes the oaks to whirl, and strips the forest bare; and in his temple all say glory!" (Psalm 29).

Pamela Christiansen wrote about a wind that lifted and sustained her after losing her children through divorce:

Wind Song
Pamela Christiansen

My babies had grown to their teenage years. I had just left them there, on a moment's notice, with their father. The stress had become unbearable and I knew I had to go in order to live. Divorce is a horrible tragedy. I had not seen them, my own flesh and blood, for several months. Since their births, I had never left them for more than a few days' time.

My heart was aching, and I would fall asleep at night, not knowing how they were, what they were doing, or if they even cared that I was gone. I had not seen them for several months, nor spoken with them. He would not allow phone calls.

I believe there are cosmic forces that come in times of need. They bring whatever we are most in need of at the time: insight, comfort, or consolation.

One morning, as I lay in a deep sleep, something woke me abruptly, much earlier than usual. It was mid-winter.

153

I sat upright in bed, shocked by the windsong that was blowing from behind my head. It reminded me of the sound one hears when a seashell is pressed to the ear, but it was stronger, louder, eerier. I could feel it blowing through every strand of my hair, a whispered message for me to cling to: "Mom! M-o-o-o-m! M-o-o-o-o-m!" It was the voices of my three daughters, calling out to me in their agony, their despair, their loneliness, all combined together in that one beautiful seashell voice. The hair on the back of my neck stood up. I began to cry. I knew they missed me as much as I was missing them. And that they needed me.

To this day, the details of their lives are a mystery to me. I can only imagine if they are sick or well, laughing or crying, asleep or awake. And yet the windsong echoes in my head. And I lift my chin to the heavens at times, and I call their names out to the wind: "Nicole! Rebekah! Jaklyn! Mommy loves you *always*! And I miss you, my darlings!" And my hope is that the very same windsong that rushed by my head in the early morning hours will carry my message to them, softly and carefully and gently.[4]

Fire And Light

> *Divided tongues, as of fire, appeared among them, and a tongue rested on each of them. All of them were filled with the Holy Spirit and began to speak in other languages, as the Spirit gave them ability.* — Acts 2:3-4

It is difficult to describe what happens when God breaks into our lives in unexpected and totally unfamiliar ways. The language we know is always inadequate for these occasions because all language is based on previous experience. Mystics and poets of every age have struggled with this as they have tried to convey the meaning of their encounters with the holy. It is necessary for every generation to find its own language for giving witness to the light. It is not that the light changes, it's that God comes to us in response to our unique needs. The Pentecost wind blows fresh in every life.

Gail Ingle told about a "metacosmic light" that came as an answer to prayer.

> *On May 19, 1989, I had a spiritual experience that I will never forget. I was at my friends' home to participate in a prayer/healing circle. We were all standing in a darkened room lit only with candles. My arms felt weightless and they involuntarily began to rise until they were above my head. Suddenly, I felt something like a bolt of lightning enter my head and go through my body. I began to cry. My friends asked me if I was all right and I nodded silently. They told me they could see the colors violet and green surrounding me. I must have stood there for about five minutes with my arms straight up in the air before they slowly returned to my side. I felt extremely peaceful long into the night.[5]*

Attorney Roy Nelson had a similar experience while praying in the midst of anguishing grief after the death of his wife.

> *My arms were lifted up to the sides and slightly in front. I felt something like electricity flowing from my heart out of my chest, up through my arms, out my fingertips, and even out of the top of my head. I felt the burden being lifted. The heaviness of the grief and depression was gone. I felt a peace and contentment being poured down through my head and filling my chest, filling my heart.[6]*

The light came to Timothy Paulson in prison after he began attending a prayer group.

> *As my faith grew, I hungered for an even deeper experience of God. One night, while fasting, I skipped supper and spent about twenty minutes kneeling by my bunk in prayer. I cried out, "Lord, reveal yourself! I really want to know you." Suddenly a light, brighter than anything I had ever seen before, surrounded me. A tingling sensation went through my body and I knew that God had*

155

touched me deeply. I was filled with God's joy and peace. When my cellmate returned from supper, he said, "Tim, what in the world happened to you?" I told him and he couldn't wait to get out of the room. The guards and other inmates could see the difference as well. Some were happy for me and others just waited for me to fall. What difference has this made in my life? The joy and peace remained during the rest of my time in prison and since I've returned home.[7]

Ellen Sherry was praying in her bed when the light flowed in.

One night in December of 2000, I was thanking God for a prayer that had been answered ... and all of a sudden, a wide band of bright, white light came down at me from near the ceiling. My first thought was "Oh my gosh, this is going to hurt." But it didn't hurt. The light flowed into my chest and all I felt was some slight pressure. The light flowed and flowed into me, filling my heart to overflowing with indescribable love. It was the most amazing feeling, such a wonderful feeling of peace filled me: peace like I had never, ever known before! And then, after what seemed like a few minutes, the light was gone ... it was as if somehow a computer chip of new ideas, thoughts and beliefs was also implanted in me at the same time that my heart was filled with love ... I no longer fear death! I don't know why. I just know that, after death, we will be at peace, we will be with God, and all will be right. I can't explain why know this, I just have an unshakable belief that this is so.[8]

Clayton Daughenbaugh tells about an unexplainable knowing that came while hiking.

My wife and I were day hiking at Guadalupe Mountains National Park in west Texas. We had completed a climb to the top of Guadalupe Peak and were on the way down. I was walking 100 yards or so ahead of her and was coming into a small ponderosa grove in what is otherwise a pretty wide-open Chihuahuan desert environment. I noticed the shade and the birds singing right away. As I walked further into it a very strange feeling came over me. It was as though I was a permanent part of that place. But there was also a feeling of imminence — as though I was on the edge or verge of an infinite place and time ... I was at once a small and seemingly insignificant part of the universe yet somehow also an essential part of it all. There was a presence of being that seemed to uphold and permeate all that was around me. This lasted maybe ten minutes. I found it to be a very strange experience. Yet it didn't seem all together unfamiliar, as though I'd experienced it before....[9]

Eddie Ensley tells how his Cherokee grandfather taught him to look for this "presence of being" in nature.

I have a vivid memory of my grandfather standing motionless on the top of the bluff, letting his eyes soak in all that came to him. Once I asked him what he saw when he looked. I still hear his answer, rhythmic with Cherokee and Appalachian intonations. "I see the dirt, the trees, the water, the skies." "Why?" I asked him. "Why do you look so long?" He paused, took his pipe out of his mouth, swallowed, then slowly said, "If you look a long time, it will all shimmer, and you will see the glory."[10]

Every living creature and every tree and bush in creation is surrounded by energy fields. I saw the shimmer and beheld the glory often in the fields and forests on the farm where I grew up in southwest Wisconsin. I heard it singing in the ripples as the creek water rolled over the rocks under the bridge, in the croaking of the frogs, and the shrill cry of the eagle diving for its prey.

I still see it and hear it and feel it when I go back to the 25 acres there where we hope to retire one day. The energy is thick, almost palpable, especially in the spring and summer. It is invigorating, empowering. It is where I go to be "clothed with power."

Elizabeth Barrett Browning wrote:

> Earth's crammed with heaven,
> And every common bush afire with God....[11]

Pentecost In The City

> Divided tongues, as of fire, appeared among them, and a tongue rested on each of them. All of them were filled with the Holy Spirit and began to speak in other languages, as the Spirit gave them ability.
>
> Now there were devout Jews from every nation under heaven living in Jerusalem. And at this sound the crowd gathered and was bewildered, because each one heard them speaking in the native language of each. Amazed and astonished, they asked, "Are not all these who are speaking Galileans? And how is it that we hear, each of us, in our own native language? Parthians, Medes, Elamites, and residents of Mesopotamia, Judea and Cappodocia, Pontus and Asia, Phrygia and Pamphylia, Egypt and the parts of Libya belonging to Cyrene, and visitors from Rome, both Jews and proselytes, Cretans and Arabs — in our own languages we hear them speaking about God's deeds of power." All were amazed and perplexed, saying to one another, "What does this mean?" But others sneered and said, "They are filled with new wine."
>
> But Peter, standing with the eleven, raised his voice and addressed them, "Men of Judea and all who live in Jerusalem, let this be known to you, and listen to what I say. Indeed, these are not drunk, as you suppose, for it is only nine o'clock in the morning. No, this is what was spoken through the prophet Joel:
>
> 'In the last days it will be, God declares, that I will pour out my Spirit upon all flesh, and your sons and your daughters shall prophesy, and your young men shall see visions, and your old men shall dream dreams.

158

Even upon my slaves, both men and women, in those
days I will pour out my Spirit; and they shall prophesy.
And I will show portents in the heaven above and signs
on the earth below, blood, and fire, and smoky mist.
The sun shall be turned to darkness and the moon to
blood, before the coming of the Lord's great and glori-
ous day. Then everyone who calls on the name of the
Lord shall be saved.' "   — Acts 2:3-21

When all kinds people are together in one place, things happen that are not otherwise possible. It may be a synergy of energies, that of all those who are present, and the divine energy that flows through all of creation. I remember seeing the glow of something holy in the shining faces of elementary children around campfires during the many years that Jo and I directed church camps. As we told stories, and sang and danced and prayed in the firelight, the Spirit was poured out on those young souls, blessing them with a lifetime of visions and dreams.

The Spirit Blows Through Dufferin
Karen de Jong-Dermann

A country church had stood by the side of the road in the roll-ing hills of Dufferin County for generations. Its first pioneers had given it the rather romantic name of Monticello ("Little Hill"). These days only about 25 faithful souls came to hear the word of God. For some weeks, a woman had been coming to worship that hadn't been there in years. The congregation had known Ellen since she was a child in pigtails, ever since she came with her grandma. But when her grandma died, the little girl was no longer sheltered from the drunken rages of her father, and though her mother loved her, she grew bitter with age, living in that old trailer with only a space heater to tame the cold winter winds that whistled through the cracks.

It is an old and familiar story. Ellen grew up, and looked for love in all the wrong places, frequently numbing her pain with a bottle. Now she was coming to church, and though she was surly, people were happy to see her. Maybe she would finally turn her life around.

One day, after the minister had pronounced the benediction, Ellen shouted at her, "You don't mean what you say! You're just a fraud."

The minister was shocked, and took a few steps toward the distraught woman only to be shoved back, hard enough that she stumbled and fell. But then a surprising thing happened — the congregation didn't gather around to help their pastor up, but quickly stood around Ellen, soothing her temper, telling her it was all right. They loved her anyway. They gathered her up in their arms and welcomed her home. And as Ellen wept, they practically carried her out the door of the church, giving her the love that she had craved for so long.

There I stood in the sanctuary all alone, gathering my sermon notes, feeling ignored, and quite out of sorts. I had preached the word, but was unprepared for the reaction. It was only later that I could see how the Spirit of the Lord was on me that day — though I rather wished it hadn't been so strong as to bruise me.

Ellen had been angered by the word. It moved her to her core, and she shouted out her rage at God.

The whole congregation had been moved by the word. No longer did they wait to see if Ellen would turn her life around; they realized that they would have to help her to do it. Now they made sure she had money for groceries. They visited her and invited her for coffee so she wouldn't be tempted to find false friends at the local bar. Ellen had come home and they wanted her to stay.[12]

Theonia Amenda tells about how the Spirit came upon a group of Christians she was with one day on retreat.

Transfigured
Theonia Amenda

We were standing in a circle in an open, mowed field on a mini-farm outside Nashville one summer day, worshiping God and saying good-bye to our retreat leader, who had just been elected by our general conference to be a bishop. As we held hands while someone prayed for him, I found I could not keep my eyes closed. I wanted to gaze at this gentle, deeply spiritual man, for whom I had great admiration and respect. He was standing across the circle from me in his blue jeans and red checked shirt. My heart was sending him a great deal of love and God's energy as I listened to the words of the prayer.

All of a sudden, a strong, golden-white light appeared at his feet, on his right side, and traveled up his body to his head, where it swirled around and around, then traveled down his left side. He was aglow with light, which was reflected off the people on either side of him. I kept blinking my eyes, trying to clear them, to see if this light was being caused by something in my eyes, but it was not.

I felt as if time was standing still as I listened to the drone of a voice continuing to pray, heard a horse neighing down in the barn, and saw a dog walking around in the middle of the circle. I continued to watch the illumination of a man as about fifty of us sent out our love and support, asking for God's blessings and power to be poured out upon him.

After the prayer had been lifted up, a deep, deep silence fell over us. It was a silence that was almost audible. I wonder if it was like what the scriptures said Elijah experienced outside the cave as he was listening for God. One version of that scripture said that Elijah heard God "in the sound of sheer silence."

That describes the deep silence at that moment in our circle of love. Eventually that silence was broken as our song leader lifted her voice, inviting us to join her in a closing hymn. I heard others say later that they wished the silence had not been broken so soon, but no one spoke of what I saw.

I kept that experience within me until the next time I saw Bishop Rueben Job, which was months later. I dared to share with him what I had seen that day in that mowed field outside Nashville as we said good-bye to him. His response was acceptance, wondering if that accounted for his high level of energy as he began his new task, which he had not sought, but had answered as a call from God.[13]

161

When Grace Gets Here

Thom M. Shuman

"Unexpected?" he told his coworkers. "That's putting it mildly."

"Whatever in the world did I do to deserve this?" she asked her book club two days after she found out the news.

The Pentecosts were the last people in the world I would have thought would have a "surprise" child. Aging Baby Boomers anticipating early retirement, folks still dealing with the death of their son, a couple who was always so cautious about everything.

Some of their friends mocked them. "How in the sam hill did this happen? You're not starry-eyed teenagers any more!"

Others assured them that they were on the road to disaster. "Having a child at your age? Don't you remember all those sleepless nights, all those diapers, all that mess?"

Their financial planner put it bluntly. "Forget your future. You can kiss the RV good-bye; the travel plans are put on hold indefinitely; and as for retirement...."

Yep, she couldn't have come at a worse time. But there she was ... nine months later. Screaming, squalling, a tempestuous new life.

Grace.

From the moment she was born, the Pentecosts knew they were in trouble. Flaming red hair (what side of the family did that come from?), always on the move, never content to be content, Grace was a handful from day one. Folks are still amazed that they survived raising her from infancy to adulthood.

Principals sent note after note home complaining about Grace's penchant for constantly challenging the assumptions of the teachers. Adults found her to be an uncomfortable presence because she always told the truth, especially in those moments and in those situations where truth was not welcome. Sunday school teachers complained to the pastor that Grace was just too much: she never sat still, she was always stirring things up, she was always asking, "Why not?" when told the class couldn't try something new.

162

Oh, yes, she was a gadfly, a consternation, a gift.

But now, now people can't wait for Grace to come home and visit, because she's the one they've been waiting for all their lives, without knowing it.

For some, it is because Grace is the one who is there for them when no one else is. She is the one who intercedes for them when everyone else is silent; the one who nurtures them when others have forsaken them.

For some of us, it is because Grace is the one who holds our feet to the fire, who reminds us that as blessed people, we have no choice but to bend our knees in serving others; who helps us to see that as gifted people, we are to share those gifts with others. She is the one who teaches us that concrete deeds of mercy do far more than all the spoken words of concern.

But it's also because of who Grace is....

For when Grace walks into a room, little children come up to her and whisper those secrets they can't tell anyone else.

She sits down at a table in the fellowship hall and an old man who hasn't said ten words to anyone in twenty years begins to speak of forgotten dreams.

Grace walks by and touches you on the shoulder and your hair stands on end, and your cheeks flush, and you look for a cold drink of water to put out the fire in your soul.

Grace whispers your name and you feel like no one has ever spoken it before that moment.

She grabs all our self-help books and throws them out of the window. She shatters all of our needs to manipulate others; she gathers up all of our brokenness into her heart ... and gives us that peace which has eluded us forever.

And we know, though we don't understand it, that even when she is not here ... she is.[14]

---

1. Morton T. Kelsey, *The Other Side of Silence* (New York: Paulist Press, 1976), p. 35.

2. Leonard Sweet spoke about the "wind-blown life" at The American Baptist Assembly in Green Lake, Wisconsin, in May of 2004. This quotation is from notes and I hope does justice to his remarks.

3. Ben Logan, *The Land Remembers: The Story of a Farm and Its People*, 25th Anniversary Edition (Chanhasseu, Minnesota: Creative Publishing International, 1999), pp. 205-206. (Published originally in 1975 by Viking Press.)

4. Pamela Christiansen is an artist and writer. Her past and present hobbies include making handcrafted greeting cards with pressed flowers and plants, gardening, needlework, soap-making, acrylic painting, bread baking, and writing poetry and prose for over thirty years. She collects rocks that she paints and decorates with pressed flowers and poetry. Pamela has worked with the elderly for the past sixteen years.

5. Gail C. Ingle, "Metacosmic Light," *Shining Moments: Visions of the Holy in Ordinary Lives*, ed. John E. Sumwalt (Lima, Ohio: CSS Publishing, 2004), p. 37. Gail C. Ingle taught in the Waukesha, Wisconsin, public schools for over twenty years. She crossed over June 13, 2004, at the age of 54.

6. Roy Nelson, "To Bind Up The Broken Hearted," *Vision Stories: True Accounts of Visions, Angels, and Healing Miracles*, ed. John E. Sumwalt (Lima, Ohio: CSS Publishing, 2002), p. 20. Roy Nelson is attending Wartburg Theological Seminary in Dubuque, Iowa, where he has relocated with his wife and two children. His home church is St. Matthews Evangelical Lutheran Church in Wauwatosa, Wisconsin. Roy is an attorney, mediator, arbitrator, and former police officer.

7. Timothy Paulson, "Seeing The Light" (as told to Robert Gossett), *Sharing Visions: Divine Revelations, Angels, and Holy Coincidences*, ed. John E. Sumwalt (Lima, Ohio: CSS Publishing, 2003), p. 47. Timothy Paulson is the father of three children and is currently co-owner of Anchor Tile and Stone. He is an active member of Grand Avenue United Methodist Church in Port Washington, Wisconsin, where he has been part of missions and evangelism. He loves people and has a strong desire to share his faith through his story. Email: elmerfud3@hotmail.com.

8. *Ibid*, Ellen Sherry, "A Day of Pentecost," pp. 139-141. Ellen Sherry lives in Ellsworth, Wisconsin, where she and her husband have raised three children. She works as the Community Education Director for the Ellsworth School District.

9. Clayton Daughenbaugh is a Field Organizer with the Southern Utah Wilderness Alliance. He was previously employed with the Sierra Club on its National Public Lands Team. He serves as a volunteer on the Sierra Club's National Wildlands Committee. Clayton lives in Berwyn, Illinois, with his wife, Lisa, and their two sons, Luke and Sam. They are members of First United Methodist Church in LaGrange, Illinois. Clayton serves on the church's environmental justice committee.

10. Eddie Ensley, *Visions: The Soul's Path to the Sacred* (Chicago: Loyola Press, 2000), p. 40.

11. Elizabeth Barrett Browning, *Aurora Leigh*, Book 7, lines 821-822, ed. Margaret Reynolds (Athens, Greece: Oxford University Press, 1992), p. 487. (Originally published in 1857.)

12. Karen de Jong-Dermann is an ordained minister. She resides in the city of Barrie with her husband. Karen holds a double masters, with a specialty in Hebrew/Old Testament studies.

13. Theonia Amenda, "Transfigured," *Vision Stories: True Accounts of Visions, Angels, and Healing Miracles*, ed. John E. Sumwalt (Lima, Ohio: CSS Publishing , 2002), pp. 67-68. Theonia Amenda is a retired diaconal minister in The United Methodist Church. She continues in ministry in the area of spiritual formation as the leader of a three-year covenant community events, retreats, and as a spiritual director. She lives at 3612 Birnamwood Drive, Slinger, Wisconsin 53086.

14. Thom M. Shuman is a poet and pastor of Greenhills Community Church, Presbyterian, in Cincinnati, Ohio, and an associate member of the Iona Community. His website, "Occasional Sightings of the Gospel," is visited by people every day from all over the world. Thom's writing is humorous, passionate, rooted, and always deeply human. www.occasionalsightings.blogspot.com.

Miracle 7

How To Stretch A Meal

My mother's people, the Longs of Longfield House, County Tipperary, came from Ireland to southwest Wisconsin after the great potato famine in the 1840s. Over a period of five years, a fungus known as the black rot destroyed the potato crop that 75% of Irish farmers depended on for their livelihoods. More than a million people died of starvation and disease. About 30% of the population, nearly three million people, left Ireland to seek a life elsewhere. Most of them, like my great-great-great-grandfather, came to the United States where land was plentiful.

We always had plenty of potatoes on the farm where I grew up, just over the hill from where my Irish ancestors settled — boiled, baked, twice baked, mashed, hashed, in pancakes and bread, fried, scrambled with eggs, frittered, roasted, or diced in Mom's wonderful potato soup. We had potatoes at almost every meal. When my mother said to me, "Johnny, eat your potatoes," the urgency in her voice came from a memory handed down from a time when there weren't enough potatoes to go around. "Food mustn't be wasted; there was a time when we didn't have enough to eat," she was trying to tell me.

Mom was also deeply affected by the lean times her family endured during the Great Depression of the 1930s. She tells about packing bean sandwiches for lunch at school and eating bread and butter sandwiches for supper. Sometimes there was just bread and milk and they were glad to have it. If there wasn't quite enough to go around, her mother would say, "Here, you take my bowl, I'm not very hungry tonight." Grandma knew how to stretch a meal.

Jesus knew how to stretch a meal, too.

167

In The Midst Of Grief ...

Now when Jesus heard this, he withdrew from there in
a boat to a deserted place by himself. But when the
crowds heard it, they followed him on foot from the
towns.   — Matthew 14:13

Jesus' day began with unexpected news. John the Baptist was
dead, killed under some of the most horrific circumstances imag-
inable. Matthew's description is like a scene out of a modern horror movie. John had been arrested by Herod because he had the
audacity to suggest that Herod was living in an adulterous relationship with Herodias, his brother, Philip's, wife. Herod wanted to
put John to death immediately, but was afraid to for fear of the
crowds who followed him and called him a prophet. Then came
Herod's infamous birthday party and the sultry dance of Herodias'
daughter, which affected him so much he made an oath in front of
all of his guests to give her anything she desired. Herodias whispered in the girl's ear and she asked that the head of John the Baptist be brought to her on a platter. What was Herod going to do? He
could not afford to lose face with his guests, so John lost his head
and Herod's guests were served up a ghastly entree that must have
ruined their appetites for years. John's followers were allowed to
bury his body, and then Matthew writes, "... they went and told
Jesus" (Matthew 14:1-12).

Jesus must have felt like we feel when we get that dreaded
phone call. "Oh, no, it can't be!" We feel like we've been kicked in
the stomach. We can't breathe, we can't think, we just want to be
left alone, to get away from everything and everyone. There is little
energy for work or relationships when our hearts are breaking. But
life pulls us onward, often before we are ready.

Tiger Woods went back to playing golf a few months after the
death of his father: the father who had mentored him every step of
the way in his amateur and professional career, and win or lose,
had always been the first to greet him when he came off the course.
After winning the British Open in July of 2006, Woods broke down
in a most uncharacteristic way. There was the number one golfer in

the world "bawling into his caddie's shoulder." He left the green in tears. "I've never done that before ... I'm the one who bottles things up and tries to move on ... But at that moment, it just came pouring out, all the things my father has meant to me and the game of golf, and I wish he could have just seen it one more time."[1]

Life will not wait for us, and so our grief sometimes pours out at the most unexpected times. We've all been there. We want to take a time out for a while to grieve, but duty calls; we are needed at work, the family still expects dinner on the table, there is the laundry to do, and another committee meeting at church. Even God will not let us mourn in peace, calling us to serve others who are hurting as much or more than we are. Jesus wanted to be alone in his grief, too, but when people got wind of where he was they crowded up to the lakeshore to wait for him.

Perhaps a grieving heart is more open to the needs of others. When we have experienced pain we are more sensitive to the wounds and scars others carry.

Rachel Naomi Remen tells about meeting the Dalai Lama at a luncheon at an exclusive San Francisco hotel. Many of the city's wealthiest, most powerful people were present. She describes a scene when the friend who accompanied her had the privilege of speaking to the Dalai Lama and showing him some pictures of her work with cancer patients. He gave her his full attention, as if there was no one else in the room. And, when their conversation was concluded, he reached down to pick up the bag she had dropped when she removed the photographs. The Dalai Lama simply opened the bag and offered it to Remen's friend, but the way he did it was filled with an unexplainable power:

> *It was not so much what his holiness had done, but the way in which he had done it. In this tiny intersection I felt something purely joyful in him go forward to meet with her ... Of all those in the world who could have picked up a string bag and held it out, I doubt anyone else could have done it in quite this way. For some inexplicable reason, a place in me that has felt alone and abandoned for all of my life felt deeply comforted, and*

169

I had a wildly irrational thought, "This is my friend."
In that moment it seemed absolutely true. It still does.[2]

This may be the way people were drawn to Jesus, by some indescribable power that filled an empty space in their hearts. A look, a simple gesture, a nod, a word, a story, the touch of his hand, healed their bodies and fed their souls for a lifetime. This is a story about hungry people who find, in Jesus, food that fills them full like they have never been filled before.

Hungry Hearts

When he went ashore, he saw a great crowd; and he
had compassion for them and cured their sick.
— Matthew 14:14

Jesus could not hold himself back when he saw how much people were hurting. Long before the end of the day, when the disciples came to Jesus expressing concern about the physical hunger of the crowds, Jesus recognized another kind of hunger that most of those who came that day probably would have not been able to identify. They only knew that for the first time in their lives they had encountered someone whose very presence was satisfying. Jesus sensed their deep need and, though he was tired and overcome with grief, had "... compassion for them and healed their sick" (Matthew 14:14b).

Several years ago, the question was asked in a burger commercial, "What are you hungry for when you don't know what you're hungry for?" This is, indeed, one of the burning questions of our time, and it has nothing to do with fast food.

An unknown poet has put to paper a paraphrase that strikes home. He writes:

My appetite is my shepherd, I always want. It maketh
me to sit down and stuff myself. It leadeth me to my
refrigerator repeatedly. Sometimes during the night, it
leadeth me in the path of Burger King for a Whopper. It

170

destroyeth my shape. Yea, though I knoweth I gaineth, I
will not stop eating. For the food tasteth so good. The
ice cream and the cookies they comfort me.

What is it we are hungry for when we reach for the cookies and cream? Most of us who live in the Western world are overfed; we don't really need to add any more calories to our ever-expanding waistlines, yet we are hungry ... deeply hungry, painfully hungry ... but not for anything we can buy or consume.

Have you ever been hungry? Truly hungry? Not dieting hungry? Not too-busy-to-eat hungry, but didn't-know-where-your-next-meal-was-coming-from hungry? Physically starving.

A man came into our church building asking for bus ticket money to go to Indiana for a job he had waiting there. I knew him to be an honest man, about my age, who migrated from city to city and job to job. He had stopped several times before on his way through Milwaukee to visit his brother's family. They had refused to help him again. So I went with him to the bus station to buy a ticket with money from one of our special funds.

On the way out to the car, it occurred to me to offer him a plate of cheesecake bars my wife, Jo, had made for the staff. "A little something to eat on the bus," I said. I handed him the travel package and then we walked down the stairs and through the fellowship hall toward the back door. Before we reached the door, he had eaten every one of those bars. After we purchased his ticket at the bus station, we walked across the street to a sandwich shop and I bought lunch for this very hungry man who had not eaten for two or three days and was too proud to tell me how hungry he was.

During the war in Bosnia, in 1992, the Serbian forces allowed no food to pass through their roadblocks during the siege of Sarajevo. Some families survived on a gruel made from water and nettles taken from the surrounding hills. "When two Western reporters entered the city ... one of the first people they encountered was a professor of biophysics from the medical faculty of Sarajevo University, Dr. Hamid Pasic. 'I am hungry!' he said. 'I am 76 years old, I am a professor, and I am hungry!' "[3]

171

Most of us have not known real physical hunger like that. But we know other kinds of hunger. We who live in the time of fast food restaurants and supermarkets and shopping malls, whose refrigerators and pantries are full, know another kind of hunger — the hunger of the heart, the hunger of the soul. It is a longing in the depths of our beings that cannot be satisfied by anything we can buy at the grocery store or the mall.

I remember hearing someone say in a sermon at a pastor's school that the best symbol of our consumer world is the "open mouth." We are always hungry, or think that we are; we are always wanting more. Advertisements in the media all around us are continually stimulating our appetites for super-sized meals, bigger houses, plusher furnishings, and smarter and faster technological gadgets. We are never satisfied and we don't know why.

What are we hungry for when we don't know what we're hungry for?

Mother Teresa once told about visiting a seminary in the United States, and how, after hearing her speak, they took what proved to be a very generous offering and proudly presented it to her to take back to the poor in India. She told them, "I cannot accept your offerings. I did not come to the United States to collect money for the poor in India. I came to talk about people here starving for love and starving to love."

Peter Fonda, of *Easy Rider* fame, and son of the great actor, Henry Fonda, tells how uncommunicative his father was with his family. Peter writes, "Dad could sit on the bus and talk to strangers for hours, but for us in the immediate family, he never knew how to fill the space. The more we demanded, the further he withdrew, and we misinterpreted that as anger."

Peter tells how he taught his father to say, "I love you." He said to his dad on the phone one day, "If I could, I'd write a scene for Henry Fonda and direct it. The name of it is 'I love you very much, Son.' And my dad went, 'Uggggh!' and hung up." But, it was the beginning. Before long, he had coached Henry to sign off each phone conversation with those longed-for words. Later, Peter flew to Los Angeles to visit his father, who was by then frail and using

172

a walker. "When I was ready to leave, he grabbed me by my shoulders," Peter recalled. "With tears he said, 'I love you very much, Son.' I hugged him so hard I could feel his pacemaker and said, 'I love you, Dad.' And I got in my car and wept like a baby."[4]

We are hungry for intimacy. We yearn to know that we are loved, and not just by parents and children and spouses, and siblings and friends.

Marjorie Thompson writes in *Soul Feast* about what she calls the "deeper reason for the spiritual hunger of our day ... Human beings are innately religious. We harbor a bedrock desire for a transcendent wellspring of meaning and purpose in life ... We are made for relationship with God. Therefore until that relationship is sought and found, there will always be an existential emptiness at the core of our beings."[5]

God is not unaware of this sometimes desperate need. A clergy colleague, who prefers to remain anonymous, tells a story about a desperate need that was met one day with more than a little help from the Spirit.

Desperately Hungry
One day, many years ago, I had a rather strange experience. It was back in the days when I believed in miracles, when I expected the unexpected. It was back in the days when I thought everyone should think like I did. I was dogmatic, judgmental, rigid ... well, you get the picture.

It was a bright, sunny day that particular Thursday. Thursdays were the days that Viola and I went door to door in the neighborhood (I am embarrassed to admit this, but I must), evangelizing. Yep, we had our set of questions, and though we shivered a bit at the thought of approaching people we didn't know, we tried to be courageous. Viola was a gentle soul in her seventies. She and her friend, Nellie, and I would often go for dinner at the diner down the street. I grew to love them both. Today we were headed out the door of the education wing of our Lutheran church in a neighborhood of Queens that had become home to me very quickly. We waved at the older gentleman who lived across the way, and was headed the opposite direction from us, down to the market where there were fresh fruits and vegetables, a regular grocery store, and a bagel shop (my favorite thing for Sunday mornings!). I was thinking about the bagels when the subway roared past above us. Viola and I rolled our eyes at one another. "I don't know how you have gotten used to that thing."

"I'm not sure, either. The first night I was in the apartment and it roared past, I sat bolt upright in bed, certain that the train was coming right through the bedroom. Every 45 minutes, the same thing. Now I sleep like a baby. Who would have guessed a Nebraska girl transplanted to Queens would adjust so easily?"

Just then I noticed that my left hand was tingling. Viola was turning right. I almost went with her, but decided to risk sounding a little crazy. "Viola, would you mind if we went left? I know it sounds strange, but I just have a feeling that we're supposed to go that direction."

As fervent as I was at the time, my faith began to sag when, at the first house, a large, burly, hairy man answered the door. "What do you want?" He asked belligerently.

"We are from the Lutheran church around the corner, and we have a questionnaire. We wondered if you had the time...."

"We don't want any." The door slammed in our faces. We took deep breaths and headed to the next house. This time it was a woman with a facial mask of some green, pasty-looking stuff, who answered the door.

"Hello," I beamed at her, and Viola smiled her most winning smile.

"Do I know you?"

"No, we are just out and about with a survey for the neighborhood. We wondered if you had the time to answer a few questions?"

"Not interested." And she politely, but firmly, closed the door.

"Well, Viola, maybe I was wrong."

"Let's try one more before we give up."

We rang the doorbell and a woman with long, dark hair came to the door. Her eyes were puffy, as though she had been crying. We told her about our survey and introduced ourselves. We learned that her name was Rosemary. When we started asking our questions, and she realized they were spiritual questions, she burst into tears and told us to come in. We sat with her and listened for a long time as she said that just five minutes earlier she had been praying for God to send someone. She wanted to kill herself. And there we were at her door.

We talked about our faith. We invited her to Bible study. Her life changed. It really did. Rosemary and I met every week for many months, studying scripture. Her face seemed to shine, and everyone in her world knew something had happened.

I have never had exactly that kind of experience before or since that day, but it was a holy thing to find myself sharing my love of God with someone who was so hungry. It was profoundly, unspeakably holy to watch this young woman come alive with the light of Christ.[6]

What Then Shall We Do?

> When it was evening the disciples came to him and said, "This is a deserted place, and the hour is now late; send the crowds away so that they may go into the villages and buy food for themselves." Jesus said to them, "They need not go away; you give them something to eat." They replied, "We have nothing here but five loaves and two fish." And he said, "Bring them here to me."
> — Matthew 14:15-18

The disciples had been doing crowd control all day. They came to Jesus and said, "People are restless and hungry, and there are no vendors or port-a-potties out here. We're tired; you're exhausted. Why don't you tell everybody go into town and get something to eat? They won't listen to us, but if you tell them they'll go." It was a reasonable suggestion, given the circumstances, and Jesus rejected it. "We don't need send them away. You feed them."

The disciples' blood pressure must have begun to rise at this point. It had already been an unusually stressful day. They must have thought to themselves, "Where are we going to find food for 5,000 people? Is he expecting a miracle?"

But if the disciples were thinking that, they didn't say it. They swallowed their exasperation and replied the way you and I would have replied if something like this had happened in our workplaces. "We have nothing here but a few loaves of bread and a couple of fish."

You can almost hear the strain in their voices, the unspoken complaint of employees who have been pushing themselves all day and are now being asked to work overtime. We've all been there, feeling exhausted, checking our watches, counting the minutes until quitting time. Then, when it is just about time to clean up and go home, the boss comes in and says, "Let's keep at it until we get it done. Nobody is obligated to stay. I know you have families to care for, but this order is already late and it's for our best customer."

You groan inwardly because this is what the boss always says when she wants you to work late, but you stay because you need the job — or maybe because you respect and love your boss.

> *We have nothing here but five loaves and two fish.*
> — Matthew 14:17

How often have we said this to God and to each other in the church?

"We've called everyone and there are not enough teachers for all of the Sunday school classes this year."

"You want to add onto the building? We could never raise enough money in a million years. Think of all of the members we have who are on fixed incomes and the price of gasoline keeps going up. Can't be done. And besides, we can't keep asking for money; it turns people off."

"All the church wants is our money. If that pastor preaches one more sermon on stewardship, I'm not coming back."

As I write this, I have just received a letter from our bishop asking our congregation to take another special offering on the anniversary of Hurricane Katrina in a few weeks. This, after we have already given thousands and thousands of dollars in the past fifteen months for the tsunami survivors in southeast Asia, for hungry refugees in Darfur, as well as for the survivors of Katrina. We

176

have had an overwhelming response, more than we have ever given before to needs outside of our own community. This is a time of overwhelming need.

I know, as I think about how I am going to present the request for this offering, that we are experiencing some "compassion fatigue." We have come to a point where we think we can't give anymore. Our resources are exhausted and we are emotionally drained, but the needy crowds keep coming.

We become angry, sometimes, when we are reminded of one more need in the world. Thelma Wilson, a pastor from the Isle of Man in Britain, wonders if "Jesus' command to feed the hungry makes us angry ... because he challenges our complacency," and makes "us reflect on our self-centeredness."[7]

Whatever our response, we may be sure Jesus has heard it all, and says to us what he said to his weary disciples, "Bring me what you have."

The Miracle

> Then he ordered the crowds to sit down on the grass. Taking the five loaves and two fish, he looked up to heaven, and blessed and broke the loaves, and gave them to the disciples, and the disciples gave them to the crowds. And all ate and were filled; and they took up what was left over of the broken pieces, twelve baskets full. And those who ate were about 5,000.
> — Matthew 14:19-21

There is a miracle in here somewhere, and the church is still sorting out what it is and what it means. If we allow ourselves to be pulled into a debate about miracles — with one side saying, "This literally happened: Jesus created food out of thin air, and if you don't believe that you are not a 'real Christian,' " and, the other side insisting: "This is a metaphor, you uneducated fool; it teaches us to have faith that God will provide in all circumstances" — we will not only waste our time; we will miss what the gospel writer is trying to teach us.

There is mystery in this story and therein is its power for us today. Celebrate the mystery. Learn from it. What matters more than what happened back then, is how this miracle empowers our ministry with Jesus today.

Mark Galli tells about a trip in which he had an opportunity to attend one of the most successful churches in the United States. Twenty thousand people worship there each weekend, the pastor is internationally known and a writer of popular books. It is a church with a vital and relevant ministry. "Fortunately," Galli wrote in his recent book, *Jesus Mean and Mild*, "it became impossible to attend there, and instead I was blessed to end up at an irrelevant church." He was welcomed at this second church by a woman who had been pulling weeds by the church sign. "The service, which included maybe 45 people, bumbled along — that is by contemporary, professional, 'seeker sensitive' standards." It was when the announcements began that Galli said he "... began to realize he was in 'the midst of the people of God.' " The pastor announced "... a new milestone for the church: They had served 22,000 people with groceries in ten years." Galli concluded, "... for all the good the megachurch does, this little fellowship manifested the presence of Jesus in a way that is unique and absolutely necessary in our age."[8]

Bob Stimmel, who retired from Downey United Methodist Church in southern California not long ago, said in one of his sermons, "We know the importance of food shared ... Our salvation is somehow tied up with food; I think it's always 'shared food.' And because it's shared, it is also sacred. It is not what we get for ourselves, but what we give away, and what we share with others."[9]

New York Times columnist, Nicholas Kristoff, reminded the nation on the third anniversary of 9/11 that almost as many people are dying in Darfur every week as died on September 11, 2001.

> *In my last visit to the Darfur area in Sudan, in June, I found a man groaning under tree. He had been shot in the neck and jaw and left for dead in a pile of corpses. Seeking shelter under the very next tree were a pair of widows whose husbands had both been shot to death.*

178

*Under the next tree I found a four-year-old orphan girl
caring for her starving one-year-old brother. And under the tree next to that was a woman whose husband
had been killed, along with her seven- and four-year-
old sons, before she was gang-raped and mutilated.*

Kristoff describes a woman he met on his last trip to Darfur.
Hatum Atraman Bashir

*... was pregnant with the baby of one of the twenty
Janjaweed raiders who murdered her husband and
gang-raped her. A few days ago, I received an email
note from an aid worker in the International Rescue
Committee, which is assisting Ms. Bashir, saying that
she had given birth but could not produce milk for the
baby — a common problem because of malnutrition.*[10]

When we respond to needs such as these by putting money in
the offering plate for the hungry, bringing food for food pantries,
working in soup kitchens and homeless shelters, and building Habi-
tat for Humanity homes, we discover that our own hungry hearts
are fed. In giving of ourselves we find sustenance for our souls.
That is the miracle.

*Jesus said to them, "They need not go away; you give
them something to eat."*   — Matthew 14:16

The Feeding Of The Fifty
Jo Perry-Sumwalt

Nancy Baker's cooking had become something of a legend at
Our Savior's Church. Whenever there was need for advice or action on a church dinner, Nancy's phone would ring, and she was
always happy to comply because she loved to plan and cook meals.
In part, people's high regard for her expertise came from the fact
that Nancy had taught home economics at the local high school for
thirty years. Equally important was their firsthand knowledge that
her home-cooked meals were delicious. But the most likely reason

Nancy was so often consulted was the miracle she had performed. Now, Nancy pooh-poohed the suggestion that there was any miracle involved, and her husband, Vince, jokingly referred to it as "The Feeding of the Fifty," but those who were present to assist did not take what she had done lightly. In their eyes, it had been a true miracle.

It had all come about because Our Savior's hosted an annual leadership training event for their denomination's area churches. A planning committee arranged for workshops in a variety of different leadership areas: trustees, parish boards, music, church school, finance, and so on. Our Savior's provided meeting and worship space, music, and snacks.

On the day of that most memorable of training events, the morning had dawned overcast and forbidding. Thunderstorms were forecast for the entire day. However, the church volunteers and workshop leaders arrived early and made their preparations. By 11 a.m., an hour-and-a-half before show time, the rain that had been falling all morning began to freeze. Salting and sanding trucks were out on the streets and highways, so the planning committee reasoned that, while the numbers of those in attendance might suffer, it was already too late to cancel the event.

Two hundred and fifty hearty souls had arrived at the church by 12:30, through an unseasonably late shower of heavy, wet snowflakes. The weather people on local radio and television stations were chuckling over this April snow shower, explaining that it was an arctic blast that had veered much farther south than expected. "Enjoy!" they said. "Christmas in April could be fun!"

But while the leadership training workshops kept their participants occupied, area businesses, schools, and offices began to close. Snowplows made repeated passes along major thoroughfares, but the snow was relentless. Workshop participants who had come from a distance began to slip out a few at a time. By the 3 p.m. break time, several had returned saying it was no use — they couldn't get home in the raging storm conditions.

Pastor Erickson and the planning committee called the remaining 109 participants together in the sanctuary at 3:15.

180

"We have begun calling our nearby church members and constituents to find overnight accommodations for everyone who is stranded here," Pastor Erickson announced. "As soon as the phoning is completed, you can take turns contacting your families to let them know you are taken care of."

But the phoning netted only 56 available beds, couches, cots, and rollaways within walking distance. When those people had been met and escorted away through the storm by their hosts, 53 stranded participants still remained.

"I can take four of you," Pastor Erickson announced, suggesting as diplomatically as possible that those with strong backs, muscles, and joints remain to sleep at the church, allowing four with more fragile constitutions to accompany him.

The group graciously complied. But as the telephone volunteers were being instructed on their next campaign for nearby blankets, pillows, sheets, and sleeping bags, someone brought up the problem of food.

"What will we feed those who are left here?"

City traffic was almost literally at a standstill. There were numerous cars abandoned as much off the streets as possible, most where they had become stuck or struck. Snowplows had been ordered back to the public works garages until there was a let-up in the storm, but still snow flew and blew with raging ferocity. The entire city had shut down, including any grocery stores or restaurants within walking distance. Two people whose car was stuck in a drift up the street had seen the lights on in the church and come in asking for shelter: 51 snowbound guests, four church volunteers, and no food.

"Have the phone volunteers ask for whatever food people can spare along with the bedding," Nancy Baker said sensibly. "God will provide."

So the nearby parishioners trudged out into the vicious storm one more time to deliver whatever they had to offer. While the sparse volunteer crew helped their stranded guests find the most comfortable spots in the building for making up beds, or set tables for 56, Nancy Baker shut herself in the church kitchen with the hodgepodge of food offerings. There wasn't a lot to work with — mostly canned goods, a little hamburger and chicken, cheese, pasta, eggs, and milk — but she began to rummage about the kitchen and work her magic.

The guests occupied themselves with get-acquainted conversations, and cards and board games from the youth room, after the eating and sleeping arrangements were completed. At 5:45, they were called to the tables by the clinking of a spoon on a glass by Nancy.

"Please, find a seat and let's pray before we eat," the pastor, who hadn't been able to make himself stay away, said as the group assembled and grew quiet. "Thank you, dear God, for the warmth and shelter of our church building, for the generosity of those who have provided food and bedding, and for the love and fellowship around these tables. Bless this food we are about to eat. In Jesus' name. Amen."

And then the kitchen doors opened, releasing wonderful aromas, and the four volunteers began carrying out bowls and platters and casserole dishes full of steaming, mouth-watering food, and everyone ate their fill, with plenty to spare.

The story of the quality and quantity of the food offered at that meal grew as it spread in the days and weeks following the storm. When the snowplows had done their work, and the shovelers and snowblowers had freed trapped vehicles, and everyone had returned home (after an equally amazing breakfast!), Nancy Baker was already on her way to being a legend in Our Savior's Church history.

"Such a lot of fuss!" Nancy said to Vince, "I told them God would provide!"[11]

---

1. Anthony Cotton, *Denver Post*, repeated in *Milwaukee Journal Sentinel*, July 24, 2006.

2. Rachel Naomi Remen, *My Grandfather's Blessings: Stories of Strength, Refuge, and Belonging* (New York: Riverhead Books, 2000), pp. 159-160.

3. *The New York Times*, International, June 8, 1992.

4. Marjorie Rosen, *Parade* magazine, March 8, 1998.

5. Marjorie J. Thompson, *Soul Feast: An Invitation to the Christian Spiritual Life* (Louisville: John Knox Press, 1995), p. 5.

6. The author prefers to remain anonymous.

7. *Midrash*, July 30, 2002.

8. Mark Galli, *Jesus Mean and Mild: The Unexpected Love of An Untamable God* (Grand Rapids: Baker Books, 2006), pp. 122-123.

9. Bob Stimmel, PRC-L Listserve, July 25, 2003.

10. Nicholas Kristoff, *The New York Times*, September 11, 2004.

11. Jo Perry-Sumwalt, "The Feeding of the Fifty," *Lectionary Tales for the Pulpit: 62 Stories for Cycle C*, John Sumwalt and Jo Perry-Sumwalt (Lima, Ohio: CSS Publishing, 1996), pp. 150-153. Jo Perry-Sumwalt is Director of Christian Education at Wauwatosa Avenue United Methodist Church in suburban Milwaukee. She is also the co-author of *Life Stories: A Study of Christian Decision Making* (Lima, Ohio: CSS Publishing, 1995). More recently, from 2002-2005, she and her husband, John served as the editors of StoryShare, a weekly online e-zine published by CSS.

Miracle 8

Storm Walker

The call came on a Sunday after church just as we were sitting down to lunch. "Eric's vital signs are dropping. We think this may be it. You'd better come." It was the Palliative Care Nurse, one of the dozens of hospital and hospice staff people who supported Eric and his family over the five years he lived with bone cancer. She met me as I came in the door of the hospice where Eric had lived for five months — a much longer stay than most of their patients who usually died within weeks. This 25-year-old young man who loved sports and every kind of video game was not going quietly into the dark night. The "Caucasian Sensation," as Eric called himself, had a voracious appetite for life.

The hospice cook, who loved Eric and was always coming to his room to give him hugs and make sure he was getting everything he wanted to eat, would tell later at his funeral how she would pile scoop after scoop on his butterscotch sundaes only to hear him say, "More, more." She finally gave up, she said, and gave him the pail and the scoop so he could take as much ice cream as he wanted. She was just one of the many friends Eric made along the way over those five years. Other cancer patients and their families, staff from the hospital where he was treated before coming to the hospice, along with friends from high school, college, and work, all paraded in and out of Eric's room. The hospice custodian and the chaplain stopped in regularly to chat and play video games. The nurses, aides, physicians, and social workers, many of who also came to his funeral, all took him into their hearts. None of them had ever seen so much activity in the room of someone who was supposed to be dying.

Eric was not ready to let go of this world. So, as I turned to walk down the familiar hallway toward his room that Sunday, I should not have been surprised to hear Laurie, the Palliative Care Nurse say, "Sorry, false alarm; Eric is better. And, he is not in his room. He is down here in the cafeteria." This had happened several times before, when Eric had come very close to death only to rally and call for more ice cream. On one of those occasions, he told me about two angels who came to him and told him that he could go with them if he wished. They also made it clear that it was up to him. He asked for and received more time.

I turned the other direction and walked with Laurie around the corner, and sure enough, there was Eric, propped up in a chair, eating ice cream, surrounded by his family.

As heartening as this sight was, the news was not all good. Eric was in great pain. Despite the efforts of a crack palliative team and the best pain management medicines available, his pain levels were extremely high. When they asked him to gauge his pain on a scale of one to ten, it was ten plus, unbearable. Eric said he was ready to enter a medically induced sleep. A decision was made to increase the dosage as much as possible.

I led them all in prayer, consulted with the chaplain, and then left to keep a family commitment. I came back at about 6:30, expecting Eric to be asleep. The room was buzzing with over a dozen people, not counting the two nurses, who were talking to Eric as they adjusted his intravenous lines. Though he had received enough painkillers to knock out a horse, Eric was wide-awake. He had the Tour de France on the television screen with the volume turned down low. I kept vigil with them for about four hours, taking it all in as people took turns talking to Eric, holding his hand, mopping his forehead, talking, laughing, moving in and out of the room to get snacks and soda, and watching the best cyclists in the world pedal steadily up the daunting slopes of the French Alps.

I would recall this scene in my sermon as I stood in front of Eric's casket in our church sanctuary, exactly four weeks later, on a warm Sunday afternoon in August, comparing our long vigil with

186

Eric to the plight of the disciples that night they were in the boat "battered by the waves." It was chaotic and wonderful, a strange mix of death and life like I had never seen before, and Jesus was there with us, as he always is, walking toward us over the storm.[1]

A Ghostly Tale

> *Immediately he made the disciples get into the boat and go on ahead to the other side, while he dismissed the crowds. And after he had dismissed the crowds, he went up the mountain by himself to pray. When evening came, he was there alone, but by this time, the boat, battered by the waves, was far from the land, for the wind was against them. And early in the morning he came walking toward them on the sea. But when the disciples saw him walking on the sea they were terrified, saying, "It is a ghost!" And they cried out in fear. But immediately Jesus spoke to them and said, "Take heart, it is I; do not be afraid."* — Matthew 14:22-27

Matthew passed on a story about a perilous time to people who were living in perilous times. Jesus had just received word of the beheading of John the Baptist. If there had ever been any question about him being in danger of being killed by the religious or political authorities, there was none now. Jesus went up into the mountains to grieve and to prepare himself for what was certain to come. It must have been like this for Martin Luther King Jr., who lived every day of his ministry knowing he could be killed at any moment. Robert Kennedy surely knew risk like this when he decided to run for president just five years after his brother was assassinated in Dallas.

There was a night during my own ministry in Montello, Wisconsin, in the early 1980s, when the sheriff sat next to me at a school board meeting. I had taken a public stand against a paramilitary group called the Posse Commitatus who were calling for the banning of certain books from the school library and the firing of teachers they accused of advocating subversive ideas. The sheriff told me later that he thought I might be in danger because they

187

had received a tip from an undercover agent to expect violence at the meeting. I wasn't frightened at the time, but later that night I went to bed shaking at the thought of what might have happened. The world would never look the same to me again. Danger brings everything into focus. It is easier to see what must be done, what cannot be postponed because there might not be another day.

While Jesus was praying on the mountain the disciples were in a boat being tossed by waves. The wind was against them, Matthew writes. Later Jesus would send a Pentecost wind to blow in their favor, but in this moment an unfavorable wind threatened to destroy them. Matthew doesn't say, but they must have been frightened to death. I would have been if I had been in a boat battered by waves, and if my beloved rabbi was about to go up against powers that would surely kill him and everyone around him. I would have thought twice about sticking around, just as I have often thought twice about getting out of the church before it kills me, but that is another story. The dangers I have known in my life, including my little run-in with the Posse, pale beside those of the disciples, who had seen bodies hanging on crosses.

So there they were, clinging to the sides of a boat that might be washed under at any second, and they looked out and saw a figure coming toward them over the waves. The storytellers who told this story in the house churches of Matthew's day must have loved telling this part. I love to tell it to the children in my best horror-inspiring voice. Matthew wrote that they were terrified, thinking they were seeing a ghost. They were more afraid of what was coming at them over the waves than the possibility of drowning in the deep, dark waters. Choose your terror. Which one would you rather face? I would take the ghost over the sea, but then I wasn't there and I don't much like boats.

Some of these guys were seasoned fishermen. They had been through all kinds of storms and survived. But they didn't know what a ghost might do and they didn't have the luxury of being able to call "Ghost Busters." They were in "deep doo-doo" as we might say, and probably so scared that they forgot these familiar words of the psalmist, which surely were in Matthew's mind as he recorded this ghostly tale.

Some went down to the sea in ships doing business on the mighty waters; they saw the deeds of the Lord, his wondrous works in the deep. For he commanded and raised the stormy wind, which lifted up the waves of the sea. They mounted up to heaven, they went down to the depths; their courage melted away in their calamity; they reeled and staggered like drunkards, and were at their wits' end. Then they cried to the Lord in their trouble, and he brought them out from their distress; he made the storm be still, and the waves of the sea were hushed. And they were glad because they had quiet, and he brought them to their desired haven.

— Psalm 107:23-30

How often our courage melts away in calamity. How easy it is to forget that the one who raises the stormy wind and lifts up the waves can also make the storm be still and hush the waves.

As I was pondering what to write in this chapter this morning, I came across a real-life horror story in our daily newspaper. A man who owns a tree service was pulled into an industrial-size wood chipper in a community near where we used to live. He kicked at a small limb that was stuck and the machinery grabbed him and pulled him into the steel grinders. The homeowner who had hired the tree service called out in terror but could not make himself heard over the noise of the machine. The man's nephew and four other employees did hear his cry for help and pushed down on the safety bar that was supposed to stop the machine, but couldn't get it to engage. The young father of two daughters, and another on the way, was pulled all the way through the chipper. It was all over in twenty seconds. The witnesses wept when they recounted what happened as the cameras rolled for the evening news.[2]

If I ever tell this story in a sermon I will not describe it so graphically. One or two sentences will make the point. There is so much suffering in our world. I could go on about suicide bombers and our own smart bombs that are not so smart that they can avoid blowing up innocent babies and their families, but I don't need to. We have all been in boats so battered by waves that we forget who and whose we are.

189

"I'm just trying to keep my head above water." This is what people used to say when times were tough in the midwest farm country where I grew up in the 1950s and '60s, and times were always tough. Keeping your head above water was about the best you could do most years. This is what the disciples were doing in the boat that night as a fierce storm raged all around and the wind blew them further and further from shore.

M. Scott Peck begins his first best-selling book, *The Road Less Traveled*, with three little words: "Life is difficult." Peck quotes Buddha, who taught, "The first of the 'Four Noble Truths' is 'Life is suffering.' "[3] We all know this but we go around hoping it might not be true for us, that we might somehow escape the pain we see and hear all around us. And often we can, for a while, especially those of us who live lives insulated by money and power in the Western world. Our supermarkets piled high with highly nutritious and fresh, heart-healthy foods; our gleaming hospitals and health clubs; and our investments, insurance policies, and generous pension plans give us "golden parachutes" unknown to the millions who are hungry, diseased, and living in squalor in countries whose natural resources we have exploited. Yet the poor often face tragedy and hardship with more faith and equanimity than those of us who can afford to drive to church on Sunday.

But sooner or later, cancer or heart disease, the untimely auto crash or the ghastly wood chipper gets all of us, rich and poor alike. There is a poignant death scene in the novel, *Broken Trail*, which was also made into a full-length movie with Robert Duvall in the lead role of Print Ritter. Print and his wranglers are moving a herd of 500 horses from Oregon to market several hundred miles east over rough trails. They come upon five young Chinese girls who have been sold into slavery. Print and his crew rescue them from their evil owners and take them along on the trail. They become very fond of the girls, and the beautiful young immigrants, in turn, come to love their rescuers. Sadly, one of the girls commits suicide by hurling herself from the wagon into the galloping herd after she is raped by cowboys in town. They bury her body along the trail and after the grave has been filled with the fresh dug earth, Print takes off his hat and says:

*We're all travelers in this world: from the sweet grass
to the packing house. Birth 'til death, we travel between
the eternities.*[4]

Life is hard. The psalmist got it right. We live many of our days with hearts "bowed down" and "no one to help." Our courage melts away in calamity and, like the disciples, we find ourselves calling out in fear (Psalm 107:12, 26b).

Jesus hears their cry, Matthew writes, and immediately identifies himself. "Take heart, it is I; do not be afraid." He identifies himself with "I Am." It is God walking above the storm, God in Jesus, or Jesus who is God, whichever it is. Fine theological points are of little concern when we are scared to death. Knowing God is with us is what matters, if only we can be sure. The knowing part is not so easy.

In her book, *When In Doubt Sing: Prayer In Daily Life*, Jane Redmont tells about a woman named Barbara who entered the Alcoholics Anonymous 12-step program and found she could not connect in any way with what the AA folks call their "higher power." Her sponsor told her she must pray: "You will pray in the morning and at night. Say anything you want, use prayers you know or your own words, I don't care. But you have to pray." Barbara complained that she didn't believe in God so it would be dishonest for her to pray. Her sponsor replied, "Who cares what you think? Just do it." Barbara agreed, saying, "... I'll just pray to my office wall." Each day she spoke her words to the wall, expecting nothing would come of her mandatory ritual. Then one day, the recovering woman discovered, as she prayed to her office wall, that she was not talking to herself.

*I just knew somebody was there. And that it was the
power who had been behind saving my life, that had
motivated the work of those who saved me, and whose
spirit I felt in the rooms of AA. I started crying. I was so
grateful. I had no idea that I was worth saving.*[5]

Barbara may not have known she was worth saving, but like the disciples she had cried out in fear, hoping someone might hear, and someone did. Jesus called out to the disciples in their battered boat, "Take heart, it is I; do not be afraid" (Matthew 14:27b).

No Ifs Ands Or Buts ...

> *Peter answered, "Lord, if it is you, command me to come to you on the water." He said, "Come." So Peter got out of the boat, started walking on the water, and came toward Jesus. But when he noticed the strong wind, he became frightened, and beginning to sink, he cried out, "Lord, save me!" Jesus immediately reached out his hand and caught him, saying to him, "You of little faith, why did you doubt?" When they got into the boat the wind ceased. And those on the boat worshiped him, "Truly you are the Son of God."*
>
> — Matthew 14:28-33

Peter's faith, like that of all of us would-be followers of Jesus, seems to be a little iffy at times. This incident in the battered boat foreshadows the denials that are to come on the night that he and Judas both betray Jesus (Matthew 26:69-70). Peter says, "Lord, if it is you, command me to come...." Peter, who represents all of the disciples, and all of us would-be disciples in the church, still has doubts about who Jesus is, especially in those times when he finds himself in rough seas. Who doesn't? Who of us can say our faith has never wavered. Matthew gives us a story in which we can see ourselves for who we are: flawed human beings who, in moments of weakness, are gripped by fear and doubtful about the identity of the voice that calls out to us over the storm. We are all in the same boat with Peter and the other disciples.

Peter expresses doubt, though he has just heard the familiar voice of his beloved rabbi calling out like God called out to Moses from the burning bush, "It is I," "I Am." Matthew is very clear whom Peter is being iffy about. Peter's response to Jesus is a direct quote of the words the devil spoke to Jesus when he is tempted in the wilderness: "If you are the Son of God, command these stones to become loaves of bread" (Matthew 4:3b). This is the issue Matthew raises throughout his gospel. Those of us in the boat have a decision to make. Are we with God or with the evil one? This decision is all the more difficult when we are being tossed around by the storms of life.

Matthew is writing to a church that has been tossed about by a series of calamitous events. Many in the early church, in the last third of the first century, had seen and survived many killer storms: the fall of Jerusalem and the destruction of the temple in 70 AD, the persecutions of zealous Pharisees who were trying to maintain the purity of Judaism, and the persecutions of Roman emperors when a political scapegoat was needed, as when Nero blamed Christians for the burning of Rome. Matthew is writing to strengthen the faith of believers in the church who are tempted to doubt during trying times, something the church has needed in every age.

Hundreds of Christians were attacked by local police and watched in horror as their half-finished church building was torn down and smashed one sunny afternoon in China in the summer of 2006. Simon Elegant tells what happened to this church of 5,000 parishioners in a suburb of Hangzhou, a lovely city by a lake a little over 100 miles southwest of Shanghai, in an article for *Time* magazine. Some church members were helping the construction crew and others were sitting on chairs on the perimeter of the construction site singing hymns.

> *... at about 2:30 p.m., thousands of uniformed police and plainclothes security officers ... bludgeoned people indiscriminately with nightsticks. "They were picking up women — some of them old ladies — by their hair and swinging them around like dolls, then letting them crash to the ground," says a man who watched the clash from across the street.*

The government claimed later that the Christians had attacked the police officers, who were only doing their duty, lawfully tearing down an illegal church. But one member of the church showed the *Time* reporter receipts from the hospital where he was treated for broken ribs, along with many others from the church who suffered similar wounds. "They treated us like dead dogs," he said.

"Some of them scoffed at us as we lay there, saying, 'Where is your God now? Why can't he help you? If you want to go to heaven, we'll help you get there right now.' "[6]

The author of the *Time* magazine article doesn't say how this frightening episode affected the faith of the church members who were assaulted, or that of others in the church. But who could blame them if they had called out like Peter, "If you are there, Lord, give us some sign of your presence."

My Wisconsin United Methodist colleague, Nancy Bauer-King, wrote an article for our local newspaper celebrating the fifty years that women have been allowed ordination in our United Methodist denomination, and in support of an area Roman Catholic woman who was recently ordained to the priesthood in an unsanctioned ceremony. Nancy recalled how, at age thirteen in 1953, she was told she could "... serve Jesus by being a missionary or a minister's wife but not a minister. Three years later," Nancy wrote, "the men in authority in my denomination granted full ordination to women...." Wisconsin had a woman bishop and Nancy knew several clergywomen by the time she got around to going to seminary 25 years later. But the church boat was still being rocked by waves of prejudice when she was appointed to her first charge in 1985.

> *I foolishly thought the battle — at least in the United Methodist Church — had been won. Ha! My first meeting with a pastor/parish relations committee included a verbal attack by a very angry woman citing scripture. People left the church. Two men from the small town stopped because they "wanted to see what a lady minister looked like." I quickly got used to the stares, questioning criticism, and warnings that I was going to hell (I was told the souls of the people I served were in peril, too). Why on earth would anyone — male or female — put themselves in the position of being subjected to such slings and arrows.*[7]

It is not easy to keep faith when your every move is scrutinized and criticized, and your right to be who you are is attacked at every turn in a place where everyone is supposed to be safe. Nancy points out that what is now a little less true for clergywomen in most, if not all, United Methodist churches, is not yet true for gay and lesbian men and women who are denied ordination in the United Methodist church.

> *Any institution can continue to stick with its rules and deny access to holy things, but no institution or individual can eliminate the hunger folks have within for sacred presence. No doctrine can stifle questions of meaning. No institutional rule can erase one's imagination. No threat of excommunication can prevent all creative actions — like Vandenberg (the woman who was illegally ordained) getting into a boat in an "unsanctioned" ceremony.*[8]

I don't know if Nancy's faith ever wavered in all the years she has served our beloved United Methodist church. We are still a long way from the perfection John Wesley encouraged his followers to strive for. I know my faith has certainly been tried, as over and over again I have seen dear friends excluded from their rightful places in the church. It breaks my heart. In my beloved church, whose national advertising slogan is, "Open Hearts, Open Minds, Open Doors," a majority of hearts remain closed to the movement of the Spirit in the lives of our gay and lesbian brothers and sisters. There have been times that I have been tempted to call out with Peter, "If you are there, Lord, give us some sign of your presence."

After saving Peter, Jesus says to him, "You of little faith, why did you doubt?" Does he say it sharply, with indignation, or tenderly, like a father comforting a frightened child? In chapter 9, Matthew had written about the way Jesus looked upon the masses of people who came to him seeking healing. "When he saw the crowds, he had compassion for them, because they were harassed and helpless, like sheep without a shepherd" (Matthew 9:36). Is this the tone in which the gospel writer expects this question of Jesus to Peter to be read to the little huddles of first-century Christians, gathered in secret in homes and caves, fearful for their lives, lest anyone discover who it is they serve?

195

We don't know. Jesus speaks both sharply and tenderly to his followers in Matthew's gospel. Perhaps the author would leave the choice of inflection to the reader who knows the circumstances of his or her local church.

We do know that the disciples are beginning to understand who Jesus is. In an earlier, slightly different version of this story in chapter 8, Jesus is in the boat with the disciples when the storm comes up. He is asleep, undisturbed by the fierce winds that are about to swamp the boat. The disciples wake him, begging to be saved. Jesus asks them, "Why are you afraid, you of little faith?" Then he calms the storm and the disciples say in amazement, "What sort of man is this, that even the winds and the sea obey him?" (Matthew 8:23-27). The disciples are dazzled by his power, but they don't recognize the divine in him.

But at the conclusion of this second account in chapter 14, Jesus comes walking to them on the water, and they get it. They finally have absolute clarity about who he is. As Jesus helps Peter into the boat "... the wind ceased," and "... those in the boat worshiped him saying, 'Truly you are the Son of God.' " This is how Matthew hoped and prayed everyone who heard his gospel would respond.

Get Out Of The Boat
Pamela J. Tinnin

When my father retired from the Navy, we moved to a small fishing and logging town on the southern Oregon coast. The coastline along that part of the state is as beautiful as any I've seen. It is also extremely dangerous — the shore crops away sharply and the water is broken by rocky outcroppings, some clearly visible while others lie hidden beneath the waves.

Every few years a fishing boat was lost in the storms that swept in off the Pacific, until finally the US Coast Guard opened a station there. When I was a senior in high school, I saw one of their rescue efforts. I was standing on the shore, watching through binoculars while the wind whipped my hair and the rain came in dark sheets and the Coast Guard station alarm blared behind me. Within minutes after the siren had sounded, the dock was lined with towns-people, watching the scene with anxious eyes — wives and parents and friends clasping hands, holding each other up, sending up prayers.

The rescuers didn't have a helicopter, just a small boat of their own. The little boat struggled to find its way through waves that topped out at thirty feet. Bandon was a small town, and I knew most of the fishermen. The boat in trouble was the *Cindy Kay* with five men aboard, one of them a neighbor of ours, Owen Russell, just five or six years older than I was. I'd had a crush on him since junior high, but his age, wild reputation, and my parents kept me from ever pursuing that interest.

The *Cindy Kay* was breaking up, her hull tearing into pieces as the wind tossed her against the rocks. As I watched, my hands clenching the binoculars, I saw a man swept overboard and disap-pear, almost as if he'd never been there. I could see another man standing at the rail, his yellow slicker bright against the dark sky. He was looking at the water, searching for the man who'd gone under. Then he tore off the slicker and jumped, all in one motion, and he, too, disappeared beneath the waves.

It wasn't until later I learned the man who jumped was Owen Russell, the boy who'd been nothing but trouble since I'd known him. But on that day, when Owen pulled Mickey Andrews up from the deep, he forever became a hero.

I was seventeen, standing there in the middle of that storm when the Coast Guard vessel brought in all five survivors. I re-member Owen coming down the walkway, a gray blanket around his shoulders, his blond hair wet against his head. Word came that he had been the one to jump into the water, the one who saved Mickey. All of us waiting there on the dock cheered and cheered for him, and the reporter from Channel 12 stopped him and asked how it felt to be a hero. Owen just shook his head and blinked at the lights, then moved on. That was the last time I saw him until three years ago when I was back there for my high school reunion.

In the last few years, something strange has happened. People who've known me all my life, people who knew me as a clumsy kid, as a rebellious teenager, as a struggling young adult — when

197

they hear I'm a minister, they tell me things like a confession or something, like they've forgotten I'm the same old Pam I always was.

Owen was no exception. I ran into him at the grocery store. Even with gray hair and a bit of extra around the middle, he still has that wild look in his eye and that teasing smile. When I told him I was a minister, he laughed and said, "Now that's crazy." He told me he had his own fishing boat with his three boys. We talked a while about families and work and how time goes so fast.

I started to say good-bye, then I turned back and said, "Owen, I was there on the dock that day — that was something. You were a hero."

"Nah," he said, "I'm no hero. I didn't want to get off that boat. It was breaking up fast, but we knew the Coast Guard was comin' and if we just hung on, we'd make it."

"So what made you do it?" I asked.

"I don't know exactly," he answered and shook his head. He didn't look at me while he talked, his eyes on the produce man stacking oranges in a big pyramid.

"I kept thinkin' about Mickey's wife and how they had a little kid and another on the way; how there wasn't nobody else to do it but me. Next thing I knew I was in the water, so cold and so dark I couldn't see a thing. I looked up at the boat once, then kicked hard and headed down into the darkness. I was choking for air and I almost gave up when I saw his face, all white and dead-looking. I grabbed for his hair and hung on. When I looked up there was nothin' but black water and I remember thinking, 'Jesus, help us.' *Help us* — me, who'd never prayed in my life. Then a light come on up there by the boat, a big circle of light. I kept hold of him, and swam for that light. Funny thing," he said and laughed, "I didn't even like Mickey."

Then he turned back to me and smiled. "You know, my life's not much to brag on. I'm no church man, never was. Never could stand to sit still that long. I still drink too much most Saturday nights. Been divorced twice. And I'm sure no hero. But at least I got that one thing, that one time when I did what was right, scared as I was. Maybe that counts for something, huh?"

198

His face was flushed and his eyes slid past mine. Perhaps he was seeking some kind of absolution, but I failed to offer him anything but the usual polite things you say when you meet someone from your past. "Well, good to see you ... Let's stay in touch ... Come on by and meet the family." Then we shook hands and walked away.

This past week, thinking about the story in Matthew, I've wished I could see Owen and tell him what I should have told him that night, that it's our whole life that counts for something, not just those big moments, those times when we have to risk everything. Certainly those times may come into our lives. But most of our days will be filled with those small moments, those small decisions, the ones that sometimes scare us worse than the big ones.[9]

La Ceiba
Stan Duncan

Last week a town that I used to call home — and a great many of its people who I loved, who lived there — all died.

Many years ago I lived in a sweet little seaport town called "La Ceiba," on the northern Caribbean coast of Honduras. It is named after a rare tropical tree called the Ceiba, which seems to grow forever, with huge intertwining branches that — according to the legend — hold down the earth and keep it secure in the universe. The roots of the tree seemed to reach to the center of the earth, where the center of God's spirit resided. We had one such tree in our town, and it was breathtaking. It was down by the beach in a park that I passed by whenever I would walk from my apartment to a friend's house who lived near the water. On the way to her house, I would often stop and admire the massive Ceiba tree, in all its glory, holding down the earth, and protecting it from being blown away. It was so large that it was hard to imagine anything that could dislodge its hold on the ground that it was there to secure. Its branches soared upward and outward into a magnificent canopy, broad and flat, and Harpies — the largest of all eagles — would perch from them and study our behaviors from above, searching for prey.

199

My job in those days was to do research on the work of development agencies in Honduras for a master's thesis I was writing in economics. But in the process, I met and loved — and now miss — an enormous number of people and places. I lived in a tiny upstairs apartment on Colon Avenue, in a gorgeous old Spanish villa with terraces and patios and hanging plants. My bedroom was on the second floor with a magnificent floor-to-ceiling, bricked-in arched window overlooking a busy Caribbean street scene below. I had a lush forest of nationalities and races that poured through the street below me all through the day and most of the night, buying and selling, begging and badgering one another until their faces and voices began to blend like a choir in some kind of modern abstract harmony. Often when I got in bed at night, I would turn off the light and open the curtains and lay in bed looking out at the lights and listening to the horns of the buses and the taxis singing to one another until I finally fell asleep.

My landlord was Maurico Benza, a dignified, aging, thin-lipped Spaniard, with a pencil-thin black mustache and an always-present bow tie. I loved the looks of him because he reminded me of all the Hollywood movie depictions of old world Spanish aristocracy. He had a slight smell about him of someone who wore just a touch too much cologne or hair cream. His hair had a metallic smoothness to it and I suspected that he used the better part of a bottle of Wildroot Cream Oil to get it to lie down like that.

Next door to the villa was my barber, Alfonso. I was warned before I ever went to see him that he was not fond of the influence that the American military was having on Honduras in those days, so I confess I lied to him and told him I was from Great Britain and we became fast friends. I loved Alfonso. He was an immigrant from Italy, and his Spanish was as bad as mine. We could talk well together because neither of us knew how to use big words and complicated sentences.

I remember, too, that his shop also had that same smell to it that Maurico my landlord had, and I often wondered if Alfonso was the supplier for Maurico's pungent hair products.

Down the street from Alfonso was the *Parque Infantil*, the "Children's Park." When I would get home early, I liked to go there and sit on a bench and watch the children play while I fed the pigeons. Across the street was a great place to eat called *La Pizza Barrata*, "The Cheap Pizza." The owners not only let you choose your own ingredients, but also had tables around the walls of the dining room where customers could roll out the dough and bake their pizzas themselves. It was a great hit with the children.

One day while I was sitting on my bench feeding some left-over pizza to pigeons, a man named Guillermo came up to me and begged for some money. I lied and told him I didn't have any. So he said, "Well, then, would you like to buy a map?" I thought about it and said that yes, I would like to buy a map, and I took some of the money I had just told him I didn't have, and I bought my first map of Honduras. And I still have it.

Over the next few weeks, Guillermo found me many times, and each time we repeated the same litany. I didn't always buy his products (I didn't always feel good about where he might have attained them), but often I did. He had postcards, sea shells, movie tickets, and discount coupons at The Cheap Pizza. We shared the pizzas and had a great time. One day he announced that he had found a cat and wanted to keep it, so I gave him about $10 in Honduran *limpira* to buy cat food and milk. He told me it was a loan, but I didn't think anything more about it until months later when I had moved to Tegucigalpa, and I got a letter that my landlord, Mauricio, forwarded to me. In it, Guillermo thanked me for the loan, apologized for the delay, and said he was repaying the money. In the envelope was a bundle of The Cheap Pizza coupons in a rubber band, the value of which was about $10.

Outside of La Ceiba there were a number of clinics set up over many years by Dr. Joyce Baker, a United Church of Christ medical missionary in Honduras. Joyce could have made a fine living anywhere in the world, but for thirty years she lived, worked, and raised her family among the poorest of the poor in Honduras. In town, I knew a hardware store owner named Raul Madrigo, over on a street called the Avenida de La Republica, who grew up receiving free medical care from one of Joyce's clinics. He gives one day a week volunteering at another clinic in the poor Garifuna Indian community.

About a block down Colon Avenue on the corner of Thirteenth Street there was a real live Dunkin' Donuts, where I ate breakfast almost every morning. It was a little touch of North America in an otherwise very Caribbean-looking world. It looked and felt almost like any Dunkin' Donuts in the states, except that the coffee had a blackened, ruddy texture to it, and tasted something like a mixture of tar and charcoal. Honduran coffee is a serious drink for serious drinkers, and they are amazed at the weakened, pale fluid that passes for coffee in the States. It took me weeks before I could get my tolerance for caffeine up to Honduran levels, and I finally prided myself on my ability to get down two whole cups at one sitting, though I'm sure it did terrible damage to my blood pressure each time I did it.

I got into trouble at that Dunkin' Donuts one time, on my last day in La Ceiba. I had finished my work and was moving to Tegucigalpa, the capital of Honduras. I got to the bus station early, bought my ticket, put all of my luggage on the bus, and then went down the street to Dunkin' Donuts to have a muffin and cup of caffeinated tar. But when I got back, less than an hour later, the bus had already filled up and was taking off. I waved at the driver to stop, but he refused. He'd gotten his load and was leaving early, even if my things were on his bus! I couldn't send all of my worldly possessions off on a strange bus without me, so I jumped onto the ladder on the back of the bus, crawled along the top holding onto the luggage racks, and then slid down the side by the front door. I put one foot on the running board and one on the right fender, and held onto the rear view mirror, and rode that way, like Indiana Jones, for about two hours until we finally came to a another coastal town called Tela where the driver let some passengers off and nonchalantly let me on.

Inside, I collapsed in a rumpled, dirty, smelly, heap of exhaustion and dust across the aisle from a very proper-looking little girl in a prim pink dress who was reading a book. She looked up at me and over to her mother next to her, and then back to me. She said, "We're going to visit my grandmother in Tegucigalpa, and we're all dressed up. I guess you're not going to go visit anybody."

On Monday, October 26, 1998, Hurricane Mitch began to threaten the northern shores of Honduras. It was huge at first, but for a while it dissipated and people in La Ceiba and other coastal towns breathed more easily. Then, just as they were learning to relax, it made a dramatic turn downward right into the coast, and there it stalled for six days dropping as much as four inches of rain per hour. Fifty rivers overflowed their banks in the area. In La Ceiba, every house and building from the shore for twenty blocks up the hill through the *Parque Infantil* was covered by water in the first two days. My friend's simple home on the beach was gone. The villa I lived in was gone. The Dunkin' Donuts was gone. The barber shop, The Cheap Pizza, and movie house were all gone. The mighty Ceiba tree, holding onto the earth to keep it secure, was buried in water and sand. Many of the rural clinics, that Dr. Baker had labored to build for twenty years, were gone. Destroyed. Washed away. In the first four days, 70,000 people were evacuated from their homes. Ironically, when the storm built up, people bought out the stores of medical and food supplies, and then when their homes washed away, in many cases, there was no food in the store houses to help the people who were brought to the shelters.

Days later when helicopters finally began arriving to take in some of the survivors, they saw rooftops with people lying dead on top of them. They found babies whose mothers had tried to save them by tying them to the tops of trees to protect them, but they were dead. They had survived the storm but then died of hunger.

One man survived by breaking open a hot water tank and drinking from it. A four-year-old neighbor girl washed in and lodged into the window of his house. He could wrap her up, but he couldn't get her out. So he saved her life by getting drinks of fresh water from the tank in his mouth and squirting it from his mouth into hers. Another man was caught in a mud slide next to his house. He heard the roar of the rain and the mud coming down onto him, so he lashed himself to a tree to protect himself, but the tree and all of his house were carried away with the water. He flowed for over ten miles tied to the tree before he was lodged into a mud bank and the rope broke free. His feet were buried deep into the mud, but it broke both his legs, and he laid there for two days more waiting for someone to come and dig him out.

The death toll across Honduras rose into the thousands. It is estimated that one out of every three buildings in the entire country no longer exists! Every major road was destroyed, every airport. Every major power line. Seventy percent of the economic production of the nation was ruined. At least 12,000 people, real people, died, 13,000 were unaccounted for. Over one million people were put into temporary shelters. At least a million and a half more were made homeless.

When people die far away it's terrible, but we don't feel for them because we don't know them. I didn't know anybody in Rwanda, or Bosnia, or Palestine, or Afghanistan, and it is hard to know the true impact of suffering and dying until you know somebody there. I want you to know that these people are not statistics but real people, good people, kind people, and they all died. And I miss them.

I worried and cried for my friends. I tried to contact them and was unable to reach most of them. I also prayed to God for them, not with anger but that they could reach out to God's Spirit and experience strength and courage in it, whether in this world or the next.

Perhaps in one sense God is like the mighty Ceiba tree. News reports say that when the waters receded, they finally found it — beaten and damaged — but still standing. They say that throughout the storm and its horrendous destruction, the tree gave strength to the community and all of the people who lived around it, in part because it too had suffered, right in the midst of their suffering, right along side their pain, and in the end, battered and bruised, it never released its hold on the earth.[10]

---

1. Eric Monteith was a regular in our worship services at Wauwatosa Avenue United Methodist Church. He attended the 8 a.m. chapel service with his mom, Phyllis, his stepfather, Richard Matel, and his brothers, Brent and Joel, even after he was admitted to the hospice. In the last few weeks of his life he explained to me over and over again that he would come to church but he couldn't

make it up the steps anymore. Eric was born in Richland Center, Wisconsin (where his father, Harry, still lives), June 3, 1981. He was a graduate of Hamilton High School in Milwaukee and a student at The University of Wisconsin-Whitewater when he was diagnosed with bone cancer in 2001. Eric loved people, sports, and video games. Eric loved life! His very presence was life-giving and life-enriching for his many family members and friends.

2. Erin Richards, *The Milwaukee Journal Sentinel*, August 17, 2006.

3. M. Scott Peck, *The Road Less Traveled* (New York: Simon and Schuster, 1978), p. 15.

4. Alan Geoffrion, *Broken Trail* (Golden, Colorado: Fulcrum Publishing, 2006), p. 199.

5. Jane Redmont, *When In Doubt Sing: Prayer In Daily Life* (New York: Harper Collins Publishers, 1999), pp. 94-95.

6. Simon Elegant, "The War for China's Soul," *Time* magazine, August 28, 2006, pp. 40-43.

7. Nancy Bauer-King, "Female Clergy Answer the Call," *The Milwaukee Journal Sentinel*, August 18, 2006.

8. *Ibid.*

9. Pamela J. Tinnin is pastor of Guerneville Community Church (United Church of Christ) in Guerneville, California. She is co-author of *Bit Players in the Big Play* (Lima, Ohio: CSS Publishing Company, 2004).

10. From a sermon preached by Stan Granot Blythe Duncan on December 12, 1998, at the United Church of Christ in Abington, Massachusetts, following the destruction of Hurricane Mitch. Stan Duncan is a UCC/Disciples of Christ pastor, originally from Oklahoma, now residing in Abington, Massachusetts. He has served as a pastor, campus minister, and economist, DJ, and pianist. He lived for two years in Central America researching and writing about economic development projects. Stan is the author of *Companions of Jesus* about the killing of the six priests, their cook, and his daughter in El Salvador in 1988, which he co-authored with Jon Sobrino. He has also published a number of articles on economic development and human rights, and writes a religion column in the *Patriot Ledger*. Now and then, Stan does commentaries on NPR, most recently he did one on *Market Place* about immigration.

Miracle 9

Foreign Territory

I grew up "poor" — or so I thought. My siblings and I wore hand-me-downs from our cousins, and we were glad to get them. There was one Christmas when we were the recipients of a Christmas basket of fruit, candy, cookies, and a turkey from a charity group in our county because we were on "the list." There was rarely extra money for luxuries like restaurants, movies, or vacations. I didn't stay in a motel until I was sixteen, and then only because my school paid for the room so I could compete in the sectional wrestling tournament in a distant town. After I won the sectionals and went on to the state tournament in Madison, I was very self-conscious about being the only wrestler there who didn't have proper "wrestling" shoes. I wore an old pair of black and white canvas shoes. It proved to be one of the richest experiences of my young life, despite the embarrassing shoes and the fact that I was eliminated by a pin in the first round.

It was on a trip to Mississippi in 1970, the summer after my freshman year in college, that I learned what it really meant to be "poor" in America. I went with a group called "Project Understanding," a cultural exchange program. We stayed in the homes of rural African Americans (although that is not a term used at that time) in Marshall and Carroll counties. I was in "foreign territory," like Jesus was when he ventured into the realm of the Syrophoenician woman.

When the bus pulled up at a small shack of a house outside Holly Springs, we were greeted by children with distended stomachs and herniated navels protruding from their ragged clothes.

The condition was caused by an inadequate diet and a lack of money to pay for the operation needed to correct the disfigurement. Inside the house the stench of urine-soaked dirt (animals under the house) came up through large cracks in the floors. I wanted to get back on the bus and go home. I had no choice but to stay and receive one of the greatest blessings of my life.

During those eight days of living in real poverty, I met some of the most courageous, spirit-filled people I have ever known — leaders who risked their lives in the early days of the Civil Rights Movement, who were beaten and jailed and were the first people with black skin to register and vote in their communities. Our group worshiped in a country church where few white people had worshiped before, and afterward we were served some of the best food I've ever tasted. It was a life-changing, perhaps a life-saving, experience. I was never the same after that, thank God!

When You Don't Know What To Say ...

> *Jesus left that place and went away to the district of Tyre and Sidon. Just then a Canaanite woman from that region came out and started shouting, "Have mercy on me, Lord, Son of David; my daughter is tormented by a demon." But he did not answer her at all.*
> — Matthew 15:21-23a

Seeking to avoid the crowds that surrounded him everywhere he went in Israel, Jesus leaves the country for a little rest and relaxation. Tyre and Sidon were in Phoenicia, a region in Syria that stretched north between Galilee and the Mediterranean Sea.

This was foreign territory, a dangerous place for a Jew to be. The Phoenicians were of Canaanite stock, the ancestral enemies of the Jews, the forbearers of the people we know as Palestinians today. To Jews in Jesus' time, all non-Jews (that is, all Gentiles) were considered to be unclean. Anyone who did not keep the Jewish cleanliness laws was by definition "dirty." A Jew was to have nothing to do with anyone who was unclean.

Have you heard the expression "dirty foreigner"? Some of us have grown up in families who were called that when we emigrated here from another part of the world. My own Irish ancestors were called that and worse. Irish, Italian, Polish, German, Hispanic, Asian, African, Indian, Scandinavian, Native American, Arab, and Jew — we have all had our turn as a despised minority in Wisconsin.

I am sad to say that in my childhood I heard members of my own extended family refer to African Americans as "dirty." When I was in high school, an eleven-year-old African-American girl came to stay with our family for three weeks as part of "Project Understanding," the cultural exchange program with Mississippi, I described above. One of our relatives was quite distressed about this. She said to my mother, "Aren't you worried about her blackness rubbing off on the sheets?"

That is an attitude born of fear and ignorance, a learned social prejudice that has no basis in fact, but is as common in our time as it was in first-century Israel.

Nancy Nichols tells about the shameful prejudice a family from the Middle East encountered in the United States in the charged atmosphere after 9/11.

For Shame, For Shame ...
Nancy Nichols

Ibteson and her husband, Raji, are from Jordon. When Ibteson's parents came to visit, she invited several of us to dinner to meet them. We sat around the table together — agnostics, Christians, Muslims — people from many faith traditions ate Middle-Eastern food and celebrated our connection. Ibteson's parents felt welcome and indeed loved as they visited their daughter in the United States. They were scheduled to fly home to Jordan two days later — September 11, 2001.

The joy and freedom we felt that evening were replaced with feelings of fear. Ibteson stayed at home, away from classes, and didn't send her children to school because she was afraid to be away from her home. Her parents were grounded in Atlanta. Her mother, for the first time in her married life, removed her hijab and went with her hair uncovered in a public place. She was afraid to be identified as a religious Muslim.

You remember that day and the weeks that followed, when we watched as the world we knew melted down. There were feelings of pain, sorrow, anger, confusion, blame, and most of all *shame*! How could this happen to us? And how could we, as a nation, treat people the way we were all of a sudden treating people of Middle-Eastern descent? Everyone who didn't look like us — whoever us was — and who believed in Allah rather than Yahweh, was suspect. I remember explaining to someone that Allah is the Arabic word for God and that Muslims also believe in the God of Abraham. He was stunned, and then began to argue that it must be a different God, and anyway they weren't Christians so it didn't really matter, they were, at the very least, suspect!

For shame! I felt it, and as I watched our country cycle closer and closer to war and saw politicians, and even some religious leaders, use the fear of the other to justify war, I was shamed even more.

... Jesus, for all of his connection to God, was a product of his culture, and his culture hated, and probably feared, those who lived in the region of Tyre, a rather immoral and ungodly seaport. The only woman from this area other than the woman in today's text that we hear of coming from that area in scripture is Jezebel, the wife of King Ahab, and she was anything but admired! Jesus absorbed this message, and when the Syrophoenician woman asked for his help, he answered out of his culture — you are not worthy — in fact, you are lower than the dogs! The woman, desperate mother that she was, confronted Jesus. She may as well have said, "For shame, for shame, for shame...."[1]

What is Matthew trying to teach the church by placing this story here? Was it prejudice against Gentiles that landed Jesus in this predicament with a foreign woman? It is more than just ironic that it follows directly after Jesus' little brouhaha over cleanliness

210

with the scribes and Pharisees. They challenge him, asking, "Why is it that his disciples defy the tradition of the elders by not washing their hands before they eat?" And he answers immediately, calling them blind guides, saying their hearts are far from God, that they are hypocrites for seeking a loophole in the law to get out of supporting their aged parents as the fifth commandment requires. Then Matthew describes how Jesus calls the crowd over and makes the pronouncement, "It is not what goes into the mouth that defiles a person, but it is what comes out of the mouth that defiles" (Matthew 15:1-20).

After taking this stand about the proper interpretation of the cleanliness laws, he steps into foreign territory where everyone and everything is unclean. The tension builds. Matthew is about to give us something big. Jesus himself, whom Matthew has already made clear is the Messiah, the beloved Son of God, encounters an unclean woman, a Gentile (like me) who begs him to cast a demon out of her daughter. Jesus, who had responded immediately when challenged by the scribes and Pharisees, has nothing to say, "... did not answer her at all" (Matthew 1:18; 3:17; 15:23).

When we don't know what to say, it usually means we are about to learn something — so it is really better to say nothing until we have figured out what's going on. It is disconcerting to go into foreign territory. Strange places and strange people can bring out the worst of our fears and bad behavior. And, strangely, it is in foreign territory that we often learn more about ourselves than anywhere else. Richard Rohr writes in *Simplicity: The Art of Living*, that to find a new way of life, "You have to leave the world where you have everything under control. You have to head into a world where you are poor and powerless. And there you will be converted in spite of yourself."[2]

Most of us resist this kind of conversion fiercely, refusing to consider any point of view that threatens our comfortable world. Robert Kirby had an epiphany as he watched people watching a film about Mormons, which most non-Mormons refuse to go see because they don't like what it is about, like many people refused to see *Brokeback Mountain* because it was just a "gay flick." In a discussion after a showing of *States of Grace*, a pro-Mormon film that Kirby encouraged all of his readers to see, he noticed that "Everyone, it seemed, had a personal filter that either helped or hindered the way he or she interpreted the film. Sitting on the stage like a dope, I suddenly realized that most people don't go to films for any real understanding. Most of us go to watch ourselves. And any film that doesn't give us the narcissistic view we want is smugly deemed a travesty of art."[3]

The same is true of most of us in the United States when we travel to foreign places. We go not so much to learn about the people and their way of life as to see and snap photos of the things we have heard about.

Esther Armstrong and Dale Stitt of Portland, Oregon, have an ecumenical ministry called Journey Into Freedom that, among other things, sponsors what they call "Trips of Perspective." Esther wrote in their newsletter of a "wonderfully disturbing" trip to Haiti where they met some of the poorest of the poor. They heard stories of starving people so hungry they are forced to eat emaciated dogs and donkeys, and of schoolchildren in Port-au-Prince swallowing stones to assuage hunger pangs due to poverty. Why do they go? Esther says, "We go on our Trips of Perspective not to fix the problems, to have answers, or even to make a difference. We go to be present, to stand in solidarity with the people of Haiti, to confront our real powerlessness in the face of dire need, and to be transformed."[4]

What have you learned in a foreign territory that you could not have learned anywhere else?

Christina Berry of Sandia Park, New Mexico, tells this story.

> *A dear friend's eldest son, age 31, died unexpectedly in early June in a city on the west coast. As she and her husband were planning to travel there from Arizona to attend a memorial service, his friends and partner had arranged, to collect his things, she told me that her husband did not know their son was gay. The relationship between father and son had been strained in the past, and we were sure her husband, a really traditional guy, would not handle this information well. "How could he not know?" I asked. "Are you going to tell*

him?" She said that she would wait and see. They had
so much to deal with in their preparations that we never
had a chance to talk again before their trip. Amidst
much chaos and grief, they left home. On the plane she
said something in passing about their son and his room-
mate. Her husband answered, referring to the room-
mate as the son's partner.

My friend said, "Where did you learn that?"
"Well, he told me."
"What did he say?"
Her husband related what their son had told him.
"When did you find out?" my friend asked,
shocked.
"Two years ago, that time I was in the hospital."
"Why didn't you say anything to me?"
Her husband looked surprised. "Didn't you
know?" he asked. She was so relieved she didn't have
anything more to say.

When they arrived at the home of their son's friend,
where the memorial service was being held, the first
person they saw was the son's partner. My friend said
that her big, macho husband looked at this bereft young
man, went to him, enfolded him in his arms, and said,
"Thank you for loving my son." And the two of them
wept together.[5]

Earl Kammerud tells about an unexpected detour he took into
foreign territory when he was pastor of a northern Wisconsin church
in the early 1970s.

The Day Andy Came Home
Earl Kammerud

I was fortunate to have a terrific youth group. Relationships
among members of the group strengthened and after high school
graduation, a young man and a young woman in the youth group
became engaged. Several years went by without any plans for a
wedding. In the meantime, the young man worked summers for
the fair that came to our town. One summer, after the fair, the young

man (I'll call him Andy) disappeared. His fiancée was upset, to say the least. I didn't know where he had disappeared to. Not even his parents knew what had happened.

Finally, at the end of the summer, he called me from Houston. He had spent the summer going from town to town with the fair and now had ended up at the winter quarters. He told of falling in love with a prostitute in Houston and the fear gripped him as her pimp was out to get him. I encouraged him to come home.

"Andy, we love you here. Mary (his fiancée) is waiting for you."

"But the girl down here!" Andy exclaimed.

I said, "If she really loves you she will come back with you or will follow shortly." He said he would think about it.

Several days later, Andy called again. He said his phone call had all been a lie. He ran away because he had admitted to himself that he was gay and couldn't face telling Mary or his parents.

"Please come home, Andy, we love you."

"But how can I tell my parents?" he cried.

"I'll go with you. We'll tell them together."

Several days later, he arrived at our house. We talked. We cried. We hugged. And then we went to face his parents. At first, only his mother was home. I said, "Andy has something to tell you."

"Mom," Andy blurted out, "I am gay." His mom responded, "Andy I know that. I have been waiting for you to tell us." At that time his Dad walked in.

Now, his Dad is a nice guy but Andy was so different from him. His dad was a steel worker, a hunter, and a fisherman. He worked with his hands. Andy was none of those things. But when Andy looked at this dad and told him he was gay, his dad walked over to him, threw his arms around him and hugged him. "I don't care, Andy, you are still my son."[6]

Who You Calling A Dog?

And his disciples came and urged him saying, "Send her away, for she keeps shouting after us." He answered, "I was sent only to the lost sheep of the house

214

of Israel." But she came and knelt before him, saying, "Lord help me." He answered, "It is not fair to take the children's food and throw it to the dogs." She said, "Yes, Lord, yet even the dogs eat the crumbs that fall from the master's table." — Matthew 15:22b-27

Jesus is in foreign territory, and a "dirty foreigner" approaches him. The fact that she is a woman compounds his dilemma. Jewish men were not to speak to women in public, even members of their own families, lest they risk making themselves unclean.

The Canaanite woman shouts at Jesus, "Have mercy on me, Lord, Son of David." She addresses him as the Messiah; she knows exactly who he is, something that even the disciples were not yet clear about. She yells, "My daughter is tormented by a demon."

Jesus ignores her: "... he did not answer her at all." But he must have known his little vacation was over. The disciples urge him to send her away because she won't stop shouting. Jesus finally speaks, "I was sent only to the lost sheep of the house of Israel" (Matthew 15:24).

The woman is not deterred. She comes and kneels at his feet, the proper deferential position for a woman in this time and place. And she pleads with him, "Lord, help me" (Matthew 15:25).

Jesus responds in a manner that seems uncharacteristically harsh. "It is not fair to take the children's food and throw it to the dogs" (Matthew 15:26). This is a sharp rebuke. To suggest that someone is like a dog is not a compliment. The Canaanite woman doesn't miss a beat, and I think she must have smiled as she said this, "Sir, even the dogs under the table eat the children's crumbs."

Ba-da-bing, ba-da-bang.

This woman is good at repartee. She does to Jesus what he is so good at doing to any critic who dares to engage him in oral combat. Nowhere else in the gospel accounts is there a report of anyone so clearly getting the best of Jesus. This Canaanite woman takes Jesus to school, and he knows it.

Jesus said to the Canaanite woman, "It is not fair to take the children's food and throw it to the dogs." The Canaanite woman speaks with the voice of God to the Son of God (is that possible?)

215

when she says, "Yes, Lord, yet even the dogs eat the crumbs that fall from the master's table" (Matthew 15:26-27).

In 1988, one of this Canaanite woman's descendants was on trial in Israel for "incitement and possession of inciting materials ... Samiha Khalil was known at that time as the most powerful woman on the West Bank ... perhaps the best way to describe Khalil is the way she described herself. 'I am Palestinian to the core. My wish before I die is to have a passport with the word "Palestinian" on it.' When the Israeli military governor of Khalil's district asked how she was one day, she responded dryly, 'God is with us.' Not to be outdone, the governor responded, 'No, he is with us.' Without blinking an eye, Khalil shot back, 'God was with you, but he is beginning to correct his mistake.' "[7]

Ba-da-bing, ba-da-bang!

In a sermon, titled "Even Jesus Needed To Be Reminded To Be Inclusive," that won the Lawrence J. Mickelson Preaching Prize on the Gospel and Social Justice and Human Dignity in 1999, Timothy Browning Safford called Jesus' comment a "... clear ethnic epithet — a racial slur — toward this Gentile woman."

> *Decorum prevents me from using the word related to a dog that we use in our language, and Jesus', of the word "dog" in his own language. I know it may seem too bold to suggest that Jesus is using "hate speech." No matter his motives, I respectfully suggest that hate speech is always hate speech. I think the woman in the story knows it is hate speech, as shown in her response.*[8]

What's even more surprising than the hutzpa of this non-Jewish woman is that Jesus agrees with her. He not only gets it, he admits it. Jesus does what all of us can learn to do when we are shown to be wrong; he graciously acknowledges the rightness of her position. This is, perhaps, Matthew's clearest message to both the Jewish and the Gentile churches, the gospel is for Jews and Gentiles alike. We belong to God whoever we are or wherever we are from.

216

Several months after the events of 9/11 my friend, Rebecca Coan-Henderleiter, who is Cherokee, was startled by an overt act of prejudice against a Muslim neighbor:

I was in the produce department of a grocery store picking out strawberries next to an older woman. A Muslim woman was picking out fruit on the other side of the stand. The older woman turned to the produce manager and started talking about the trouble in the Middle East and how terrible it was what the Palestinian terrorists were doing in Israel. This was said loud enough for the Muslim woman to hear. The produce manager was speechless at the insensitivity of the woman. Then I looked at her and told her how thousands of my ancestors died on the "Trail of Tears" (which she had never heard of). I told her my sympathies were with anyone who was being pushed around by bullies with tanks. She walked away rather quickly. The other woman came up to me with a tear in her eye and thanked me. She was in fact Palestinian and had received nothing but prejudicial treatment since 9/11. I was the first American she'd encountered who truly understood what was happening. [9]

An elder of one Masai tribe was talking with a well-meaning American missionary about faith. "Faith," said the elder, "is like a lion going after its prey ... as the animal goes down the lion envelops it in his arms, pulls it to himself, and makes it a part of himself. That is the way a lion is. This is what faith is."

The missionary was much taken aback by this. He realized for the first time that faith is much more than embracing certain beliefs. But what the elder said next was even more stunning to this foreigner who, as Jesus commanded, had gone forth from his own country to "make disciples of all nations ..." (Matthew 28:19).

"We did not search you out," he continued. "We did not even want you to come to us. You searched us out ... You told us of the high God, how we must search for him, even leave our land and our people to find him. But we have not done this. We have not left

217

our land. We have not searched for him. He has searched us out and found us. All the time we think we are the lion. In the end, the lion is God."[10]

Two Miracles

> *Then Jesus answered her, "Woman, great is your faith!*
> *Let it be done for you as you wish." And her daughter*
> *was healed instantly.* — Matthew 15:28

There are two miracles here. The first one is obvious and by itself no small thing. The demon that possessed this child, whatever it was, is gone. If you have ever loved a child who suffered from some debilitating, painful illness, you know why this woman is willing to risk public humiliation to get help. She will do whatever is needed to make her daughter well. She has nothing to lose and everything to gain. Jesus heals this little girl, but clearly it would not have happened except for this mother's great love.

The second miracle in this story of healing is even more significant. Jesus' immediate response to the Canaanite woman is tribal. "I was sent only to the lost sheep of the house of Israel."

We are all members of a tribe first. Who you are related to counts for something in this world. My uncle, Theron Long, hired me to work for him in his milk-testing lab when I was in college, not because I was more qualified than a dozen or so others he could have hired, but because I was his sister's son. He preferred to pay someone in his own family even though he might have found someone more qualified than me. I loved him for that then, and I love him for it now.

Families take care of their own. Blood is thicker than water and everything else. How many wars have been fought; how many millions have died in our world because of this? In 1994, 800,000 people from the Tutsi tribe in Rwanda were murdered by members of the Hutu tribe, who were then in power. "Ethnic cleansing" we now call this, bad blood between neighbors, which begins with simple disagreements about religion and who owns what territory, and ends in a bloodbath. Witness Bosnia, Kosovo, Burundi,

218

Chechnya, Kurdistan, Northern Ireland, Palestine, and Iraq to name just a few of the places where ethnic tensions have erupted in violence again and again. One wonders where God is in these places; why it seems that God cannot be heard or seems not to be known, especially where one would most expect to find God.

Alex Haley interviewed Martin Luther King Jr. for *Playboy* magazine in 1965 and asked him to recall mistakes he had made in leading the Civil Rights Movement. King said:

> *Well, the most pervasive mistake I have made was in believing that because our cause was just, we could be sure that the white ministers of the South, once their Christian consciences were challenged, would rise to our aid. I felt that white ministers would take our cause to the white power structures. I ended up, of course, chastened and disillusioned. As our movement unfolded, and direct appeals were made to white ministers, most folded their hands — and some even took stands against us.*[11]

We often find God working among and through people we would not expect. A racist crowd was taunting Jackie Robinson during batting practice before a game in Cincinnati one day in 1947. The Brooklyn Dodgers had just signed Robinson to break the ban on black ball players in the major leagues. He had agreed to take the jeering without responding in kind.

> *One Southern-born Dodger, appropriately named Dixie Walker, passionately joined in shunning him. But another, Kentucky-born Pee Wee Reese, the team captain, declined. As Robinson fielded practice grounders in a vile din in Cincinnati, Reese purposefully strolled across the infield. He engaged Jackie in a chat. He placed his arm across his teammate's shoulder casually, triumphantly sending a message to fans, players, and sportswriters.*[12]

219

There is always surprise and often shock when someone crosses accepted lines of social division. A story is told of a bearded Jew, attired in old-fashioned garb, who had some personal business that required that he leave his ghetto neighborhood. That afternoon he found himself in an exclusive area of New York's "silk stocking" district. Feeling hungry, he entered a posh restaurant. As soon as he was seated, he was approached by a haughty waiter. "I'm sorry," the waiter said, "but we don't serve Jews here." "That's all right," the old man said, "I don't eat Jews!"

President John F. Kennedy resigned from Washington's exclusive Metropolitan Club as a protest against its refusal to admit African Americans at about the same time he refused to grant an entry visa to the Congolese rebel leader, Moise Tshombe. Whereupon the *New York Times'* Arthur Krock, a Metropolitan member, took Tshombe's side and pled with the president to grant the visa. Kennedy told Krock, "Arthur, I'll give Tshombe a visa if you'll take him to lunch at the Metropolitan Club."[13]

Humor is a good way to ease the pain and salve the deep wounds caused by evil. It may also be the best way to expose the ultimate powerlessness of evil. Jim Wallis tells about a time the South African government blocked a demonstration against apartheid and how Desmond Tutu responded by speaking about the evils of the apartheid system in a worship service at St. George's Cathedral.

> *The walls were lined with soldiers and riot police carrying guns and bayonets, ready to close it down. Bishop Tutu began to speak of the evils of the apartheid system — how the rulers and authorities that propped it up were doomed to fail. He pointed a finger at the police who were there to record his words: "You may be powerful — very powerful — but you are not God. God cannot be mocked. You have already lost." Then in a moment of unbearable tension, the bishop seemed to soften. Coming out from behind the pulpit, he flashed that radiant Tutu smile and began to bounce up and down with glee. "Therefore, since you have already lost, we are inviting you to join the winning side." The crowd roared, the police melted away, and the people began to dance.*[14]

Another good way to thwart the flood of evil is to name it, to call it out whenever it raises its ugly head. This makes deep healing possible for both the wounded and those who wound. A few years ago, the district clergy met in our church parlor for our regular monthly meeting. I'll never forget one of our pastors telling about going out for supper with a new member class in her church. While they were trying to decide where to go for supper, someone suggested a popular national chain restaurant. The pastor said, "I don't go there because they have a policy not to hire people who are homosexual." Whereupon, one of the prospective new members said, "I am not going to join your church. You are a gay lover."[15]

Jesus, who himself was cured of a harmful prejudicial attitude, works through us in the church to heal these deep social wounds.

In the following stories, Larry Wassen and Randall Nulton tell about two very different experiences in foreign territory.

Prejudice Once Removed
Larry Wassen

I was raised in a little coal mining town in the foothills of the Ozarks in Arkansas. One of the high points of the history of this little town, its sense of its importance, was a simple statement that floated around the community almost like an ambiance; and that statement was, "No n_____ ever stayed overnight in this town" (I will say "N word" in the pulpit).

My parents didn't particularly promote that statement. They were neutral about it, and I thought that I was not affected by it. I thought that I was fairly free of any kind of prejudice. I grew up, went on to high school and college. In college, the janitor in our dormitory was an African American, liked and respected by everyone on campus, including me. So, I went on assuring myself that I was free of any kind of racial bias.

After we married, my wife and I came to Milwaukee, and in due course, we became chairpersons of the commission on Christian social concerns in this church. As a part of our responsibility to the commission, my wife suggested that maybe it would be a

221

good idea for us to visit one of the African-American United Methodist churches in Milwaukee. I agreed to it without any major reservations.

So, one Sunday morning we went down to one of the African-American neighborhoods. We parked our car and walked over to the church, about a block away. And I found myself struck by a tremendous sense of dread. It's nothing I can put a name to, even now. It was just a dread I felt of going into that church. It amazed me, because I still didn't think of myself as prejudiced. But if I had had any kind of excuse with which I could have saved face, I would have turned around and gone back home. But my wife didn't let that happen! She took my arm and we went on into that church, where we were accepted like long-lost kinfolk.

That's the story of how I became aware of the fact that I had been tainted by the racism I grew up with; that I had carried around an internal bias that I had not even been conscious of. Having a spotlight shone on something in yourself that you don't like is very helpful in taking steps to remedy it. One thing I did was to sing part-time in the negro church choir. Our church had two worship services, so it was easy for me to visit the African-American church and still attend my own congregation.

And a few years later, my wife and I became members of the board of directors of Northcott Neighborhood House, just about four years after it was formed, and while it was in the process of trying to find its role in the African-American community in Milwaukee. We worked closely there, got well-acquainted with many people, and one woman in particular became a close friend. She invited my wife and me to her home one week for Sunday dinner. After dinner neighbors and friends came in and we had a delightful conversation. It wasn't until about 11 p.m., when the group broke up and we were getting in the car to go home, that I became conscious of the fact that my wife and I had been the only white people present.[16]

Randall Nulton found himself in foreign territory when he followed the call he received in a dream.

Go To Manhattan ... Go To Manhattan ... Go To Manhattan
Randall Nulton

On Friday afternoon, June 4, 1992, I met with Phil Wynn, director of the Regent University conference and seminar department. Having done a stellar job the past three months coordinating and marketing the Dennis Waitley business conference (I learned that even the big boss — Pat Robertson — was pleased with the number of Platinum cosponsors involved — ten — and the number of attendees at Dr. Waitley's main session — 600), I assumed that I would be offered a full-time coordinator position with the Regent conference and seminar department.

However, Phil made it clear that while everyone was pleased with my performance, he was *not* going to hire me. To put it in his words, he was afraid that I would "melt down" under the weight of juggling ten or twelve conferences at once in their various stages of process. He projected that my "intensity for making things happen" would get the better of me when I was producing and promoting a full slate of conferences.

I had looked forward to leaving the pizza delivery business and believed a job at the Regent conference and seminar department would be the perfect fit. Many of the conferences I'd be running point on were spiritual warfare training related, something I had a real heart for. Of course, only God knew that afternoon that the university would shut the department down within six months and everyone would lose their jobs. Nonetheless, I was bummed thinking: "What does a person need to do to get hired around here?"

That evening I was still wallowing in self-pity when I arrived home and got my mail. Not coincidentally, there was a package from my good friend from Marion, Illinois, Diana Crosson. It contained four cassette tapes and a fifty-page study guide from the fasting and prayer seminar she had just attended. The seminar featured an Australian evangelist named Dr. Steve Clarke who taught occasionally at Asbury Theological Seminary. Her note said that the Holy Spirit had strongly prompted her to send this to me and right then I thanked the Lord and thought: "I can take a hint. Looks like I'm going to be doing some serious fasting in the next week or so."

I started a juice fast the very next day — a fast that I believed was for direction and the revelation of what God had in store for me for the next season of my life. The following Thursday, June 10, I experienced a breakthrough as I prayed. For almost an hour I travailed with groans and sighs, believing that I was on the precipice of hearing clearly from the Lord about his plans for me. Then suddenly the travailing ended and was replaced by the Shekinah glory of the Lord. I was full of joy. I was at peace. And I may have even danced for a few minutes as I praised the Lord for his goodness.

That evening, while I was still surrounded by an extra dose of peace, I popped one of the teaching tapes into my cassette player and listened while the instructor, Steve Clarke, explained that the Lord sometimes uses dreams to give us directional instructions. "It's scriptural," he said. "Four different times in Matthew 2, alone, the Lord gives directional instructions during dreams," he said. He then went on to tell a story of what had happened to him five days into a fast that his entire Australian Bible College had participated in together.

Tired because of the week of fasting and blessing, he had gone to bed earlier than usual on a Friday evening. Almost immediately he fell into a deep sleep that included the following dream. In it he was told to go to a back alley behind a row of bars and night clubs in a town about fifty kilometers away. He knew where it was because, he noted, he used to frequent some of those establishments before committing his life to Christ. The dream carried with it a sense of urgency.

Not quite sure what to do when he awoke, he threw some clothes on and knocked on the Bible college president's door. "This dream is definitely from God," the president counseled. "Take my car and the keys that go with it."

Steve went on to share that he had arrived at the alley at about midnight, not really sure what the Lord was up to. All he knew was that he was being obedient. Suddenly, a harsh, low-pitched voice rang out into the cool night air. "Who are you? What are you doing here?"

The darkness and shadows made it difficult to see, but Steve ascertained that the questions had come from a big, bearded fellow sitting on a Harley Davidson. "The guy could kill me," Steve thought. But then he remembered that the Lord had brought him that far, so he decided to pointedly answer the questions.

"My name is Steve Clarke and I attend the Bible college in the next town over," Steve candidly told the rugged biker. "I had a dream earlier this evening and I believe the Lord spoke to me with instructions to come here and come here right away."

The moment of truth had arrived, but instead of getting his face beaten in, he watched in wonder as the leather-jacketed tough guy broke down weeping. It took several minutes to find out what was going on, but Steve Clarke eventually learned that just about everything had been going wrong in the life of that biker, or so that motorcyclist had thought. Earlier that evening he had determined that he would commit suicide before morning. However, just about the time Steve Clarke had gone to bed, he had cried out to God, if there was a God, to send somebody to help him. *If not*, he determined, he would make good on his suicide threat.

Steve Clarke went on to say that he had the privilege of leading that man into a saving knowledge of Jesus Christ that very night and was able to stay connected while he went through pastoral training. That big, burly Australian biker is now a big, burly Australian pastor.

Not that it needed any help, but that true story really stirred my faith. So I told the Lord before dosing off to sleep, "If you want to give me my directives in a dream, I'm ready."

Sure enough, that night I had one of the most vivid dreams I've ever experienced. It started out with a voice, which I believed to be the voice of the Lord, saying, "Go to Manhattan. Go to Manhattan. Go to Manhattan."

Three specific times that three-word instruction was repeated. Eager to please the Lord, I responded by saying, "Okay, Lord, I'll go to Manhattan. I'll go."

Fully expecting to find myself in Times Square, or maybe Central Park, I was surprised to find myself standing in rolling prairie grass hills for as far as the eye could see. This wasn't New York. It was Kansas. I knew it was Kansas because I had ridden through Kansas on a 1974 coast-to-coast bike trip and these hills had the distinct look of Kansas written all over them.

In the dream's next scene I was with my best friend in high school, Rob Falk — someone I had visited just twice in the past ten years. Rob and I were in Manhattan, Kansas, at a Kansas State University dormitory lobby and though I'm not sure why, we were supposed to walk from that spot to downtown Manhattan. Know this. I had never been to Manhattan, Kansas, before. Nor did I know anyone from Manhattan, Kansas. I did, however, know that Manhattan was a town of about 40,000 and the home of one of the great universities of the Great Plains. I knew that because of my interest in college sports as well as my tenure as communications director for International Students Incorporated. At any rate, as Rob and I walked toward our downtown destination, we had a conversation about the street we were on.

"Kearney Street," I noted. "I've been to Kearney, Nebraska. Must not be too far from here."

Rob and I never did find downtown Manhattan. It was one of those dreams where you're trying to get somewhere, but to your frustration, you can't quite seem to get there. So Rob and I retraced our steps, went back to the dormitory, found a map, and figured out what we had done wrong.

In the next scene of the dream, my friend, Rob, was gone. I was alone, sitting on a hill overlooking what I assumed was downtown Manhattan. Immediately below was a wide, murky, brown river and a bridge for car and truck traffic. On the other side of the river was a mall, downtown buildings, and in the distance I could see university buildings at KSU. At this point, I had a little chat with God. "You told me to come to Manhattan, Kansas," I said. "Well, here I am. I've been obedient. Yet, I still don't have the slightest clue as to why you've sent me here. About all I know to do is get in my car and drive back to Virginia."

So I got into my blue Mazda and drove just a little ways — perhaps even less than a mile. "Pull into this parking lot," the Lord instructed. As I obediently followed the instructions and stopped the car, I was cognizant that the lot was at the edge of town. I didn't know why, but the dream seemed to include an exclamation point as to the parking lot's location at one end of Manhattan. "See that man walking this way," the Lord said. I could see him, but I couldn't quite make out his face. "He's going to give you a directive that will help you understand why I've sent you here."

And with that, before I could meet the man, I woke up. The dream was over, and for all intents and purposes, so was my night's sleep. So profound was the dream that I got up early and journaled it. I also shared it first thing that morning, Friday, June 11, 1992, with Jack Bailey, a good friend who had helped rebuild my self-esteem during my pizza delivery days. I had dinner later that day on the outer banks of North Carolina with my Asbury College class-mate, Cliff Ann Perry, and I gave her a detailed blow-by-blow of the dream as well.

But actually "going to Manhattan, Kansas" based on nothing more than a dream proved easier said than done. I wanted hard evidence that this truly was a directive from God. So I dilly-dallied for a few weeks, hoping to receive some kind of confirmation. However, other than sensing a peace every time I prayed about taking a leap of faith and going to Manhattan, Kansas, none was forthcoming. Then one morning in early July, I had breakfast with John Chappel, a vice president at CBN who had assisted me when I was working on the Dennis Waitley business seminar. John had lived on Manhattan Island, New York, for more than twenty years while working in the banking business. Though it didn't quite jive with the dream, I wondered if he might be the "man from Manhattan with a clear directive."

"Nope, I'm not that guy," John said. "But I do believe this dream is literal. I think God is going to give you a Word when you get to that university town on the plains.

"I'm a little surprised you haven't left already," John went on. "What's it going to cost you, a few hundred in gas and lodging at the most? You're single. You don't have any obligations right now. What's the hold up? I think God is going to show you something that might very well impact much of the rest of your life. But even if he doesn't, what have you lost? Almost nothing. And you can sleep at night knowing that you've been obedient with his command to 'go to Manhattan.' "

"Now, what's it going to be?" John continued rather authoritatively. "I'm not leaving this table until you look me in the eye and tell me one way or the other if you're going to go to Manhattan or not."

I knew John meant business. And I knew he had me in a corner. I needed to make the decision and quit procrastinating. "All right. All right!" I responded. "I'll get in my car and go."

Two days later, July 5, 1993, I was on the road. Unfortunately, I had hardly passed Charlottesville, Virginia, on I-64 when I coasted to a stop with smoke coming off my engine. Three-and-a-half days later, and $885 poorer (thanks to the miracle of credit cards), I was finally on my way again. Before I could get to Louisville, Kentucky, my little car, now with 197,000 miles on it, was acting up again. This time the problem was with the catalytic converter. That's when it hit me. My friend in my dream, Rob Falk, was a medical doctor in Louisville. "The least I can do is call him while I'm waiting for my car," I thought.

It turns out that Rob was thrilled to hear from me and invited me to stay the night with his family. When I told him why I was "going to Manhattan," Rob didn't think I was weird. "My grandma used to have dreams all the time that she attributed to God," Rob said as he affirmed me in what I was doing. Nonetheless, at this point in the trip I was really discouraged. I had thought two good days on the road would get me to Manhattan. But now I had been traveling for five days and I still was only halway there. Financially, because of the major repairs, the trip had been a disaster. And there was no telling whether or not something else would go wrong with a car that was obviously on its last legs.

My emotions were on edge, in part, because I had committed myself to fasting all the way to Manhattan until I received the promised "directive." It had now been the better part of a week since I had eaten and I was emotionally and physically tired. As I tossed and turned that night in Rob Falk's guest room, I decided that all of this was really nothing more than a wild and crazy spiritual goose chase. And by the time morning arrived, I had made up my mind to turn my car around on I-64 and head back to Virginia Beach.

So was my state of mind when Rob Falk bid me adieu that morning. As he left for his radiology practice, he stuck his finger in my chest. Rob then looked me in the eye and said, "I want to know what you find in Manhattan. You tell me what you discover when you get there."

And with that, I knew I needed to make it to Manhattan. I knew I would be letting Rob down if I didn't see this trip through to its fulfillment. So, I abandoned the plan to turn around, and later that morning, when I picked up my car, I somehow found the motivation to keep going.

I made good time that day, Friday, July 10, 1993, and found myself in the eastern suburbs of Kansas City at about 9 p.m. The map showed that I had a good three-hour drive ahead, which was fine with me. "I'll arrive in Manhattan shortly after midnight, get a motel, and check the place out tomorrow," I thought. However, that plan changed abruptly when I sensed a directive from the Lord in my spirit.

"Vineyard. Go to Vineyard. Go to Vineyard now," the message noted. It wasn't an audible message, but it was coming through loud and clear. I believed that meant a church, Metro Vineyard Fellowship, which I had heard about in south Kansas City. So, after finding the address in a convenience store phonebook and matching the address with my atlas, I detoured off of I-70 and arrived at the church at about 9:40 p.m.

A prayer meeting attended by about thirty people was in progress, so I simply walked in and sat down like I was part of the group. To my amazement, the leader was sharing his thoughts on Joshua, chapter 5, and the circumcision of the children. He was saying virtually everything that I had previously discerned about the passage and more. What a comfort and blessing!

The meeting ended at about 10:30, after another round of prayer. I introduced myself to those sitting near me and was invited to stay the night on the couch of a nearby apartment. That, in turn, put me back on the road for Manhattan at about 8:30 the next morning, Saturday, July 11. My intention was to leave I-70 about 55 miles east of Manhattan in Topeka and take US 24 through a number of small towns before arriving on Manhattan's east end. However, just as I was about to take the exit I heard, "No! Stay on I-70," loud and clear in my spirit. So, at the last moment, I did just that. I stayed on I-70, which brought me into Manhattan from the south. Little did I realize just how important that final act of obedience would be.

That's because the parking lot directly across from the "Manhattan City Limits" sign included about a dozen people standing around a handful of cars. It was a church parking lot — a church that called itself "Living Word." Once I drove in to say, "Hello," I discovered that it was a ministry to single moms and other economically challenged people in the church — free oil changes — free radiator flushes — and other minor maintenance.

I introduced myself as Randall from Virginia Beach and immediately stated that I believed the Lord had a purpose for my coming to Manhattan. "I've just now arrived," I told them. "Are there any meetings going on in town this weekend that I should know about?"

"Not that I'm aware of," one gentleman responded. "Tell us a little more about yourself."

"I'm a published author," I replied. "I've done writing for Pat Robertson at CBN and most recently ran point on an event for the Regent University conference and seminar department. I've also done communications work for several prominent Christian organizations."

"Say no more," the same gentleman interrupted before I had a chance to include some details. Rather authoritatively he continued, "I know whom you ought to see. His name is Ken Canfield. He's the president of the National Center for Fathering and he's going to speak at Promise Keepers in a couple of weeks."

I had no idea what Promise Keepers was, but the man had my attention. "Come with me to the pay phone in the church and I'll call Ken for you," the man continued excitedly. "In fact, my daughter is at his house right now at his daughter's birthday party."

So, without having been in Manhattan, Kansas, for even five minutes, I found myself on the phone with a man the man in the parking lot seemed certain I should see — Ken Canfield. "Today is really hectic," Ken Canfield told me, "but if you can drop by early tomorrow evening, I'd be glad to meet with you."

I agreed, got directions, and just like that had an appointment with a gentleman who seemed to be an up-and-coming national Christian leader. At least that's what I ascertained after the gentleman in the parking lot, who introduced himself as Jim Hermesch, Ken Canfield's insurance agent, told me a little more about his friend's vision and then filled me in on what Promise Keepers was all about. "They'll probably have 25,000 men at their rally in Boulder, Colorado, later this month," he said. That got my attention, because next to a football game, I didn't know of anything that could draw 25,000 men together at one time.

"Hey, there's somebody else I think you should meet," Jim Hermesch authoritatively went on as I rapidly tried to process the information I was receiving. "He's a pastor, Mark Irvin, and he lives at Living Water Ranch, about fifteen miles northeast of town. I'll go ahead and call him for you as well."

I had two hours to kill before Mark Irvin's appointment, which was fine with me. That would give me some time to get acquainted with Manhattan, I thought. And then it started happening. Within a half-mile of leaving the church parking lot, I found myself crossing the bridge I had seen in my dream. Everything was there. The hill overlooking the murky, brown river that turned out to be the Kansas River. Then there was the mall in the foreground and the university buildings in the distance. It was the exact same scene, from a little different angle, as I had seen in my dream. As I finished crossing the bridge I said to myself, "This is getting spooky!"

While driving further into Manhattan, I thought of the dream and some of its highlights. "The dormitory," I thought. "Let's see if I can find that dormitory where my friend Rob and I rendezvoused." And with that, I circumvented the Kansas State University campus, approaching it from what most people would call "the back side." Sure enough, I found a building that looked just like the dormitory in my dream. And that got me thinking, "What did Rob and I do? Oh, yes, we took a walk downtown."

I have to admit, I was too lazy to walk, but I decided to drive in the direction that I thought downtown was in and see what happened. I don't know what made me take a left turn, but the street I was driving down looked awfully familiar. To my astonishment, I looked up at the street sign and realized I was driving down Kearney Street — the very same street that had been featured in my dream. I missed downtown by about seven blocks, and I had to look at a map in a convenience store to find what I had done wrong, similar to what my friend Rob and I had done in the dream.

"Lord, you are truly amazing," I thought as I killed an hour or so in Manhattan's downtown mall. But he wasn't finished yet. On my way to Living Water Ranch, I took a turn onto a different highway. And there it was. The same rolling prairie grass hills for as far as the eye could see. It was exactly what I had seen in the dream.

Shortly into my conversation with Pastor Mark, I asked him what he would be preaching on the next morning. By this time almost nothing surprised me anymore. So when he said he was a fan of a man from Mississippi, the Reverend Don Wildmon, who encourages Christians to stand up for righteousness by boycotting companies that sponsor large amounts of immorality on television, I simply smiled. He said he was going to challenge his people to take action for righteousness and join a boycott.

"You may find this ironic," I said, "but I worked with Don Wildmon for the better part of two years and I wrote his autobiography called *The Man the Networks Love to Hate.*"

"Well, why don't you join me and preach for part of the service tomorrow?" Pastor Mark responded. "Sounds like you know a lot more than I do on the subject and as an outsider, my people will probably listen more to what you have to say. I'll put you up for the night and you speak tomorrow. How about it?"

And that's how I filled most of the hours until it came time to meet Ken Canfield back in Manhattan on Sunday evening, July 12. Figuring that I had nothing to lose, I started our get-together by telling Ken about my dream and how every scene in the dream had been fulfilled since I had arrived in Manhattan. "The man in the parking lot seemed to be adamant that I talk with you." I candidly acknowledged. "So here I am."

I didn't intend to put Ken Canfield on the spot, but in retrospect, I can see how he might have felt that way. Nonetheless, we had a wonderful discussion. I told him some of what I had done professionally over the years and he told me about the National Center for Fathering and its vision to be a part of the fulfillment of Malachi 4:5 and 6. I wasn't familiar with Malachi 4:5 and 6, so I had him quote it for me: "Before the great and dreadful day of the Lord I will send the prophet Elijah and he will restore the hearts of the fathers to their children and the hearts of the children to their fathers," he said.

"What a noble cause," I thought to myself, "helping men be the involved, loving, nurturing, affirming, and spiritually equipping father figures they were ordained by God to be." The more passionately Ken Canfield shared, the more excited I got about the possibility of joining him in this endeavor.

Over the years, I've learned you can tell a lot about an organization by the makeup of its board. So I asked Ken to name some of the names.

"Well, there's Paul Heidebrecht, a Wheaton College professor," he said. And with that I interrupted him.

"Heidebreath is on your board?" I exclaimed. "I lovingly call him that because he's a very good friend of mine. He was my first boss out of college when I worked as managing editor of publications for Christian service brigade. I have a list of references and he's the first name on it. Who else?"

It turns out, I personally knew, or was aware of, every man he named.

That knowledge was helpful to Ken Canfield. I mean, how would you feel? Here's this guy that comes out of nowhere, sitting on your front porch, saying, "I'm here this evening because God spoke to me in a dream." Ken realized that he could get on the phone right then and talk to people who knew me and knew me well.

"I'd like to pay for your motel room tonight," Ken said. "National Center for Fathering business expense. Tomorrow I'd like you to come by the office, meet the staff, and then we can talk some more."

Motel 6 was fine with me. The inexpensive room was clean, quiet, and comfortable. That night, I marveled at God's goodness as I realized that the real reason I was in Manhattan was for a job interview. "If nothing else, I can write the whole trip off on my taxes," I thought.

I also reflected more on the dream and what I had seen with my natural eyes the previous day. And that's when it dawned on me: the succession of scenes in the dream and the succession of what had actually happened, was like a mirror image. In the dream, the man in the parking lot was last. In my experience, that parking lot and the "man with the directive," came first. In the dream, the hill, the bridge, the wide, murky river, the mall, and the university buildings in the distance was second to last. I had come upon that scene second. In the dream, the university dormitory lobby, the walk down Kearney Street, and looking at a map when we missed downtown, came right after the opening scene of the rolling prairie grass hills as far as the eye could see. I had experienced all of that in precisely the opposite order. It made me marvel at the orderliness of God. I also reflected on the actual role that my friend in the dream, Rob Falk, had played when I got to Louisville. I realized that if it hadn't been for him encouraging me to stay the course and continue to Manhattan, I might have missed an incredible blessing.

The next afternoon, Ken Canfield offered me a job, "pending board approval," along the line of what I had been trained for in my professional experience. And to make a long story short, in July 2004, The National Center for Fathering gave me their first-ever "Lifetime Achievement Award" for services rendered, above and beyond the call of duty, to the cause of effective fatherhood. What a journey! A journey that for most of those years saw me doing the exact same thing that Phil Wynn of the Regent University conference and seminar department didn't think I could do — juggling ten to twelve seminars at a time. And to think, it all started with a dream. "Go to Manhattan ... Go to Manhattan ... Go to Manhattan!"[17]

1. From a sermon preached by Nancy Nichols at Broadway Christian Parish United Methodist Church, South Bend, Indiana, September 10, 2006. Nancy Nichols, a United Methodist minister, has written teenage pregnancy prevention curriculum, worked in a welfare-to-work program and taught parenting skills to at-risk parents. In addition to her pastoral work, Nancy has finished course work toward a Doctorate of Education and is starting her dissertation on United Methodist women clergy ordained in North Indiana from 1974-1990. Nancy's call story was published in *Vision Stories: True Accounts Of Visions, Angels, And Healing Miracles* (Lima, Ohio: CSS Publishing Company, 2002), and her story, "Not Left Behind," appeared in *Shining Moments: Visions of the Holy In Ordinary Lives* (Lima, Ohio: CSS Publishing Company, 2004).

2. Richard Rohr, *Simplicity: The Art of Living* (Crossroads, New York 1990), p. 113.

3. Robert Kirby, *Salt Lake City Tribune*, January, 2006.

4. Journey Into Freedom, 4620 SW Caldew St, Unit E, Portland, Oregon 97219-1573.

5. Christina Berry, "A Time To Weep," *Shining Moments: Visions of the Holy in Ordinary Lives*, ed. John E. Sumwalt (Lima, Ohio: CSS Publishing Company, 2004), pp. 142-143. Christina Berry is a member of St. Andrew Presbyterian Church in Albuquerque, New Mexico, and a student at Austin Presbyterian Theological Seminary in Austin, Texas. For the past fifteen years, she has served Presbyterian churches as a volunteer, as children's ministry staff, and as a preacher and pastoral intern. Christina was the writer for the PC (USA) *Children's Mission Yearbook* for 2003 and for 2004, and a contributing writer to *Seasons of the Spirit* curriculum for 2005.

6. Earl Kammerud is a retired pastor in the Wisconsin Conference of The United Methodist Church, from 1974-1990. Earl's story, "Born of the Spirit," was published in *Vision Stories: True Accounts of Visions, Angels, and Healing Miracles*, (Lima, Ohio: CSS Publishing Company, 2002), pp. 114-115.

7. *The Christian Century*, November 23, 1988.

8. Timothy Browning Safford, Christ Church, Philadelphia, 1999. www.christchurchphila.org/prizesermon.html.

9. Rebecca Coan-Henderleiter is a Native American Catholic and attends the Congregation of the Great Spirit in Milwaukee, Wisconsin. She is a recovering addict, clean since 1989. Her life is devoted to her sons, Tony and Matthew, and to working with addicts and mentally ill persons seeking recovery. henderleiter@cs.com.

10. Vincent Donovan, "On Faith With The Masai," *Christianity Rediscovered* (Chicago, Illinois: Fides/Claretain Press, 1978).

11. Alex Haley, interview with Dr. Martin Luther King Jr. (1929-1968), *Playboy* magazine, January 1965, http://www.playboy.com/features/features/mlk/.

12. Francis X. Cline, *New York Times*, October 1, 2005.

13. Thomas Borstelmann, "Hedging Our Bets and Buying Time: John Kennedy and Racial Revolution in the American South and Southern Africa," *Diplomatic History, 2000*, Volume 24, Issue 3, p. 435.

14. John Ortberg, "Roll Call," quoting Jim Wallis in *Christian Century*, August 9, 2003.

15. Cindy Thompson is a United Methodist Pastor in the Wisconsin Annual Conference currently serving at United Methodist Children's Services of Wisconsin, Inc. in Milwaukee.

16. Larry Wasson, "Prejudice One Removed," *Lectionary Tales for the Pulpit*, John E. Sumwalt and Jo Perry-Sumwalt (Lima, Ohio: CSS Publishing, 1996), pp. 117-119.

17. Randall Nulton was born October 25, 1956, and raised in a pastor's family in Wisconsin. He graduated from Asbury College in 1978 and received a Master's Degree in Mission Development from Wheaton College in 1982. He worked for several evangelical para-church agencies, including thirteen years for the National Center for Fathering in Kansas City. Randall died of cancer October 16, 2004. With thanks to Randall's brother, Pastor Paul Nulton of Ripon, Wisconsin, who is glad to discuss how this vision was a part of his brother's faith life as a prophetic/charismatic Christian. pnulton@sbcglobal.net.

The All Of Love

Not out of earth,
But out of love itself,
Arises everything that is:
Each atom, every cosmic pull and tug,
Each burgeoning leaf on every ancient tree,
Each wren and oriole singing its own rare tune,
Each ant moving the planet one particle at a time,
Each humpback whale slipping through the sea,
Each root and seed,
Each wing and fin and hand,
Every eye and heart and hidden soul,
Each newborn baby crying for dear life,
Each woman, each man waking to creation
In every single morning,
Yearning, sighing, smiling, healing,
Each grace, each goodness,
Each miracle
Most amazing, most joyous,
Most holy,
Each surges from the All of Love,
The One who was and is and ever shall be,
World without end.

Timothy Haut, May 21, 2006

Timothy Haut is pastor of the First Congregational Church
(UCC) of Deep River, Connecticut. He is a graduate of Yale Divinity School and was ordained in 1972. Timothy has several books of
poetry in the works and waiting for publication.

Appendix

John Sumwalt is collecting miracle and vision stories for a new anthology. Write to him at 2044 Forest Street, Wauwatosa, Wisconsin 53213. Phone 414-339-0676. johnsumwalt@sbcglobal.net.

WARNING
Removing or tampering with the card on the back side of this page renders this book non-returnable.

Title: How To Preach The Miracles, Cycle A

ISBN: 0-7880-2457-4

INSTRUCTIONS TO ACCESS PASSWORD FOR ELECTRONIC COPY OF THIS TITLE:

The password appears on the reverse side of this page. Carefully cut the card from the page to retrieve the password.

Once you have the password, go to

http:/www.csspub.com/passwords/

and locate this title on that web page. By clicking on the title, you will be guided to a page to enter your password, name, and email address. From there you will be sent to a page to download your electronic version of this book.

For further information, or if you don't have access to the internet, please contact CSS Publishing Company at 1-800-241-4056 in the United States (or 419-227-1818 from outside the United States) between 8 a.m. and 5 p.m., Eastern Standard Time, Monday through Friday.